SEVENTY SUMMERS

The Story of a Farm

SEVENTY SUMMERS

The Story of a Farm

Tony Harman

BBC PUBLICATIONS

This book accompanies the BBC Television series *Seventy Summers* first broadcast on BBC 2 in 1986. The series was produced by Lucy Parker.

Published to accompany a series of programmes prepared in consultation with the BBC Continuing Education Advisory Council.

Diagrams by John Gilkes

Typeset in 10/12pt Sabon and printed in Great Britain by Butler & Tanner Ltd, Frome and London

Published by BBC Publications,
a division of BBC Enterprises Ltd
35 Marylebone High Street,
London W1M 4AA
© Tony Harman 1986
First published 1986

ISBN 0 563 21203 9 (pbk)
     0 563 21224 1 (hdbk)

Contents

Best Leys

1916 Nine Acres

1951 Well Field

Slip

Further Flax Field

1884 Pond Field

1881 Crab-tree Field

1880 Lower Field

1879 Long Leys

1917 Nine Acres

1949 Great Hanging

Stoney Field

1952 Leathers

Upper Leathers

1943

1957 Honour Croft

512

Sale's

B.M. 526.7

1883 Four Acres

1882 Middle Field

1878

1920 Middle Hangings

1947

1948 Sales Dell Field

1944 Long Ley

1942

1945 Grove Field

527

1939 Long Orchard

1877 Dell Field

516

500

1918 Bottom Field

1919 First Hangings

1921 Six Acres

1935 Pond Field

△Sun 538·1

1937 Little Newlands

522

187b

Ashley Green Field

490

1874 Ashley Green Meadow

Gap

1936 Great Newlands

533

1873 Wethereds Piece

1872 Two Acre Field

1871 Deans Wood at The Grove

1933 The Banks

1934 Rick Field

1927 Further Meadow

1928 Hither Meadow

192b

534

2116 Calves Close

70 Great Bassetts

B.M. 454.6

1870 Dell Field

1922

Deans Wood

The Banks Piece

1922 Stock

Chapel Remains of Great Meadow

1929

1930 Courtsthire Orchard

523

2146 Briary Close

ts Spring

1922 Seven Acres

1869 Dell at the Grove Farm

1923 Spring Close

1931 Banks Wood at the Grove

1932

Grove Farm

2117

1823 Further Field

465

1867

1868 The Lagger

Little Grove Wood

1854 Wood Field

1924 Wood Field

1925

B.M. 520.0

ts Spring

1824

1865 Pond Field

482

1859 Hill Field

1858

1855 Spring Field

1856 Back Orchard

1853 Rick Orchard

2147 Outwood

2145 Sharpes Croft

819 Little ye Field

Middle Field

1863

Twodells Wood

1860

1851 Pond Field

1852 Rick Orchard

Little Grove Farm

Field

2149 Little Cheers

2148 Middle Cheers

2144

2143 Hither Pond Cl or Ten Acres

82b Upper lors Field

1825 Lower Taylors Field

1862 Two Dells Field

497

1861 Seven Acres

1849 Great Dell Field

1850 Rick

1848 Little Dell Field

524

Grove Lane

2150 Great Holly-bush Field

Barn Field or Great and Little Leys

2153 Church Field

2152

1836 Bottom Field

512

1837 Home Field

1846 Pond Field

Torrington House

B.M. 527

2151 Little

Little

The Canvas

This is the story of one farmer and one farm – Grove Farm, Whelpley Hill near Chesham, Buckinghamshire. When I was born in 1912, Whelpley Hill was a small and very ordinary village where the whole population either worked on farms or had jobs connected with farming. It was a closed agricultural community only 30 miles from London, though it might have been 300 miles for all the difference it made. Now it has all changed. Today, very very few people in Whelpley Hill work on the land, and Chesham itself has grown into a busy commuter suburb of London. The commuters are housed in estates that cover fields I ploughed during the Second World War when the country needed food. Now, if the same need arose, that land is lost, for although farmers as well as builders alter the landscape, the builders' changes are the ones that are not reversable.

Farming changes *can* be reversed. The trouble is they can't be reversed as fast as the politicians and the urban population want them to be. When food is short it takes time for farmers to get into gear, to build up skilled labour and to increase the fertility of their existing land and bring more land into cultivation. And however much their efforts alter the landscape, traces of the old patterns will still remain.

To me the countryside is like a canvas with one picture drawn on top of the last, nothing ever quite rubbed out. The picture of the countryside when I appeared on the scene was one of sixteenth-century field names and boundaries, eighteenth-century farming methods and nineteenth-century people. When I first remember, every field had its own name and its own secrets. The name might be a description of the place: First Hangings – the steep field at the back of the farm; Dabberfield – dabber is the Chiltern name for a pebble. Some fields carried the names of their owners from as far back as Tudor times, like Wethereds, which was given to Edmund Wethered when he married in 1585 by John Partridge who lived in my house then. Many farming techniques had changed little since the Agricultural Revolution, like mining chalk from 25 feet down with a windlass to spread on the fields and correct the soil balance. The implements were the same too: the seed drill had not changed

The canvas around The Grove. Although this map was printed in 1878 it has been amended by a local historian, Dr Arnold Baines, to show the field pattern as it was in the 1840s.

much since it was invented by Jethro Tull in the early eighteenth century, and the horse-drawn plough with which one man could work only about 100 acres had hardly altered at all. (Now, with a tractor, one man can easily manage 400 acres.) The people around me, like George Larkin, who managed our farm in my childhood, reflected the staunch non-conformity of the Chilterns in the nineteenth century, and you can still spot traces of their independent and decided frame of mine in their grandchildren today.

In the seventy years that have passed since then, more changes have taken place in farming than in the previous three hundred. Part of the reason for this is that in farming the limit of the market is the limit of the transport available. The first cows I bought in the early 1930s I walked home from market along country lanes. There were few cars on the road then. Now the cattle go on great trucks across England and up to Scotland. We have even sold bulls to New Zealand and America.

Other changes have been brought about through improvements in machinery. Small, irregular-shaped fields of 6 or 7 acres have given way to great expanses of 60 acres or more so that combine harvesters can work them more efficiently. Still other changes have been produced by the botanists and chemists. When my father bought Grove Farm in 1919, 18 cwt to the acre was a good yield of wheat in this area. Just before World War II we got it up to 35 cwt, nearly double. Now we're disappointed if we don't get 70 cwt to the acre. So the yield has quadrupled in my lifetime.

All these changes – changes in landscape and farming techniques, crops and crop yields, people, occupations and transport – I have experienced at first-hand in one spot in the Chilterns. But it was not until I bought a book in a second-hand bookshop a few years ago that I thought of recording my experiences. The book was called *The English Gamekeeper* and it was written at the end of the last century by John Wilkins, who had been a gamekeeper all his life in this area. In many respects he described a scene which was a lot like the one I first remember, a scene which is fast disappearing; I decided to carry on where he left off. So this is a story of one farmer and one farm. But it is also the wider story of the changes in farming and the countryside in Britain over the past seventy summers.

Tony Harman
Grove Farm, June 1986

A Farmer's Prayer

Lord, give me another seventy years. It ought not to be too difficult
for you. As the hymn tells us – a thousand ages in thy sight is but
an evening gone. After all, you give tortoises and trees much longer
than us and we are supposed to be made in your image. I don't
want immortality – just another seventy years – and not to do
anything very extraordinary either. I would like seventy more
autumns, the ripe fruit, and the chance to contemplate the harvest
that is past. Seventy more miserable winters during which to look
forward to beautiful springs, which so rarely come. Seventy more
chances to sow and seventy more harvests; and seventy more years
to see the trees that I have planted grow, to see them mature
enough to cut down, prove that it was worthwhile and plant some
more. It is not really very much to ask.

Hawridge
Moor End
Pippards Green
Bellingdon F.
Ashridge F.
High Spring
Crowfoot
Flamstead
Ashley Green
Bellingdon
Ash ridge
Thorn
Captains Wood
Charteridge
Hazloden
Mount Nugent
Presmoor
Sloughland
Nash Leigh
Twodells
Chesham Bottom
Chesham Bottom F.
Leigh Green
Porto Bello
Hobbs Hole
Brokice
Lit. Brokice
Nash Leigh
Godmore
Maple Tree
Hollybush
White Hill
CHESHAM
The Bury
Dry Dell
Halfway Ho.
Bungrove
Round Green
L. Germans
Amy Mill
Brick Kiln
Hill F.
Canons Mill
Warehouse Mill
Mill Hall
Broadwater
Back Moor
Brays Green
Weedon Hill
May Hall
Chesham Bois
Bois F.
Bois Wood
Blackwell
Stubbs
Blackwell Hall
Ivy Ho.
Elliotts Mill
Weedon Hill F.
Brays Wood
Pipers Wood
Mill End
Shardeloes
Mantles Green
Bowers
Batchelors
Woodside
Herrings
Raynes
Rectory
Cold Morcham
Lit. Shardeloes
AMERSHAM
Silk Factory Mill
Reeves
Bendrose
Bel Ho.
Loudhams
High Ho. F.
High Ho.
Post Ho.
Hoved
Cokes
Woodrow F.
Brickwick
Cold Harbour
Quarrendon
Mill
Adams Barn
Burtons
Nightingales
Heaven Orchard
Cottage
Claymoor
Brentford Wood
Stock Place Field
Coleshill Gram
Winchmoor Hill
Kiln
Pollards
Ivy Ho.
Wood
Harwood Downs
Bottom F.
The Hut
Warren F.
Rough Wood
Brentford Barn
Bottom Spring
Up Bottom
Hobbs Hole
Lowlands
Luckings
Hertfordshire
Hill Wood
Hunger Hill
Stockings
Hill F.
Frog Hall
Dodds
New House
The Vach
Chalfont Hill
Stonage
Pheasant
Gorelands
Botwells
Post Ho.
High Wood
Hodge Wood
Chalfont St. Giles
Shrubs Wood
Newlands
Beards
Owls Ears
Hill
Broadway
Tridey Street
Harestock
Bottom F.
Droppings
Mounts Hill
Harrats End
Bourn End
Bovingdon Hay
Lit. Hay
Bourn Grove
White Hill
Dells Wood
Whelpley Hill
Grove
Lit. Grove
Bush Wood
New Ho. F.
Bovingdon Bury
Bovingdon
Colliers
The Moors
Frog Lane
Lane F.
Bovingdon Lodge
Cross
Peekels Dell
Whelpley Ash
White Hart Cross
Mary F.
Bovingdon Green
Pudds Cross
Jason Hill
Marchants
Botley
Tylers Hill
Layhill Com.
Cowcroft
Spencers
Fewinens
Chantock Hall
Maldens
Venus Hill
Holly Hedges
Cottingham F.
Woodmans Wood
Hoop it Bottom
Lit. White End
Pinner Green
White End Park
Godmore
Hockley Hole
Whites End
Flaunden
New House F.
Moulds Croft
Mumshoms F.
Rose Hall
Thrift Wood
Old Barn
Martins End
Flaunden Grove
Surratt Bottom
Latimers
River
Flaunden
Cheneys
Mill
Halfway F.
West Wood Spring
Cheneys
Golding
Surratt Mill
Old Field
New Hanging Wood
Old Hang Wood
Green Street
Cheneys Lodge
Grove Wood
New Ho.
Currants Bottom
Charley Wood Common
Old Kiln
Black Cot F.
Kings F.
Long Hill
Mumfords Herring Gate
Phillips Hill
Bulls Land
Hunt Ash
PART OF

The Road to Wooden Babylon

If you want to get to The Grove, Whelpley Hill, which is my farm, come to Hemel Hempstead and look for the B4505 road. People might think they have been put on a particularly dull road where nothing is ever likely to happen. It is not quite like that.

When you leave the traffic lights at Hemel Hempstead, if you have managed to avoid the speed trap that is frequently there for the first few hundred yards, you come across a common on the left-hand side of the road. This is Sheephanger Common; years ago, locals pronounced it Shipangle Common. It is not particularly special, although recently, when there was a public enquiry for the diversion of a projected motorway, one self-appointed environmentalist got up and stated that its flora and fauna were unique and that a motorway in that position would destroy these things for ever in the whole of Herts and Bucks. Apparently, if the motorway were to be routed slightly further from his own residence and garden, the effect on this environment would not be so disastrous. I do not think this was true but it added a little levity to the proceedings.

The route I am taking you on must be the route which, many years before, William Cobbett followed on his rural ride from St Albans to High Wycombe in 1827. He mentions the large number of commons which he saw on the way and this is the only route between the two towns which would pass many commons. One of them must have been Sheephanger Common. Of course, he was obsessed with the wickedness of landowners at that time who were enclosing commons and depriving the general public, particularly cottagers, of their use. The cottagers won with Sheephanger Common. It was never enclosed. Now, if you take a look, it is a golf course. Today's urban middle-class, no doubt people of the highest principles, have succeeded where the wicked landowners failed and the common is no longer freely available for people to graze stock. Fortunately they no longer want to do that anyway.

After Sheephanger Common, and just before you get to Bovingdon, you will see a restaurant called *The Bobsleigh*. In a sense this is a memorial to the destruction of a major pleasure of a large part of the population of the town of Chesham. Chesham

The dotted line on this 1830s map shows the route that I believe William Cobbett took on his rural ride from St Albans to High Wycombe. He commented on the number of commons on the route, also on the hedge greens – a permanent headland all round a field for the machinery to turn on. It was never cultivated but just cut for hay.

used to have its own brewery and its own special beer. This was bitter and cloudy and nobody liked it particularly, except the inhabitants, who loved it. When the brewery closed down in the fifties, many of them cried their eyes out. The owners, the Nash family, sold it to Benskins of Watford and the last brewer, Bill Nash, set up *The Bobsleigh*, named after the only Englishman ever so far to win the Olympic Bobsleigh Championship – a member of his family.

You then come to Bovingdon itself, now seemingly a prosperous suburb of Hemel Hempstead, where middle-management families live and where shops have grown up catering for the housewives who are prepared to pay slightly more than the supermarket prices in Hemel Hempstead. It is a bustling, busy little place, but not long ago it was not like this at all. Forty years ago, there was no drainage; many of the houses were not even provided with septic tanks. It was like the eighteenth century. Once a week, a cart came round and collected buckets from the earth closets. The atmosphere was appalling. Any elderly countryman will know, without being told, what the carter who provided this service for the community was called.

During the war, Bovingdon was occupied by the Americans in the air base nearby and hundreds of American servicemen lived on the spot. American racial troubles spilled over into Bovingdon so that, of the four pubs in the village, two had to be put out of bounds to white Americans and two out of bounds to black

Bovingdon village in 1903. Just past the village well, round the corner to the right was the pond known as 'Bovingdon Docks'.

Americans. In my experience, most of the locals who remained during the war, tended to use the black American pubs, either in the hope of seeing some action or else because they instinctively sided with those they believed to be the underdogs.

Bovingdon is more or less on top of a hill – perhaps 500 feet above sea level, but, remarkably, it is subject to floods every hundred years or so. A year or two after the war, there was a cloudburst on level land just behind Bovingdon where the American air base was. The water poured through the village about 9 feet deep swamping the little pond in the village, which is rather eccentrically known as 'Bovingdon Docks'. Thence, it ran down by the church, through Bury Farm, of which I was then the tenant, 4–5 feet deep, washing away brick and stone walls and destroying everything in its path. Unfortunately, my bank manager was due to look at the farm the following morning because I wanted an extra loan out of him. He arrived to see a scene of destruction all round – somewhat surprisingly he still gave me the loan. The old people said that this had happened a hundred years before too, so if it is going to happen again, it will presumably not be until the middle of the next century. When it does, a lot of the newer properties will, presumably, be in danger and one can imagine the middle-management wives floating down the fields towards Hemel Hempstead trying to retrieve their three-piece suites.

Following the route that Cobbett must have taken for a little while longer, you come to a fork. He must have gone off to the left. There are more commons that way. (The next one has also been appropriated by the golfers.) We, however, go off to the right. Where the road forks is, to me, 'suicide corner', though not, I expect, to anybody else. There you can see the farm where Whistler Smith worked. He cut his throat. When his only son was asked by the police the following day why his father had done it, he answered, 'I don't know, he's never done it before'! He added, 'He drank a gallon of homemade wine last night and wasted the bloody lot'! Just across the field towards Bovingdon Green, there is a big house. This is where Mr Dobson shot himself. A bit further over is another barn where an unknown man was found hanging. I cannot see anything particularly depressing about the place, but there were three suicides in a period of thirty years or so.

Over to your right until recently lay a great open space which was the site of the American air base during the Second World War. Before that, it was little fields with high hedges, all closed in and particularly good land for this area. In a short space of time during the war, everything was swept away and great concrete runways made. Some have now been broken up and the land restored to agriculture – the rest is occupied by a new prison. In the corner of the aerodrome was a cage which the Americans erected, complete with floodlights, a watchtower and guardhouse to house top-level German prisoners en route for questioning at Latimer. As far as I know, the only prisoner ever to occupy it was me, but that is another story.

For some months after the war, when the airport was being used for civilian purposes, people of the surrounding area were able to augment their income as a result of a few minor air crashes there. Nobody was ever killed but plane-loads of cherries came down and everybody had cherries. A little later, a plane-load of furs came down and somebody suddenly appeared in a fur coat. For a brief period, there used to be a crazy old lady called Dora who, day after day, would stand on the end of the runway, hurling abuse at the planes as they came over, standing as though a policeman on traffic duty, trying to send them in the wrong direction. In the end, they just took her away.

On the next corner, as a reminder of the past, there is a little house that was once a chapel. This marks the turning to Whelpley Hill. In the last century, Whelpley Hill had twenty cottages, seven

This converted chapel (one of many in our area) on the corner of the turning to Whelpley Hill village is a landmark on our route. There was a non-conformist chapel in Whelpley Hill long before there was a church.

farms, one church, one chapel and a pub. They must have been both very religious people and extremely heavy drinkers to keep all these establishments going. The chapel was converted a long time ago, but the church is kept going by a few stalwarts. The pub is still busy, the headquarters of the local pigeon club now and full of people who come to the village in their cars. The village itself used to be quite a pleasant little place, but it was totally destroyed, probably for ever, by the presence of the aerodrome during the war. Concrete dispersal points for the airplanes were grouped all round the village, and since the aerodrome closed down these have been used to park old lorries, as a scrapyard and, in another part, as a caravan site. It all looks rather unhappy now.

So, keep on the main road. This goes downhill on what was originally a green lane, only made up as a hard road in the 1920s. (Green lanes used to abound in the area but now very few of them are left.) On the left, Pockets Dell, which doesn't exist anymore and wasn't a dell but a little house standing in a cherry orchard, is mentioned in documents as long ago as 1600 and therefore, one would have thought, worth preserving. Nevertheless it was allowed to fall down just about the time that rural slums were suddenly transformed into historic buildings which had to be preserved at all

One of the few examples of a green lane left in the area, now rather overgrown. It leads from Pudds Cross to Soldiers Bottom.

costs and became immensely valuable. Then, a little further down, is Soldiers' Bottom. Why Soldiers' Bottom, I haven't the slightest idea. Now it ought to be called Lorry Drivers' Bottom because a layby has recently been constructed and there are almost always lorries parked in it and somebody selling tea and sandwiches.

For a little while, the road goes up again with farm land on either side. Then, for about half a mile, the road is like a frontier between one sort of countryside and another. On the left, or south side, it is all built up with houses and bungalows of every conceivable shape and size. These were obviously built over quite a long period and many have quite large gardens. On the other side, that is to say the north side, are open fields and in the distance you can see a wood or two and The Grove. The contrast is really very marked and it doesn't relate to any planning decision by a local council or anything which has happened in the last sixty years. It

The frontier between developed and undeveloped land caused by financial problems in the twenties. In the distance you can just see Orchard Leigh and Grove Lane.

results from the fact that in 1921 or thereabouts, land to the south
of the road was farmed by a Mr Ford who was a tenant of Lord
Chesham, the limit of whose estate this was. Mr Ford had been an
arable farmer with quite a modern attitude towards farming.
Concentrating solely on grain production, he had used tractors and
chemical manures before anybody else in the area and the fields on
his farm, known as Shepherds Farm, were quite big. Then, with the
repeal of the Corn Production Act in 1921, the price of grain
collapsed. Having no other irons in the fire he very soon had to
give up the tenancy and retreat to a very small poultry farm
somewhere in the Chalfonts area a few miles away. Simultaneously
his landlord, Lord Chesham, must have been under some sort of
financial pressure because he decided to sell the farm and the only
people who would buy it were a bunch of speculators in Chesham
who had dreams of developing the whole thing into something
approaching a new town.

The speculators made plans (which in those days did not have
to be passed by anybody) showing roads criss-crossing the whole
farm, which was a big one. The major part of the land and all the
road frontage was shown on the plans as plots for building, with
just a few smallholdings which they thought they would sell to ex-
servicemen or people of that sort who were getting government
help to set up on their own. Of course, in the atmosphere of the
twenties and the gathering general depression, few plots were sold,
but those that were were developed higgledy-piggledy, here and
there along the frontage of the road. In effect, this sterilised most of
the land from the agricultural point of view for ever more, and
now, in the last few years, the planning authorities have allowed
the odd spaces to be filled in with new houses.

So, you have got suburbs on one side of the road and, on the
other, open country which has been farmed ever since the First
World War by the same family, the Mashes. Why did they succeed
where Mr Ford failed? The Mashes' farm was run on very
traditional lines, using little chemical manure. It was well
cultivated, as was Mr Ford's land, the main crops being fruit and
vegetables. Of course, the Mashes' success and Mr Ford's failure
was interpreted by many of the older people in the area as a failure
of science. Mr Ford had gone wrong, had gone bankrupt or nearly
so, because the artificial fertilisers had poisoned his land and the
tractors had ruined the drainage on it, whereas Mr Mash, keeping
on with his traditional methods of using animal manure and horse-
drawn implements, was obeying the laws of nature and survived.

A circular from 1896 giving the auction particulars of cottages at Wooden Babylon and Grove Lane Farm, now called Torrington Farm – home of the Mashes.

Actually, it was something a bit more than that. It was that Messrs Mash had a wonderful contract in Covent Garden where a branch of the family had a sales organisation; they also ran a greengrocer's shop off Piccadilly and so always had both a wholesale and a retail outlet for their produce. In the last few years, the most recent member of the Mash family has swept the hedges and orchards away, so now even he has made the sort of modern changes to the environment which everybody is at present complaining about. But the changes he has made are not so permanent or so irreversible or so damaging ecologically as those that were made by accident on the other side of the road in the twenties.

This road will eventually land you in Orchard Leigh. What an inappropriate name! Just as inappropriate as the urban-looking Victorian villas which stand there. I always felt it could not be the real name of the place and, sure enough, when I looked at an Ordnance Survey map published in 1883 the place is shown as 'Wooden Babylon'. This conjures up in my mind a wonderful picture of dilapidated wooden cottages, occupied by wicked people. Perhaps the area was inhabited in the last century by people who neither went to church nor chapel and that was why their houses were christened 'Babylon'. Such a pity to sweep this away with the rather boring name of Orchard Leigh.

The largest of the, to me, hideous Victorian buildings at Orchard Leigh is now a private school. It is a house with a past. It was there that a Doctor Lieff – a refugee from Czarist Russia – started what must have been one of the first health farms in Britain. They call them health farms now, but in those days, it was called *Lieff's Nature Cure*, or occasionally, *The Healthatorium*. There, people paid to be starved and be given various unusual treatments to reduce their weight. Such places are far more common and expensive nowadays. The well known establishment of *Champneys* nearby – probably the best known of all health farms – was also started by Doctor Lieff. His son told me once that his father had been a very enterprising man with no capital at all who, when he decided to move from Orchard Leigh to *Champneys*, had prescribed as treatment for his wealthy clients the carrying of his furniture from one house to the other (all of three miles). So he got his moving done for next to nothing and, no doubt, his patients lost a lot of weight in the process.

Orchard Leigh, in its time, has had its full share of eccentric inhabitants. One lady exhibited an intelligent form of eccentricity. Driven to distraction by her housework and fed up with everything,

Orchard Leigh that once was Wooden Babylon.

she took all her washing and threw it into the bus which stopped outside her house. The bus driver, knowing her reputation, was too frightened to argue with her and took it all to the laundry in Chesham, which was not even on his route. Another lady, whose name was Rose, caught one of the ponies I used to use to draw the milk floats on my rounds in the 1930s and rode it round and round our fields with no clothes on whatsoever. A third eccentric - a dear old man called Will Chapman, quite crazy but absolutely harmless - used to sleep all day in the barns and hedges near here and play a squeaky violin in people's gardens at dead of night: very frightening. These days such people would be given heavy doses of Vallium and we should hear no more of them.

So, this 'dull' bit of road, if you cram in everything that has happened along it into one short story, turns out not to be so dull after all. In fact, so much seems to have happened, that I have forgotten to say in my directions that you must turn right down Grove Lane before you get to Orchard Leigh in order to reach The Grove, at a point where the only eccentric memory I have is of my own stepfather standing on his head and talking to the ants about Maeterlinck.

The First Commuters

Though Sydney Harman, my father, wasn't the first commuter from Chesham into London every day, he was certainly among the first because the railway only opened about five years before he moved out to Chesham in 1894 or 5. Of course, the railway from Berkhamsted to London had been open many, many years before and I expect a few people did commute in from there if they lived close to the station. But it was simply not on to get from Chesham to Berkhamsted in a pony and cart or on a bicycle first thing in the morning to go to London, and do the same thing back at night. The time taken getting to and from the station would have made it impractical and, in any case, in the winter when the roads were bad it would have been impossible.

I am not quite sure how, or why, my father came to this particular area. He told us that he was bicycling down from London and took a fancy to it, so I suppose that is true. (When I was very small I always imagined that he had come down on a penny-farthing.) His first property was a very small farm called Sloughlands at the top of Nashleigh Hill in Chesham which he rented from Alf Gee, a farmer. Because he was still a bachelor then, he called it *The Hermitage* for the brief while he was there. (I don't think he named it quite correctly because in the only picture I have ever seen of the house at that time, there was also a girl who wasn't my mother and wasn't one of his sisters . . .) Five days a week he commuted to London to the business he had first started at the turn of the century. He had been working as a salesman in a silversmith's shop till someone had lent him the money to start up on his own in Bond Street. One can hardly imagine that sort of thing happening nowadays. His father had been in the same type of business too and, although he never rose above the position of a senior salesman, he must have been extraordinarily good at it because he managed to educate all my aunts extremely well long before most women received much schooling.

After he had lived at Sloughlands for a few years, my father saw and bought, very cheaply, Little Grove Farm, a larger smallholding further out of Chesham. It looks in the photographs I have to be a pleasant house of timber and red brick, which he

My father in around 1911 with my sister Lola outside Little Grove House which he had bought in 1903.

A back view of Little Grove post-renovation.

Little Grove House before it had been altered, renovated – and spoilt.

The opening of the railway in 1889 linked Chesham with the main line to London. My father used this line to commute up to his Bond St business during the week.

proceeded to renovate. He altered it in a manner which has been followed by many people since to bring it up to modern standards, losing a bit of the character in the process and finishing up with a much larger house which he had painted black and white. (This was a style which subsequently became very popular in the twenties and thirties.) He supervised a lot of the work himself apparently. I remember an elderly bricklayer, Charlie Wallis, telling me in the 1930s, that he had worked on it and that my father had come along with a note of what the mix should be for the cement in the chimneys. He personally supervised the mixing, and then got up on the roof and personally supervised the chimneys. I am not sure that he really knew what he was doing though because the chimneys have cracked very badly in the succeeding half century.

The farm consisted of about 25 acres when my father took up occupation and it was all grass except for a small wood. On it he kept four cows, the calves from them, some pigs and quite a lot of poultry. At the time when first I remember it, which was during the First World War, Alf Newland, who was really the gardener, was the only farm help he had, but previously a local farmer's son, Simms from Moors Farm, had looked after the cows and the land. The grass cultivation must have been quite intensive because enough hay was produced to keep the cows all the year round and my father only bought in a few concentrates for them and for the pigs. Even forty years later, the agricultural advisory services would have considered that a high production from so small an acreage.

Despite having taken on this extra responsibility, my father continued to travel in to Marylebone Station every day, using the new railway. There must have been a rapid development of the roads leading into Chesham during this period, especially from the north and east, and a lot of medium-sized houses were built near the centre of the town for people who could then walk to the station and travel up to London. Simultaneously a number of businessmen, like my father, bought or built houses just outside the town. These were people such as Mr Skinner who, I have a feeling, was the Skinner of Lilley & Skinner, Mr Morford who managed a department store and Sir Frederick Dunbar of Torrington House, next to Little Grove. This first wave were all in a fairly high income bracket, but later a flood of people came out from London looking for cheaper houses, either new houses built on the edge of the towns and villages or, whenever they were available, old farm cottages which could be modernised and converted. This was partly possible because the farming depression of the 1920s meant that less labour was required on the farms and, as soon as people died or moved, the cottages became vacant and were a cheap source of housing. This developed so far that now there are probably not one tenth the number of houses in the countryside occupied by people actually working on the farm as there were in 1920. They are nearly all occupied by people going into towns to work.

The last development in this trend is that now, because they are not allowed to build new houses in the countryside, people are so keen to live there that they are busily converting old barns which, because they have been there a long time, are acceptable to the planning authority. Most of these make quite large and extremely expensive houses, including the one on my own farm which is now nearing completion. Presumably, all these people who have come to live in the countryside have come because they liked it the way it was when they found it. I notice that almost all of them resent the arrival of any more people and oppose bitterly attempts to develop any more of the land within the area. It would appear that theirs has always got to be the last house built. The original, indigenous population is not nearly so much bothered.

It was several years after he took on Little Grove that my father married my mother and, according to the Visitors' Book, which I still have, he doesn't seem to have led a very active social life during that period. I imagine he was working very hard in London and did not spend all that much time down in Chesham to

Left: Sales Farm at Whelpley Hill in the early 1930s – three cottages abandoned and derelict.

Right: The same building in 1986 converted into one desirable commuter residence.

start with. Then, in 1906, my mother paid her first visit to Little Grove. She had been brought down to stay with my father by her older half-sister, Maud, who had married Sam Ryder, a cousin of my father's. It may well have been that they had first seen each other at Sam and Maud's wedding a few years previously. In the Visitors' Book she signed herself, in big, girlish writing, Jess S. McCleod. The Jess went out within a few years; she went, so to speak, up market and decided to call herself Jean.

My mother had been born in Canada at Guelph, just outside Toronto, where my grandfather, Patrick McCleod, was a Presbyterian minister. As was quite common in those days he continually moved westwards, apparently falling out with his church elders from time to time. He finished up building the first Presbyterian church in Victoria Island, Vancouver. There, following his normal pattern, he fell out with his elders after about ten years and, since there was nowhere further west to go, came back to England and took charge of a church in Tooting; and that was where my mother and father were married.

Her family apparently disapproved strongly of the match to start with, as they considered the age difference (my mother was nineteen, my father thirty-five) too great, but they could not have caused much delay as the couple were married in, I think, the October of 1906, only three months after my mother's first visit to Little Grove. Three children followed: my brother Sidney (always known as 'Bobby') in 1907, my sister Lola exactly three years later to the day, August 3rd, and I in March 1912.

The old threshing barn at Grove Farm being converted into a rather large house.

My mother at Little Grove not looking at all like a farmer's wife.

Just like the commuters who moved out from London, I liked the world the way I found it. The countryside seemed so much more varied than it is nowadays with every field shut off from its neighbours by high hedges. Most of them had a pond or a dell or a small wood somewhere adjacent to them and, it seems to me, in my memory, an enormous variety of wild flowers and wild life as well. Even the people seemed to be more interesting and more varied. Of course, if you looked into it, you'd probably find it wasn't as wonderful as I picture it at all. Certainly many people were poor and unhealthy, housing was bad and there were few opportunities for young people. But nostalgia is a tremendously powerful thing. So much so that the OS map for 1883, which represents things almost exactly as they were forty or fifty years later, has come to be an almost romantic thing to me – a pictorial representation of the enchanting landscape I think I remember.

Fifty years on again in 1985 the picture has changed enormously. Grove Lane, for example, which led to Little Grove, used to be rather a secret place. Because of the thick, high hedges, you could not see much from the road at all, but you knew that on either side were orchards belonging to neighbouring farms. Now it is just about like any other road in the home counties. All the fields are quite large, the hedges are cut short, the orchards have been removed and you can see all around you where it used to be so closed in. You might now see some big white cows in the fields, which are Charolais, replacing the original red and red-and-white Shorthorns of the area. These represent changes I have made myself, sweeping away the obstructions to economic farming when under financial pressure, and they include pulling up the hedges during the Second World War when we were trying to produce as much grain as possible. Some people may say that doing this has ruined the environment, but, when it came down to it, I didn't have much choice, just as my neighbours had no choice in cutting down their orchards, which used to be so beautiful, because of fruit tree diseases and the falling demand for cooking apples.

The farming land around Little Grove has always been good for this area. In 1804 Arthur Young, a Suffolk farmer, made a survey of this part of the Chilterns when he was covering Hertfordshire on behalf of the Board of Agriculture. He and other people reported to Lord Sheffield, the Chairman of the Board, on the state of agriculture in various counties of Britain. The idea seems to have been to exchange information so that each area could improve itself.

Grove Lane then and now. The left-hand photograph was taken around the start of the First World War. The road is not made up and the high hedges are right on the edges of the road. In the right-hand picture you can see how the hedges have been moved back and the road is, of course, now tarmacked.

Young was full of admiration for the system of crop rotation in use in Hertfordshire at that time. It was as follows: first year turnips, second year barley, third year clover, fourth year wheat and fifth year oats, and it was in general use around Berkhamsted and Hemel Hempstead. (He quotes one man in the area who substituted fallow for the turnips, and peas for the clover.) Rotating the type of crop grown was necessary in those days because plants suffer from diseases and those diseases are passed on from year to year. Therefore, if a farmer grew the same crop every year there was a rapid build-up of infection in the soil and yields declined. But if he varied the crop each year in any particular field there was less carry-over of disease because different crops have different disease patterns. Although they were unaware of it, this was one of the main reasons why even in the Middle Ages men left land fallow for a year or two – they just *knew* that when they brought it back into cultivation the yield would be better.

Another way of improving the yield was to introduce fertiliser into the soil in the form of manure. This was traditionally done by feeding livestock on the root crop in the field where it was grown. In order to make sure the dung was evenly distributed, the animals were penned into a small area at a time with hurdles that had to be moved every day. This was known as folding, and Young mentions that everybody around Berkhamsted had a flock of sheep to fold on the turnips. In addition, large quantities of night-soil from the towns, especially London, were ploughed in, together with soot and ashes from the same source.

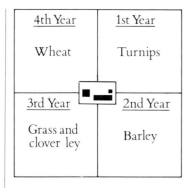

4th Year	1st Year
Wheat	Turnips
3rd Year	2nd Year
Grass and clover ley	Barley

The classic Norfolk four-course rotation system which was widely adopted during the eighteenth century. The turnip crop replaced the fallow period which had been used since the Middle Ages to restore fertility to the land and, later on, to destroy weeds. With the new system the weeds could still be eradicated by hoeing and the turnips were fed to the livestock. The grass and clover also provided fodder in the form of hay and these two crops were returned to the land in the form of manure.

There was one other way in which the soil here was treated to improve its chemical composition. Curiously, within sometimes only a few feet of the chalk subsoil in the Chilterns, the clay land on the top is extremely acid. It must have grown very poor crops until farmers found that, if they dug the chalk out from down below and spread it on the clay on top, this corrected the deficiency and made it possible to grow much better crops. This digging of the chalk and spreading it over the land has had a bigger influence than anything else on the Chiltern landscape. Everywhere you look, there are chalkpits – big chalkpits cut out of the side of a hill where the chalk was drawn out by horses, and little pits dug down into the top of the hill where the chalk was lifted out by manpower with a bucket and windlass and spread about the land. Careful and efficient eighteenth-century and early nineteenth-century landlords and farmers planted all these pits with beech trees to supply the local industry, and the unique landscape of fields dotted with very small spinneys and woods results in a great part from this. Of course, there are a few woods deliberately planted for sporting purposes or for commercial purposes on bad land to serve the timber industry in Chesham. But, for the most part, if you stand on top of the hills here and look around the valleys you will see little spinneys. Go and investigate them, and you will find each one has the remains of a hole in the middle where people laboured away, drawing up the chalk and spreading it on the land, making it possible to grow better crops.

All this added up to what Young in 1804 considered to be a good system of farming. But over the following century it began to decline. Labour was increasingly attracted into the towns as the Industrial Revolution took hold, which meant that farm help became more expensive. Then the repeal of the Corn Laws in 1840 allowed foreign grain to flood in and the price of corn fell in relation to the cost of labour. Soon the labour-intensive method of cleaning crops – hand-weeding – had become uneconomic and farmers therefore began to replace the root break (turnips) with a fallow one again every three or four years. The weeds on the land which was left fallow could then be destroyed by turning the soil over using a horse-drawn cultivator during the summer period when the weather was dry.

Another advantage of reintroducing this fallow break was one which farmers at the time may not actually have appreciated. Land without anything growing in it, if it's kept loose and aerated, becomes heavily populated with bacteria which fix nitrogen from

Sheep being folded to ensure the land was fertilised evenly.

The Hertfordshire five-course system admired by Arthur Young added another grain crop – oats. By the mid-nineteenth century labour had become too expensive to be used for hand-hoeing root crops so the fallow break was reinstated in place of turnips.

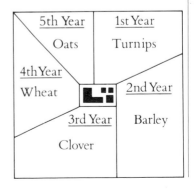

the air as nitrates in the ground, resulting in an actual positive build-up of fertility. This was a particularly important reason for having a fallow break in the Chilterns because it is such a dry area. Before 1920 there was a total absence of water – no springs, no rivers, no streams – in the whole of the parish of Ashley Green, our parish. A few farms had very deep wells which yielded a supply, but these were in the minority. Consequently, keeping livestock was always very difficult and, as labour became more expensive, so the flocks of sheep which Young reported in 1804 gradually dwindled; folding sheep was too labour-intensive to be economical and so they had to go, along with the manure they provided.

The other important source of fertiliser was the night-soil collected by 'scavengers' from households in London and the dung from the cab and dray horses which could be traded for hay and straw. Some of the farmers in this area who were near the Grand Union Canal had their own wharves and they transported both their fodder and their dung on barges. They were the lucky ones. Such farms retained their fertility far better than those on the hills which were dependent on road transport. But even this system of restoring fertility had come to an end by the First World War, when horses gave way to motor transport, and there was really nothing to replace it. In any case, it was not a very effective method; there was always more taken from the soil than was replaced.

Loading crops, in this case potatoes, on a barge on the Grand Union Canal. On the right you can see the weighing machine used, many of which survived until very recently.

So, introducing a fallow year helped to restore fertility to the land in the absence of livestock and also enabled the farmer to clean the soil of weeds through cultivation. Against this, there was a slight price to pay. One disease, I think called 'Take All', actually multiplies in empty land in the summer and crops of wheat following fallow can have whole patches wiped out by this the next year.

By 1918 artificial manures had become available, but they were expensive, unreliable and unpopular. With insufficient livestock to return enough fertility to the land and, at the same time, hand labour for cleaning crops of corn having gone right out because it was too expensive, there was still a strong case for having part of every farm fallow each year and almost every farmer did so. Moreover it spread the work of the farm. You worked the fallow in the early summer and killed all the weeds; then there wasn't too much else to do and it was ready in good time for planting in the autumn. It was nearly always followed by a good crop of wheat.

Some elderly farmers still believe in this system. One operating in this area now, Maurice Brown of Marchant's Farm, still continues to have a proportion of his farm in fallow. When asked why he does it, for it quite obviously isn't necessary nowadays

RANSOMES, SIMS & JEFFERIES, Ld.,
NEW PATENT COMBINED
STEEL CULTIVATOR, RIDGER AND HORSE HOE.
THE "TRIPLEX."

All the farmers in the Chilterns would have used this type of horse-drawn cultivator to aerate the soil and kill the weeds.

when you've got artificial fertilisers, sprays to kill the pests and an infinite variety of crops you can grow to break any cycle of disease, he said: 'Because it's the right way to do things' and went on to argue with me that it would be a way of controlling grain surpluses. Of course, if it's a method of increasing production it is not a way of controlling grain surpluses. Basically he meant that because it had always been done that way and had worked, it was the right way to do things – and so he continues to do it.

By the First World War, both the farming system and the countryside I remember with such nostalgia and which had so impressed Arthur Young had fallen into decay. Cheap labour and natural fertilisers were no longer available and the continuous drain on the fertility of the land had left it severely impoverished. The good rotation system of 1804 had degenerated into a simple sort of fallow and grain rotation which left farmers vulnerable. They were too reliant on a stable price for corn and because of the lack of water, unable to switch to livestock in times of hardship as farmers in other parts of the country could.

Just as the countryside itself was in a static or declining state, so were the people. They were close people. Families had been there almost since the Reformation and though the population had grown, the number of families remained the same. In particular, the little villages like Whelpley Hill and Ashley Green had hardly changed. Considering that it is quite close to London – only 30 miles or so – the population was extraordinarily detached from the rest of the country. I can remember an old man living at Ashley Green, who had never seen a railway, although he was only three miles from Berkhamsted. He used to say that, maybe when he retired, if he ever did, he would visit Berkhamsted Station. Normally, however, he never went any further than the pub at the other end of the village. He did this every Saturday night; his wife always had to fetch him back in a barrow.

The countryside in those days was much more self-contained because transport, with a pony and cart, was relatively slow. Therefore, the village shops stocked all sorts of goods and groceries, which they could never afford to do nowadays. In Ashley Green, there was a baker called Mr Palmer – nowadays pronounced 'Parmer' but in those days pronounced 'Pallmer'. He used to bake and deliver three or four times a week. The bread was a nasty pale grey colour. At times you found grey bits of cobweb and stuff in it and, it was reputed, occasionally mice, though we never found any ourselves.

Of all the farms in the area, the one that appeared to be the most run-down, the most closed-in and the most difficult to see from the outside because of the size and overgrown state of the hedges, was the one next door to us at Little Grove. The hedges were almost the size of the woods – thick and encroaching into the fields. The fields were not properly worked, and the farm itself was surrounded by thick trees and under-growth consisting of holly and yellow broom, which looked pretty in the summer but ensured you could not see in at all from the outside. This was The Grove, also known as Grove Farm. Like most of the farms in the area, its buildings were inadequate even though they did not need to be big because of the absence of livestock. They consisted of a pleasant farmhouse built of local brick; a stable block of the same brick for the working horses with a loft over; a few black-boarded loose boxes and a big barn with a tiled roof and boarded sides, which had originally been used for threshing by hand under cover. They were all old and in a state of disrepair.

The farmer was a man called Benny Wingrove – stout, with a red beard and a bad temper. There were 'TRESPASSERS WILL BE PROSECUTED' signs everywhere. When you popped your nose

The stack-yard around the half-ruined 'chapel' on Grove Farm looking as neglected as when I first saw it. The trees crowding in on the buildings gave the farm a secretive mysterious air.

through a hedge, Benny Wingrove would roar at you to get out at once and, of course, this made the place rather exciting. My brother, who was five years older than me, was full of romantic tales about everything. He used to keep me entertained with stories about the moat which ran round The Grove and some old ruins nearby. The stories were actually true but he used to embroider them by saying the place was haunted. In fact quite a lot of people in the neighbourhood did consider that the ruins must be haunted because of their age – they dated back to medieval times.

In the middle of the wood which surrounded The Grove there was an old stone building, then used as a barn, which is marked on old maps as a chapel. (I never thought at the time that I should finish up living in it.) One day, when my brother was home from boarding school, he agreed to take me over to have a look. Terrified of meeting Mr Wingrove, we crept through the wood. The first thing I remember as I cowered behind my brother was a privy which hung over the moat. It was a three-seater like those you sometimes see illustrated in stories about the American backwoods – a simple wooden construction, sticking out over a dry piece of the moat, with three doors, each with a heart-shaped opening cut out of them. Two of the privies were full-sized and the third one was for children. Moving on through the wood and around the farm, we suddenly spotted an old man, dressed in an off-white smock, sitting on an upturned bucket with a gun between his knees and an umbrella folded up beside him. He was very pale and appeared to be asleep. This was not Benny Wingrove but 'Old Uncle'. He was a mysterious old man who apparently spent all his daylight hours sitting in the wood, waiting for pigeons to alight on the trees. If they came, I do not believe he ever saw them and, if he had seen them, I am sure he could not have shot them. My brother claimed Old Uncle was over a hundred years old and that his gun was a muzzle loader. He sat there every day of his life. I remember thinking to myself at the time, 'Will anybody know when he dies – will they even notice?' That set me to thinking, 'I wonder if he is already dead'. I longed to go and prod him to see if he was alive, but did not dare to do so. Eventually, in 1920, Old Uncle disappeared so I suppose he did finally die or disintegrated into a pile of dust.

How I Found It

I never remember my father being particularly strict with us, though we did have to work for every penny of pocket money we had. We were also expected to eat every bit of food put in front of us – whatever it was – whether we liked it or not. I liked most things and, therefore, it was not too hard on me. But there was one thing that I absolutely loathed and this was tapioca pudding. Times without number, I would be shut up in a room with the tapioca that I had refused to eat and told that I would not get anything else to eat or be released from the room until I had eaten it up. The effect of this was that I became, in my own view, the world's greatest expert at disposing of tapioca without actually eating it. First, I tried throwing it out of the window but, of course, it hung in great strings down the wall outside. Even in pouring rain, it remained there for hours and hours and could be clearly seen. Therefore, I was fed yet more tapioca to teach me that good food must not be thrown away. In the end, after various methods had been tried, I discovered that you could rub it into the underside of the carpet and it would never be found until spring cleaning, by which time, nobody would be able to identify exactly what it was. There were just some nasty slippery stains under the carpets every time they were taken up to be spring cleaned.

When you were with him, my father always made you feel more grown-up than you were. He talked to you like an adult about interesting things and listened to what you had to say. I think this was quite rare in those days. I remember being on the beach at Carbis Bay in Cornwall one year just after the First World War and, having heard so much talk about farming, not surprisingly I was playing farms not castles. I had some ordinary yellow sand which I was ploughing up and down with my spade, a wooden spade made in Chesham, and, of course, turning it over and making it a slightly darker, damp colour. My father asked me what I was doing and I said I was ploughing. He approved and showed me the way you started and finished ploughing a field. A few minutes later, I was spreading some different colour sand on the field. He again asked me what I was doing and I said 'I am spreading sulphate of phosphate'. Quite sharply he said, 'There is

Shire horses going into the army at Ivinghoe. My father bought some when they came out at Watford.

Me, aged about two, Lola and Bobby.

no such thing, there is sulphate of ammonia which you use and there is sulphate of potash which you may use. If you want to put on phosphate, you would probably use basic slag', and he went and got some dark-coloured sand and said 'That will do for basic slag'. Basic slag was the commonest source of phosphate in those days and is a by-product of iron foundries. Although I didn't understand anything about chemical compounds, I never forgot that basic slag was what you used for phosphate. Although he spoke sharply, he spoke as though he was talking to somebody much older than the seven years that I then was.

Most vividly of all, I remember being woken by my father quite late at night during the same holiday, and being taken up on a cliff-top to see a ship which was stranded on the rocks below. He thought, quite rightly, that I would never see anything of this sort again in the rest of my life and, therefore, should be woken up to see it. It was the most dramatic scene – bright moonlight on the top of high Cornish cliffs with the stricken ship on the rocks below being buffeted about.

When the First World War broke out my father tried several times to join the army, although he was over age. He was not accepted as being fit enough, which is hardly surprising since he died almost immediately after the war. One or two friends of his who did see life in the trenches came down when they were on leave. I remember one friend coming who had had his leg off. Another cousin of mine had very serious wounds. They seemed to take it all with extraordinary cheerfulness. They played with us and joked about their injuries and we looked forward to their visits. Their cheerfulness has always struck me as quite extraordinary.

In 1917 the country's food supplies were being threatened by the German U-boat campaign and the coalition government thought it necessary to do something to increase food production at home. It's quite remarkable really how late in the war this happened. Up until that moment they must have had complete confidence in the market system – that is, that a shortage of any commodity will result in high prices which will cause people to produce more. In actual fact production of wheat fell in the first two years of the war and by the autumn of 1917 the government was worried enough to pass a bill giving guaranteed prices to farmers for wheat, oats and potatoes. Nothing else – nothing for barley for example. The prices were even made to be retrospective so that the 1916 harvest and the 1917 harvest were covered and all harvests up to 1922 at a gradually reducing price level. The fact that the Act, known as the Corn Production Act, fixed a final date for the measures shows that the government did not regard this as a permanent feature of agricultural policy. Unfortunately, many farmers did not take the hint.

The price for the first two years was 60 shillings a quarter for wheat, which is £13.50 a ton. In comparison with modern prices of over £100.00 per ton this doesn't sound very much until looked at in comparison with wages which were also guaranteed under the Act at 25 shillings a week. So, in effect, a hundredweight of wheat would easily pay a man's wages for a whole week and now in 1985 one ton of wheat would barely do it. This is a measure of how much cheaper grain has become over the years because of modern technology.

In our particular area some farmers seem to have responded to the Act's encouragement and the unfortunate Mr Ford at Shepherds Farm, Ley Hill, probably started his large usage of artificial fertiliser under that stimulus and had his entire farm ploughed for grain. On the other hand Benny Wingrove at Grove Farm apparently didn't alter his methods in the least. He made no effort to plough up the areas of uncultivated land, which had to wait for my father before anything was done about them, and seems to have gone on in his usual way, as did the other traditionalists among the local farmers. When the Act was quite suddenly repealed in 1921 and the price of grain collapsed over-night to less than half, no doubt the traditionalists thought that they had been right not to alter their ways. The unfortunate people like Mr Ford who had tried to enter into the spirit of the thing and increase production came badly unstuck.

So much in farming is a matter of confidence. The government introducing a guaranteed price structure so late in the war was unlikely to have had any dramatic effect on production, and the failure to do so earlier reflects the *laissez faire* attitude of politicians at that time. They believed that, left to itself, the market would take care of everything. But the real damage to agriculture was caused by the repeal of the Act which really knocked the stuffing out of all the more progressive farmers. Some went out of business altogether, and those that survived didn't recover their confidence until well into the Second World War. Even then, the older ones always had at the back of their minds the fear that immediately the war was over the same thing would happen again and all government support would be withdrawn.

The Corn Production Act's guarantee seems to have been given without any limit on quantity and, as far as one can see, with very little effort to maintain quality. I suppose the quantities which were going to be produced were quite small anyway, and in those days, when corn was produced in the traditional manner, there wasn't the same trouble with quality as there is now. The main outcome of the whole episode was the feeling among farmers and farm workers that: 'They never want us except when there's a war on' and this attitude was maintained right up until the time when I started farming in 1931 and thereafter.

The attitude of local people during the First World War was strange. Though miles away from any action, they were extremely nervous. All the young men were away at the front, having nearly all volunteered. On the war memorial at Ashley Green there are twenty-two names from the First World War, when the population of the area was small, and only four names for the Second World War when the population was much larger. That twenty-two must have been a high proportion of the men eligible for military service. The other people and the children who were left behind were not well-informed and, I suppose, in that atmosphere they became more nervous and suspicious than they otherwise would have been.

Anybody who was suspected of being a German was in a certain amount of danger. There was, at that time, a family living in Lye Green House called Teschmaker, who were of Austrian extraction, but the village was convinced they were German. One night, straw, tar, paraffin and so on were assembled and people gathered in the dark. They were going to burn the house down. Fortunately somebody fetched the police out from Chesham and the locals disappeared into the darkness. Mr Teschmaker subsequently changed his name to Lockton and, after that, people seemed to leave him competely alone.

I remember being out in Grove Lane with my sister, Alf Newland and a roadman at about this time. An observation balloon drifted slowly over us at tree height and one of the two men in the basket called out 'Where are we?'. Everybody answered differently. One person said Orchard Leigh, which was true. Somebody else answered Chesham because that was where they were coming from. Yet another person called out Berkhamsted because this was the direction in which they were going. The balloon men drifted on looking helpless and none the wiser. Then, as they drifted north-west of us, they passed over Grove Farm and I could hear loud obscenities about the Kaiser and Germany, etc. This was obviously Mr Wingrove in his usual temper. Following this there were the sounds of two shots, which must have been either Mr Wingrove or Old Uncle shooting at the balloonists because they were convinced they were Germans about to invade the country.

The only clue I had at that time that somewhere or other there was a wider sort of countryside than that of the Chilterns, with larger fields and better tended hedges, was from Mr Newland, the gardener. He came from Norfolk, and when I was playing in the garden he would regale me with stories of how much better farmers worked their land in Norfolk, how much bigger the fields were and how much heavier the crops. He had an extremely poor opinion of farmers in Bucks and he thought the very worst was Ben Wingrove. He used to say that before Ben Wingrove took over Grove Farm it had been quite well farmed and that the previous tenant – Duke Batchelor – had had record crops.

Newland was quite an interesting character. He was, in a sense, the first influence under which I came, because he was there all the time in the garden, and children play in gardens. Little boys always listen to gardeners and I listened to every word he said. He was by way of being a Methodist lay preacher. Every weekend he used to go off to preach in one of the little chapels which then abounded in the villages. He considered himself a great expert on the Bible and told me so. For a while, I believed him in preference to whatever I might have been taught by anybody else. As well as being a lay preacher, he was also a radical politician fond of slogans such as, 'God gave the land to the people'. This made me

The Chesham Allotment Holders' Association having an annual meeting at Little Grove. Alf Newland is the second from the left sitting down, not a member but a judge at their vegetable shows. My mother was presumably presenting the prizes that year.

think 'Thank God God gave my father a bit because otherwise I should have nowhere to be' and 'Why did God give Mr Lowndes [who owned a lot of the surrounding land] and Lord Chesham quite so much? Why didn't he give other people, including Alf Newland himself, a bit?' I did not actually ask Mr Newland these things. He would have had a political answer if I had.

Although a radical in politics and a lay preacher, Alf was the most terrible snob. He made it absolutely clear to me that, although my father was all right, he was grossly inferior to the people he used to work for in his native Norfolk, all of whom were called Squire Somebody-or-other and lived in Something-or-other Hall. All these people had two or three gardeners and they certainly would not have expected him to look after cows and pigs as well. They also had large greenhouses for propagating, whereas my father had only a small one. As he was satisfied to work for my father for quite a while, I suppose there was some reason why he did not go back to his native Norfolk. I later suspected he had been involved in some scandal unfitting to a lay preacher.

Another thing he used to say against my father was that Squire So-and-so always provided his gardeners with green baize aprons, which was the proper dress for a gardener. When he mentioned this to my father, he just laughed and said, 'That's what porters in my London business wear for cleaning silver and you don't clean any silver.' When Mr Newland insisted that he should have a green baize apron, my father brought a shop-worn one down from London which he refused to wear. I suppose other people were the same in those days but he had a curious formality about what he would and wouldn't do. He always wore a dicky – a detachable stiff shirt front – to work. When he started work, he would take it off and hang it on a tree. It was always very grubby, but I suppose it was a badge of respectability, rather like the way that, in those days, foremen on building sites always wore bowler hats. Wherever Mr Newland was working in the garden, you would see, hanging on a bush or a tree nearby, his dicky.

One night, very soon after the war was over, my father, who had now decided he wanted to farm on a proper scale, came home and told my mother he had bought Grove Farm – just like that – with the disagreeable Benny Wingrove as temporary farm manager. I don't know what it was that made my father so interested in farming, born and brought up in London as he was. It may have been a family memory handed down through three previous generations of ancestors who had been farmers in Sussex. It may have been contact with Charles Weld Blundell, the man who financed and started the family business in Bond Street, who had an estate in Lancashire. It may just have been that his experience at Little Grove Farm led him to want to farm on a larger scale. He had obviously applied his mind to the theory of farming long before this point because I remember when I was very young that the house was always full of *The Farmer and Stockbreeder* and there were books lying around about fertilisers and seeds.

I only remember my father having one farming friend, a Doctor Reeve, who had Bury Farm, Chesham, at the time. He didn't farm it for long, but I remember hearing him laying down law to my father who was, on the whole, listening and I also remember my father trying to impress him by having a large heap of enormous mangel-wurzels piled in our hall, to my mother's disgust, when Dr Reeve came to dinner. These had been grown by Alf Newland under garden conditions, mangels of a variety called 'Golden Tankard', but I think my father wanted to give the impression that they had been grown as a field crop.

The front page of The Farmer and Stockbreeder *the week war broke out. To my mind no farming paper has looked as good as this since.*

> Mr Benjamin Wingrove of Grove Farm Ashley Green agrees to sell
> to Mr. Sydney Bellamy Harman of Ashley Green who agrees to buy
> for the sum of £1600 all his interest in the tenancy of Grove
> Farm Ashley Green and all the live stock and dead farming stock
> and effects cultivations manures hay straw and other things
> whatsoever thereat excepting only the two stacks of Hay sold to
> the Government and the Wheat in Stack which Wheat is to be
> threshed at the expense of Mr. Wingrove who is to have the use
> of the necessary farm hands and horses when threshing or deliver-
> ing same. The said sum of £1600 is to include any moneys due to
> Mr. Wingrove from Mr. Harman at the date hereof whether for
> work and labour done or otherwise and also all claims by Mr.
> Wingrove under the Agricultural Holdings Acts or otherwise how-
> ever on Mr. Harman. The sale and purchase shall be completed
> on the 28th April 1919 up to which day all outgoings shall be
> discharged by Mr. Wingrove, excepting only the rent and rates
> in respect of the said Farm which shall be paid by Mr. Harman
> as from the 25th March 1919.
>
>   It is further agreed that Mr. Harman shall engage Mr.
> Wingrove and Mr Wingrove shall serve Mr. Harman as Farm Bailiff
> as from the said 28th April 1919 until the 29th September 1920 and
> thereafter from year to year determinable on the 29th September
> in any year by either party giving to the other six calendar
> months previous notice in writing. The remuneration payable by
> Mr. Harman to Mr. Wingrove for such service shall be the sum of £3
> per week and the said Mr. Wingrove shall during such service have
> the use of the said Grove Farm House as a residence for himself
> and his family.
>
>   Dated this 26th day of April 1919

When my father bought Grove Farm the valuation of the live and dead stock (i.e. animals and equipment) was not drawn up by an agent in the normal way. Instead my father negotiated directly with Benny Wingrove – a typical display of his distrust of professionals.

Grove Farm had belonged for a long time to the family of Lowndes who lived in Chesham. The member of the family who was in control in 1918–19 was known as Toby Lowndes because of his appearance, which was like a funny little toby jug. My mother always said that my father must have caught him at a time when he was pushed for a bit of money and, against all the rules, offered him some immediate cash instead of waiting for normal solicitors' arrangements to buy the farm. This was at a time when a lot of landowners were panicking about the value of their estates. They probably saw, which their tenants didn't, that the war-time

From Toogoods

315 lbs Cocksfoot
105 " Hard Fescue
52 " Sheeps do
315 " Meadow do
105 Rough Stalked Meadow Grass
52 Smooth do do
105 Foxtail
25 Yarrow
___
80 lbs Alsike
52 " Perennial White Clover
50 " Wild Clover
___
1 years lay Grasses + Clovers
20 lbs per acre 15 acres
180 Pure Red Clover) for 15 acres
30 Alsike   ) 1 years lay

My father's list of the grass and clover seeds he ordered from the Southampton firm of Toogoods for sowing down the farm. It was a much more complicated mixture than would be used today.

arrangements for the guaranteed price of grain were going to be removed sooner or later.

Very soon after my father had bought Grove Farm, a small estate of four or five farms belonging to some people called Curtis and running through Whelpley Hill up to our land came on the market. The nearest one was Moors Farm and my father arranged via Charlie Simms, who was the tenant at the time and therefore in a strong position to negotiate, to buy the 27 acres nearest to us, in addition to Grove Farm itself. I remember Charlie Simms, who was a rosy-faced bearded man, coming to see my father about it, and I

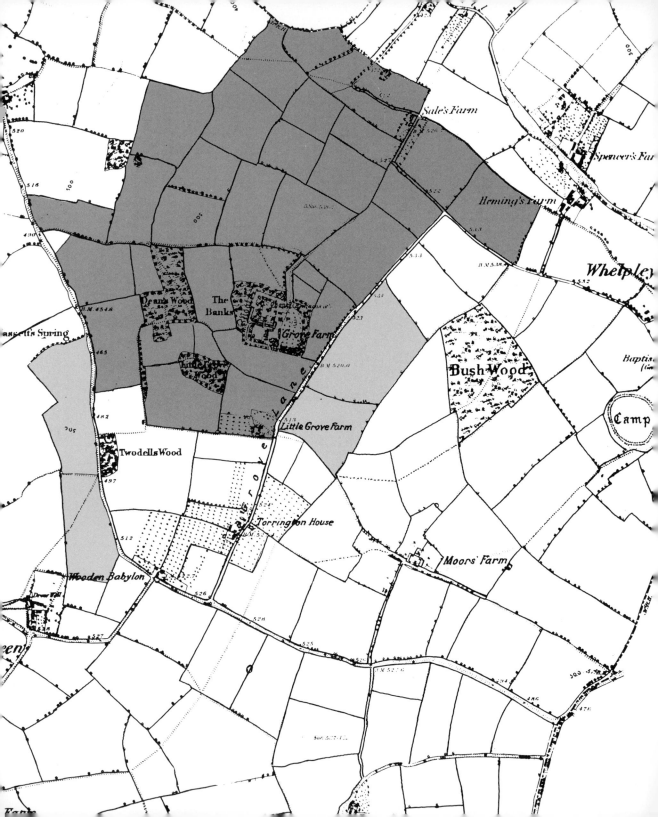

can also remember walking over to Moors Farm with my father. At the same time, 20 acres or so on the other side of the farm owned by a man called Moses Payne came up for sale. He was an enormously fat man who, I always understood, was the illegitimate son of one of the previous tenants of Grove Farm, Duke Batchelor (he of the record crops). Moses came over in his pony cart to see my father. My memory is of thinking how on earth would he get out of his governess cart which he filled from side to side like a cork in a bottle. My sister's memory is that of my father who was very, very thin, getting up beside him in the pony cart, and them looking the most ill-assorted couple as they went down to see the fields.

So, within a very, very short space of time, the whole scene had changed. My father was poised to add quite a fair-sized farm, plus these additional acres, to his 25 acres at Little Grove, and I think he went in for intensive reading of all the advisory literature he could get, particularly as to the sowing down of arable land to grass since he intended to go in for livestock. There were a lot of leaflets lying about the place and I still have some notes in his handwriting of the mixes of seed he intended to use and I remember the seeds being mixed on the floor of an empty cottage.

Opposite is the 1883 Ordnance Survey map with Little Grove plus all the land my father bought from Toby Lowndes in 1919 indicated by the dark shading, and the fields he bought from Mr Curtis and Moses Payne indicated by the light shading. The countryside had changed little in the intervening years and the map shows so much detail that it conjures up in my mind an actual picture of how everything then was.

Businessman turned Farmer

Grove Farm was in a pretty run down condition when my father took it on. Benny Wingrove had not taken advantage of the war-time situation to pull it up, and quite a lot of the land had not been worked at all for very many years. It was actually quite a poor farm, much of it steep and sticky stony land, but the extra land my father had bought from the other two vendors at about the same time was a good deal better.

Before Mr Wingrove, the tenant of Grove had been the legendary Duke Batchelor, whom Alf Newland had so admired. Although Alf blamed all the poor state of the farm at that time on Mr Wingrove, I think it was more likely to have been because the farm had an even worse water supply than most of the surrounding farms, having no deep well. Consequently very few animals had been kept and, the straw and hay trade to London having stopped, no fertilisers to speak of had been applied for a great number of years. Benny Wingrove had also originally been a butcher on the side and I think he kept a few cattle there for a very short term, buying them and finishing them up ready for use in his shop. At the time my father took it over, all the stock that was there were two cows, one red one and one blue one (actually a sort of grey colour), five heavy horses for working, not at all in good condition, a cob, one sow and, of course, her progeny from time to time.

In addition to the 200 acres of arable and woodland, there was an orchard of extraordinarily large apple, pear and walnut trees, the largest I have ever seen in my life, as big as the big beech trees which surrounded the farm. In the season, Mrs Wingrove would take the fruit in the pony cart down to Chesham to sell and, some years, there were literally tons of walnuts. But, on the whole, the farm was not productive and my father had to set about improving it with the knowledge he had gained from books and from his short experience with a very very small farm indeed. There was no advisory service that I know of then that would send people round to see you as there is now, only various agricultural leaflets which he apparently did have.

The labour on the farm, apart from Benny Wingrove himself and his son Albert, who was a very delicate forty-year-old on the

The moat around Grove Farm. This was the sole source of water for the livestock before my father had mains water laid on in 1919.

Walt Batchelor, according to his son-in-law, 'pissed on his way to a wedding'.

point of death, comprised Walt Batchelor (no relation to the famous Duke) and his son, George, who had just come out of the army. They looked after the horses and did all the ploughing and were known as 'horsemen'. There was also a little old hunchback, Joe Elborne, who did the odd jobs around the place, and my father took on Arthur Waller as a tractor driver. There had previously been a man called Dick Blunt who, for reasons I have never been told, hung himself in Cowcroft Wood about that time and he had been replaced by George Batchelor, who remained there until about 1937 when he left the area. There has been considerable continuity of labour on Grove Farm. For example Walt Batchelor originally started working there at the beginning of the century and one of his daughters, Flo, married Will Barnett, who started working for me when I took over the farm, and they are still with us. This sort of continuity of employment within a family is quite common in farming, and not all that common in other industries.

The rotation system in use on Grove Farm when my father took it over was just about as simple as a rotation could be. It was fallow, followed by winter-sown wheat, followed either by winter-sown oats or by spring-sown barley. In the case of the spring barley it would be under-sown with clover. This would grow up under the protection of the barley and provide a crop of hay the following summer. In the case of the winter oats it would be followed by a fallow and both the clover break and the fallow break would come back into wheat again. So it was a simple three-course rotation. But it did have the effect of enabling Benny Wingrove to keep the land clean and to get some sort of a crop with a minimum of bought-in fertilisers. The only variation that ever took place was that just sometimes a little of the fallow land was planted with mangels to store for the winter for the one or two cows. This 'mangel-land', which would never have been more than about 2 acres, would be sown late with wheat after the mangels had been harvested so as not to disturb the rotation.

Very little produce was sold off the farm. The yield of wheat was never more than 18 cwt to the acre and probably didn't average more than 15 cwt, so if Benny had 50 acres of wheat he would have been selling only about 36 or 37 tons of wheat a year. The oats would have been kept to feed the horses and perhaps 10 or 12 tons of barley could have been sold. So, like everybody else in the district except those who had adequate water and could keep dairy cattle, he was extremely vulnerable to the rapid decline in corn prices which took place after the First World War.

The farm hands were paid something like 30 shillings a week a piece – not a lot but it must still have been quite a struggle to keep the farm going. I suppose the rent was low and it was possible to live off the land a bit. Benny kept some poultry and Mrs Wingrove didn't sell all the eggs. They probably killed a pig twice a year. Also there were rabbits galore and a bit of garden so they grew their own vegetables. Altogether it was a very simple uncommercial sort of farm, as were most of the farms in the area at that time.

It was a pretty simple sort of life all round. There was no real water supply on the farm, so no baths, just a wash with a bucket of water drawn up, not from a spring well but from a water tank which collected the water off the rooves and in a dry year it must have been pretty awful. There wasn't even any fresh drinking water so you drank milk or beer and beer there always was both for Benny Wingrove and for his men. They were quite obsessed with it, so much so that when Walter Batchelor inherited a small sum of money from a distant relation, he spent almost all of it on barrels of beer and one was set up in the field when they were ploughing so that he or the other ploughmen or Benny Wingrove could stop at any time during the day and have a swig if they were minded to do so. Almost all the small legacy went in this way, according to his son George, except that he had a bicycle out of it, and all his life George felt that the legacy might have been spent better.

I don't know what those people thought when my father, a businessman, who they knew already as a neighbour, took over the farm. They may or may not have approved of it. But what he did must have immediately improved their lives no end because in a matter of months water was laid on both to the cottages and to the farm house and to some of the fields so that they could start to have baths, drink clean water and more livestock could be kept. Water is the key to everything in a dry area like the Chilterns.

There were 40 acres of land on Grove Farm which were steep, or in small enclosures, which were just not worked at all. If there was a good growing season, the grass was cut for hay. If there was a bad growing season, I don't think anything was done with it at all. The rent Benny paid to Mr Lowndes had been very low so I suppose he could afford to behave in that way. Around the farmhouse itself, where he and his family lived, were about 12 acres of very small old meadows which were quite good and these were used to graze the working horses. The arable land that was cultivated received practically no bought-in fertiliser. The farm was a long way from the canal and even in the booming days of the

When anyone died in Whelpley Hill Mrs Batchelor laid them out.

early nineteenth century it probably didn't get the manure out of London that farmers nearer to the canal did. Certainly a little hay and straw had once been sent up by road and dung brought back, but that had finished years before and the only fertiliser of any consequence used was soot, ordinary industrial soot. In those days this was quite plentiful from factories, all of which were coal burning. It had two beneficial effects on the land: firstly, it contains quite a lot of ammonia, which is a form of nitrate, and some other chemicals, and secondly, it darkens the soil which makes it warm up quicker in the spring. It used to be applied in early spring to the winter corn and would help it forward. Benny might also have bought a little sulphate of ammonia but I suspect nothing else whatsoever. Therefore there would have been a steady drain on the fertility of the farm.

Altogether, then, a low farming picture, probably nowhere near as good as it would have looked a hundred years previously at the end of the Agricultural Revolution, and a picture that my father set about with a will to try to change but didn't live long enough to do so. As soon as he took over, things became quite different. He had looked into the requirements of the crops and with the limited knowledge then available, proceeded to try to supply their needs artificially with bought-in fertilisers. In fact, starting to farm seriously for the first time, it turned out that my father had a natural gift for anticipating problems. He was only to be in occupation of Grove Farm for two years before he died, but in that two years he achieved the most tremendous changes. He threw himself into the business of farming with extraordinary enthusiasm.

As I have said, one of the problems with Grove Farm was that, like every other farm in the immediate area, there was hardly any natural water. The moat which dates back to medieval times, provided enough for the five working horses and the two cows which Benny Wingrove kept, but no more. So the first thing that had to be done was to get water laid on from the public supply so that more cattle and livestock of all sorts could be kept. Then, of course, when that was under way, the accommodation for the livestock had to be improved and extended. There was an open yard where the two cows lived which had space for a great deal more and my father put in hand the covering of the whole of this area. All the timber work, which is still there, was locally grown oak, which he insisted on using. In a rather bizarre fashion he then used corrugated iron for the roof, which hardly matched the top-quality oak trusses underneath. The work was done by a builder from Chesham called Mr Keen, who was also an undertaker and there were continual absences of himself and his men from their work. Usually we were told this was because there was a 'flu epidemic and he had funerals to do, so he would have to leave the roof for another time.

The other building work which was put in hand was accommodation for pigs. Twelve second-hand army wash-houses were bought and converted into pig-styes. This was never really a success but it seemed a good idea at the time. The pigs had already been bought and were looked after in the meantime by Alf Newland at buildings which were near our house at Little Grove. The pigs were a breed called 'Large Black', which is not all that common nowadays. There was a boar, an enormous, fearsome-looking animal with great long tusks called 'Ally Sloper' (which, I gather, was the name of a character in an early strip cartoon) and twelve completely anonymous sows. Imagine our delight when Ally Sloper ripped Newland's trousers with his tusks during feeding.

The working horses at Grove when my father took it over had a rather unpleasant disease called 'greasy heel', possibly because they

A Large Black. The breed was booming at the time so my father established a herd; now they are quite rare.

walked into the water in the moat, which was pretty dirty, to drink, or just because of the generally insanitary conditions in which they had been kept. The disease affects Shire horses and causes them to develop big, nasty-looking lumps amidst the hair on their feet, which is known in Shires as 'feather'. It does not affect horses of other breeds with cleaner legs. These horses were a pretty horrifying sight and soon after he took over my father had the local vet up from Berkhamsted to see them. The vet's name was Captain Wilson and he was absolutely stone deaf. He had a man called Mr Wiltshire to drive him round and interpret for him. Anything you said, you said to Mr Wiltshire, who then put an ear trumpet in Captain Wilson's ear and bellowed in what you were saying. I remember Captain Wilson examining these horses and giving his opinion. At this point, the man who looked after the horses said, 'They stink like buggery'. The interpreter, Mr Wiltshire, turned to Captain Wilson and shouted through the ear trumpet 'He said they have an evil smell'. The man who looked after the horses said, 'That's not what I said, tell him what I said'. The horses turned out to be untreatable and two of them had to be slaughtered. Benny Wingrove then went to a sale of surplus army horses at Watford and two more large Shire horses were bought. I remember their names were 'Dolly' and 'Darling'. Dolly lived for

Walt Batchelor's son, George, holding Darling, one of the ex-army horses bought at Watford. George's son, John, is the rider.

some fifteen or sixteen years afterwards and bred several foals
which remained until my time in farming.

Having attended to the livestock my father's next task was to
improve the cultivation of the land. This he could not do with just
two men and five Shire horses so he bought a tractor, one of the
earliest types marketed on any scale. It was called a 'Titan' and
was a crude-looking thing by modern standards. The plough it
pulled was not operated from the tractor as they are now but by a
man sitting on a seat on the plough itself, lifting it up and down at
the ends.

My father also had contractors in to do a fair amount of work
with other sorts of tractors. I remember there was a land girl from
some firm with another Titan tractor and a neighbour called Pop
Simms, another early tractor-user, with a Fordson. Between the
three tractors and the horses, the work was gradually brought up
to date. This really represented the best part of the first year's work
because extra stock could not be bought until the buildings had
been completed.

At that time, feeding stuffs were still quite dear and, for the
pigs, my father used the contact he had with a cousin of his whose
family ran a wharf in London – Bellamy's Wharf. He bought from
them all the sweepings of the dock where food stuff of various

*My father bought a Titan
tractor like this to help bring
the farm into full production.
This one is pulling a binder.*

sorts was unloaded. Truck loads of mixed brown sugar, dates and Lord knows what came into Chesham Station to be carted up and mixed with the pig food at home. Scientific it certainly was not. Nowadays, pigs are very carefully rationed as to what is good for them, but then things were very much more casual. Pigs were expected to eat what you gave them, regardless of its nutritional value.

For the long-term production of feeding stuff, a large, paraffin-driven stationary engine was bought – a Blackstone – and put in a small, new stone shed at the side of the original large barn. This, through various shafting and pulleys, was to drive a mill, a roller to roll oats, a grinder to grind roots and a chaff cutter. For its time, it was up to date and would have worked well if it had ever been fully put into operation, but my father died within a short time and the farm was never fully stocked. Obviously he had not expected to die so soon judging by the many plans he made for Grove Farm, even though he had been an invalid for a long time.

One aspect of my father's character was that he never really accepted what anybody told him. There were constant arguments with Benny Wingrove about the size of the fields. It was not good enough that the Ordnance Survey gave the acreage. My father used to go and measure them with a long tape, and my sister and I were expected to hold the other end and to understand what he wanted us to do.

In the first year's programme, which had been pretty successful from the harvest point of view, one area had been left out. Thirty acres of steep land known, as steep land often is in the Chilterns, as 'the hangings' had not even been ploughed during the war. It was just going to waste. There were a few plants of sainfoin, grown originally for sheep, but as there had not been any sheep for many years, it was not of much use and was not thick enough for hay. Benny Wingrove said, 'No power on earth would ever make me plough it – it is too difficult' and, sure enough, when they tried to plough it with the 'Titan' tractor, it could not get enough grip. The horses could have done it but only very slowly. So, at that stage, my father brought in ploughing engines, which in those days used to travel the country. There would be two very big steam engines and underneath a drum with a steel cable. One engine would stand each end of the field while they wound the plough, suspended on the steel cable, backwards and forwards, gradually moving the engines up the edges of the field.

The men that ran the steam plough travelled about from farm

to farm. Rather rough and peculiar people, they usually worked in a gang of five, with one on each engine, one on the implement – plough or scuffle (a type of cultivator), whichever they were pulling – one cook and one spare man. The farmer had to provide coal and water for the engines, which used a lot. This kept one farm man busy all the while. The team ploughed the 30 acres in about two days, working all the hours of daylight. This was much faster than any other method available at that time.

I remember the day they arrived, clattering down the road with a great huffing and chuffing of steam engines and rattling of the things behind them. This was all very exciting and I rushed over to the far end of the farm to see them start late in the afternoon. I watched them ploughing up and down the hill for quite a long time until it was nearly dark, then started to walk home and half way across the field practically tripped over their cook, who was lying absolutely dead drunk in the field.

The ploughing of the hangings brought the whole farm into reasonable cultivation and my father then started to put into operation his long-term plan. Right up to that period, the price of

First Hangings, one of the steepest fields on Grove Farm. Horses could only plough this type of land one way – downhill. Over a period of time this resulted in the soil banking to the right because the plough always moved the earth in that direction.

To bring the steep land into cultivation my father hired steam ploughing engines from Boughtons in Amersham, which could pull six or eight furrows both up and down the hangings. The machine shown here ploughed ten furrows at a time - not possible on the difficult Chiltern soil.

grain had been quite good, particularly following the Corn Production Act of 1917, and nobody had bothered to think much about what was going to happen in the future. My father must have guessed that there would be a complete collapse in grain prices within a year or two of the end of the war and, in the spring of 1920, he made arrangements to sow the greater part of the farm, including the hangings, down to proper grass for livestock, rather than the wild stuff which had previously been grown there.

At that time very little scientific research had been put into grass growing. Nowadays, livestock farmers only plant one or two varieties which have been raised by the Welsh Plant Breeding Station or an establishment of that sort. Then, however, you used a great variety, maybe twelve or fifteen different sorts of grass, to make sure that at least one or two would fit the job you wanted them to do. I still have the list of the varieties and mixtures that he used. It would make quite extraordinary reading to a modern farmer. As far as I am aware, nobody else in our particular area was making these sorts of plans, and a good many of the neighbouring farmers, such as poor Mr Ford, were hit by the decline in grain prices two or three years later. Many farms were then just abandoned and allowed to fall down to natural grass, thereby becoming unproductive. In fact, this probably applied to the majority of farms in the Chilterns. Very few of them were properly sown down.

In the September of 1920 my father was operated on for a duodenal ulcer, which had been troubling him for some time, and developed post-operative pneumonia. He came home, but with little hope of recovery and we three children were sent away to an aunt of mine who kept a girls' school in Malvern. He died while we were there and I hated Malvern for it, somehow blaming the town for his death. My stay there meant very little to me. I only really remember two things.

One, I was taken for a day to see a farm at Upton-on-Severn. On the farm were Tamworth pigs, which are red or sandy coloured. They were also growing runner beans for seed, as a crop. I tried both these things later in life. Maybe seeing them in Worcestershire gave me the idea. The other thing I remember was a girl called Trixie Ford. The girls were all much older than I was and I thought Trixie was absolutely beautiful, the first girl I had ever noticed. I don't think I ever spoke to her - I was much too shy, but everything she said and everything she was seemed right to me. I have since heard that she never married - perhaps other men did not agree with my standard of beauty.

When we finally came to leave Malvern after my father had been buried a new friend of my mother's came to fetch us by car, Miss Alice Warrender. She was a formidable spinster lady who lived in a rather dreadful house in Lye Green Road called Bayman Manor. (It was certainly never a manor, just a large Victorian villa.) There she lived in some style with horses, grooms, a car and a chauffeur. Not long after we arrived home, my mother, who was a fairly conventional person, arranged to have us baptised, which my father would never have done. He had strong views about religious matters and was always, I remember, arguing with the vicar of Ashley Green against baptising children when they did not know what was going on. Probably my mother had always disagreed with this. Anyway, soon after he died we were rushed off to London and baptised out of the view of the vicar of Ashley Green so that he should not think he had finally won a victory over my father. Miss Warrender was godmother to us all. It was actually quite a traumatic experience to be baptised at the age of eight at St Paul's Church, Knightsbridge by Prebendary Gough, a rather grand sort of clergyman. I found it all extremely embarrassing, especially as he got my sister's name wrong three times before he finished the job.

The Year for Discoveries

1921 seems to me to have been the year for discoveries. After a sad and dismal winter, everything suddenly opened out and the world around me was filled with an enormous variety of interests. The spring started, with flowers, such as polyanthus, and with Mr Newland telling me about cross-pollination and the breeding of new varieties. So, I made up my mind that I would raise new varieties of polyanthus, because these spring flowers seemed to have more intensity and variety of colour than almost any other flower I could see. Energetically, under his direction, I worked away with a small paintbrush cross-pollinating the different colours, hoping to collect the seeds and breed new varieties. Again, under his direction, I carefully covered the plants with muslin so that the bees should not get at them and undo my work but, of course, I did not take into account the fact that the bees had already been there and the flowers had probably already been pollinated before I started. I duly saved the seeds but did not label them very carefully so that, when they flowered the next year, the results were much the same as before and I bred no new varieties.

I had previously thought of potatoes as being simply something roundish one ate, something white and raw, or yellow and cooked. Suddenly I discovered that there was an enormous variety. People grew them in their gardens with almost as much enthusiasm as they did flowers. There were potatoes with red skins, potatoes with red patches on white skins, purple potatoes, purple and white potatoes, long potatoes, round potatoes – all shapes, sizes and colours. I had a small garden and I planted every variety of potato that I could obtain. Nurserymen then catered for children's gardens by selling collections of two or three potatoes of each of maybe half a dozen different sorts, which I found quite fascinating. I then realised that you could raise your own varieties if you were sufficiently clever and I dreamt of being able to do that one day. I realised though that this took several years in which you had to collect the actual seeds from the flowerheads of the potatoes and grow them. I dreamt of being a great discoverer of new potatoes.

Hardly were the potatoes in and growing than I began to see great variety elsewhere. Chickens then were not as they are now – rather

A Cochin, one of the many fancy breeds of chickens kept in the 1920s.

The Yokohamas, with their immensely long tail feathers, are now very rare.

indeterminate-looking birds which live in cages, laying hundreds and hundreds of eggs. Then there was a wonderful diversity of shape and colour and people kept them in small numbers in their back gardens as a hobby. There were several newspapers devoted to the fancy of poultry-keeping. Some may still exist. I was given a copy of one called *The Poultry World* by somebody and was fascinated by the enormous variety. There was a French breed called Houdans, which had tufts of feathers like hats on their heads. There were breeds called Brahmas and Cochins, which had feathers on their feet – useless, of course, but they were bred for showing in competitions. There were brightly coloured breeds – white, yellow, black, black and white, breeds with combs in the shape of a rose on their head, breeds with great, floppy combs hanging over their eyes – every sort and shape of bird that one could imagine. They had been carefully selected and bred by generations of backyard poultry keepers without regard solely to egg production. There was even a breed said to have been imported from Japan, which had such long tails that they had to spend the whole of their lives on perches, except when they got off to lay eggs. These were called Yokohamas. All these breeds have now disappeared, probably destroyed by scientific investigation aimed at developing the best egg-laying or broiler strains now that poultry keeping is a factory concern.

In those days, in the countryside and even in the towns, many ordinary working households had poultry pens in their backyards. They had full-size hens, bantams and the former fighting breeds of game poultry of which there were also innumerable varieties. So I soon gave up my dreams of potato breeding fame and planned a vast poultry farm with pens of any number of different varieties of chickens. I would place large advertisements in *The Poultry World* every week and export world-wide. I never dreamt at the time that chickens would come to be kept in batteries purely as food-producing machines.

My interest in poultry lasted for many years and I did manage to obtain some as birthday presents or with such pocket money as I had. The trouble was that, when I was sent away to school in the autumn of 1921, I had to rely upon Mr Newland to feed and look after them. He may have been a lay preacher and radical politician but he was not strictly honest and tended to cheat me and my sister, who had by then also joined in the operation. They never seemed to lay as many eggs when we were away as when we were there and always seemed to eat much more food.

In the same way as with poultry, there was a great fancy in those days for backyard rabbits. Nowadays, these too are kept in batteries. They are usually white hybrid New Zealand rabbits which are sold to Sainsburys or the like in their hundreds, frozen, but in those days, although they were kept for the table or their skins, it was on a small scale and there was an enormous variety. So I tried my hand at keeping rabbits too. There used to be shows in Chesham where you would see maybe a hundred different sorts of birds – hens of all shapes and sizes, hens with feathers in all the wrong places, hens with very long legs, hens with very short legs. In the same way, there were blue rabbits, brown rabbits, sandy rabbits, rabbits with long ears hanging down to the ground and rabbits with ears sticking up in the proper way, large rabbits, small rabbits, black and white rabbits, black and white divided vertically, black and white in spots – any sort or pattern you could think of, man had, by that stage, bred as a hobby. I think the search for variety must have been going on for a long time in this country and had reached an extraordinary level of success by 1921. I was certainly fascinated by it all and my chicken and rabbit keeping lasted from 1921 until the time I started farming properly in 1931. Of course, in the end, just as the whole country did, I fell into more practical ways of having one variety of chicken and one variety of rabbit which best suited what my sister and I were trying to do but, in the beginning, it was an exciting hobby.

In July my brother came home from school for the holidays and he introduced me to the mysteries of the moat which surrounds Grove Farm. We felt there must be something of some interest buried there since it was so old and energetically started digging at every conceivable point to see what we could find. Not surprisingly, we found nothing. I remember the farm men coming by and laughing tolerantly. Some said, 'You won't find anything. Fifty years ago, old Peter Reeve went off one lunchtime with something he found and never worked again, so there is nothing else to be found there – he had it all.' Another would say, 'Them old Romans had more sense than you might think – they never left anything laying about'. We probably thought, even at that age, and certainly our elders would have said, 'Ignorant fellows, it is nothing to do with the Romans – don't they know the difference between the Romans and the Normans', for it was generally acknowledged that the moat's origins were medieval. But the Romans had the last laugh. Fifty years later, in a dry year, we cleaned out the moat. I notified the county authorities that I was doing so in case anything

The moat clogged up with leaves and mud long before we cleaned it out in 1976.

of interest was found. A very dogmatic young man came down in an awful hurry, barely got out of his car, had a look and said, 'Oh yes, typically medieval, a moat and bailey – you might find some objects dating from the thirteenth century but nothing any earlier'. Well, when we sorted through the mud after it had dried, we found several lots of small pottery shards. The first ones which we sent off to the County Museum were identified as Romano-British, about 300 AD, and the second lot from another situation was identified as Belgic, i.e. pre-Roman. So perhaps the country people knew something that other people did not. For two thousand years folklore remembered that there had been a Roman camp on the site, obliterated later by a medieval moated dwelling.

There were very few other children for me to play with in the immediate area. I had one friend, Raymond Waller, who was the son of Arthur Waller, the tractor driver my father had employed who was still working on the farm. I used to go around the countryside with him, but my mother always forbade me to go into the Wallers' house. At the time, I thought it was some sort of snobbery, but I now realise it was probably for fear of infection.

This Cambridge ring rolls would have been used to level the ground in the spring. You could hear the singing sound of the wheels on the stones for miles around. Rolls like this are still used – three of them strung out in a line to cover 20 or 30 feet – but now you can't hear the sound they make because of the noise of the tractor that pulls them.

Two or three of the Waller family died within a short time of tuberculosis, including my friend Raymond.

One thing I remember about the countryside at that period was that everything was so very, very quiet. There were no aeroplanes and few lorries or cars. Miss Warrender had a car but very few other people had and the normal method of getting about was by pony and trap. However, you could hear quite clearly the trains in the distance, and people used to say that when you heard the trains in Berkhamsted, it was supposed to herald fine weather and when you heard them in Chesham, it meant wet weather. Of course, it only really indicated the direction in which the wind was blowing.

It was so quiet, you could hear what other farmers were doing some distance away. In the springtime, you could hear the singing noise that the ring rollers made on the stones, when the land was being levelled after sowing. At haytime, you could hear a sort of juddering noise that a hay mower makes. Despite the fact that tractors had been available since the beginning of the First World War, by 1921 the only one operating in our area belonged to Pop

Simms. They were too expensive to buy and to run for most farmers during the depressed agricultural period of the twenties and thirties. Pop Simms' tractor was an old Fordson with a peculiar whine, so everyone knew when he was ploughing. Our Titan was now deemed to be too heavy for our land and was used only to power machinery in the farmyard. The only other machinery I would have heard across the fields would have been the steam-driven ploughs and threshing machines. The threshing machine was pulled by a traction engine from farm to farm. This made a great noise when it was at work and you would know from this exactly who had the machine at any particular time as it travelled round the neighbourhood.

Several people who had been friends of my father's had rallied round to help us after his death. In particular, there was a Colonel Hugh Montgomery, a bachelor living in a little cottage in Pednor Road, Chesham. From time to time, he took my brother out shooting and also took me to show me things he thought of interest. I remember that one day he came and picked me up to take me to the other side of Chesham to show me a badger's sett. In those days, badgers were relatively rare in the Chilterns. He took me to a wood about a mile and a half out of Chesham in the Pednor direction where they had found the sett and they were going to dig the badger out that day. There were two men with a pair of tongs with which to grip the badger and a couple of terriers. I thought the badger must have done something

A badger on Cowcroft Farm, Ley Hill, taken by Raymond Franklyn, a local amateur naturalist. Rare in the 1920s, there are now plenty.

particularly wrong – eaten chickens or something like that and I said to the men, 'What's he done?' I remember one man replied, 'He ain't done nothing – he's just a badger' and it struck me that it was rather unpleasant to be digging a harmless animal like a badger out of his hole and handling him with these great iron tongs, then handing him over to the terriers. Hugh Montgomery spotted that I wasn't very happy about it and so he did not keep me there until the end. He just showed me how a badger lived and what the badger's sett was like. We had no badgers on Grove Farm until nearly twenty years after that, but now there are dozens of them, so it rather makes nonsense of the sort of letters you see in the national press saying that badgers are completely dying out – certainly there are far more of them here than there have ever been.

The other thing I remember Hugh Montgomery taking me to see was a rabbit-ferreting operation in the early morning. It was not done in a casual, haphazard way as it would be nowadays, but was quite an organised affair. There was a big rabbit warren some distance out into a field. The men went the night before and arranged a long net right round the warren, propped up on sticks so that the rabbits could get out from their holes and get under the net and go and feed during the night. Two or three men set out in the early morning, and I went with them. They had guns to use when it got light and also the ferrets. First of all, they dropped the net down to the ground and then we were all told to make a noise in the surrounding fields so that any rabbits which were out feeding would run back to get to their holes. This we did and they ran into the net and were caught. When it became light, they started putting the ferrets into the holes to drive the remaining rabbits out, which were then either shot or trapped in the net. This was before the days of myxomatosis and it was unbelievable the number of rabbits there were. Now there aren't a tenth of the number.

The rabbit-catching took place on a mild but foggy morning early in 1921 and, before it became light, I remember hearing across the valley men and horses coming out to plough on the next farm. I could hear the chink of the plough chains and the sort of stretching sound of the harness. The men came out and tied their horses up to the hedge and then took out their sandwiches to eat because, being winter, it was quite impossible to start work – it was far too dark. There was a most curious attitude among farmers in those days that it was almost their moral duty to make people get up early for work even if they could not do anything. The next door farm, Harriot's End Farm, was well run, but the

Catching rabbits was not always done with a long net. The man in the top picture has a purse net which could only be used on one hole at a time. Nevertheless, with a couple of good ferrets you could soon build up a very large catch in those pre-myxomatosis days, and in the depressed thirties half the

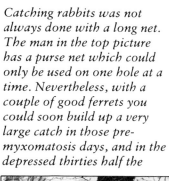

industrial workers of Chesham joined the farmhands in using rabbit-catching to supplement their income.

farmer, Arthur Puddephatt, still had this old-fashioned belief that his men, whatever the weather and whatever the conditions, had to be out early even if they could not work. It was just accepted as the proper way to do things.

There were other differences between the numbers of wild animals in the area then and now. Not only were there hardly any badgers, but there were far fewer foxes and absolutely no deer. Now, in 1986, there are two or three species of deer running in the area. On the other hand, there were then a great many pheasants reared by gamekeepers and set free. At that time, almost the entire countryside was looked after by gamekeepers. Either it was still part of an estate where the owner had kept the shooting rights and employed gamekeepers or, if they were owner/occupiers, as we were, the rights were let to a syndicate. Several local farmers specialised in rearing pheasants for sale to the shooting syndicates and it used to be said that they would entice the pheasants back with trails of raisins and sell each pheasant more than once.

There were also a lot of partridges, whose nests the keepers protected from vermin of one sort or another and, surprisingly, there were many more owls than now. I really don't know why this was because the keepers used to shoot them then whereas now they would be left alone. Perhaps it is that they eat a lot of rats which are full of poison put out by council pest officers and are killed off by this.

The keepers had then, as now, a strange custom. All the vermin they shot, they would hang up on a piece of string between two trees or on a piece of wood stuck up on pegs in a prominent place near a footpath where everybody could see. I was never quite sure why they did this. Was it to demonstrate their efficiency – a form of boasting, or was it so that their employers could see how diligent they had been? Everywhere you went, there were these hideous gallows with creatures hanging on them that had been left there for weeks – birds of prey, stoats, weasels, the occasional fox – everything which preyed upon their game.

Birds and animals are very tied up with superstition in the countryside. If you heard the curious and distinct cry of a green woodpecker, for example, it was supposed to be a forecast of rain – hence its local name 'wetoil'. The odd thing about this was that more than half a century later, talking to a farmer in Burgundy in France, I discovered that there too it is considered to be 'une bonne prévision météorologique', so perhaps it is not just a superstition. A more gruesome belief was that, when a mare had a foal, it was

important to put the afterbirth on a hawthorn tree. I asked old
Walt Batchelor why and he said 'The foal won't suck if you don't'.
This seemed to me rather weird but I took no notice at the time.
When the same thing happened about five years later I was a bit
older and more confident, so I said to him 'Don't be bloody
ridiculous – it can't make any difference'. I made him take it down
and the old boy went off muttering 'Silly young bugger, he thinks
he knows everything just because he's been away to school'. Of
course, the foal, for some reason or other, would not suck and, for
weeks after, the old boy continued muttering 'Silly young bugger,
thinks he knows everything'. Doubtless he thought the old
superstition had been proved correct.

The person who my father had appointed as our joint
guardian and the trustee of his estate was somebody called Sir
Lionel Fawdell Phillips. He was no help at all. I think he was much
more interested in my mother, who was a good-looking woman of
thirty-three, than he was in we children. We hardly ever saw him
and he never, in fact, offered any help or advice of any sort. But
there were other people who did come in and help. There was a
Mr Ward, who had been my father's solicitor. I remember he
invited my sister and me down to Reigate in Surrey for the day,
where he had a very neat, model sort of farm. He was a jolly, stout
man with a red face and a bright-coloured waistcoat who looked
much more like an old-type country solicitor than a City solicitor.
Unfortunately, as I subsequently found out, he was a pretty poor
solicitor and made an unholy mess of my father's affairs.

In fact, Hugh Montgomery and his family were the only
people who were really helpful to us. Hugh's father was a former
Liberal Member of Parliament who had retired to Bacton in Norfolk,
and my sister and I went down there for a holiday in the summer
of 1921. He took me round all the farms in the area, introduced me
to the farmers and talked to me, not exactly as an adult, but as
somebody rather older than I was, and the farmers treated me in
the same way. I therefore learned a lot about a wonderful farming
area. Everything they did in those days in that part of Norfolk
made everything we did in the Chilterns look rather silly and
untidy and incompetent (just as Alf Newland had always said).
They did have the advantage of very good soil though.

My year of discovery continued. Back at home the fruit was
starting to ripen and, just as with the potatoes, the chickens and
the rabbits, there seemed to be an infinite variety. In our own
garden, the one which surrounded Little Grove, there were twelve

varieties of plum, twelve of pear, three of peaches, two of nectarines, two of apricots and, I should think, as many as fifteen of apples. They were not all particularly good but they were all different. One variety of apple, 'Peasegoods Nonesuch' was grown because it was the biggest apple in the world. Others, like 'Beauty of Bath', were grown (and still are) for their wonderful colour and the fact that they are very early, although they have no taste. Other great big green apples were grown purely for making dumplings. Nowadays, I suppose, the average large garden may have three or

This aerial view of Grove Farm, Orchard Leigh and the edge of Chesham, taken in the 1960s, shows the many orderly orchards of the Mash family's business.

four sorts of apple. We had a bonus. As well as the fruit trees growing in the garden which were the results of Victorian and Edwardian nurserymen (people like the Lanes at Berkhamsted, who raised one of the most famous apples, Lanes' 'Prince Albert'), we also had the old orchard on Grove Farm with varieties which were probably bred and raised locally at the end of the eighteenth or the beginning of the nineteenth century. I remember there was a tree with a cone-shaped yellow apple. This was a type of codling, which was very light in weight and, if you shook it, you could hear the pips rattling inside. It was supposed to be the very best early cooking apple. There was also a russet, brown all over, of course, which always had a cross mark on its skin, said to be the mark of the crucifix. It had no particular culinary value; it was just another variety. There were perhaps half a dozen other varieties grown on trees so tall that people could barely pick them safely.

In addition, there were on the farm just three of four very old varieties of pears, all but one of which had no practical value. You had to keep the fruit from some of the trees until the following spring before you could eat them, which nobody would bother to do nowadays. Others were so sweet and sugary that the wasps always took them. Just one was very good and I managed, years afterwards, to get some grafts from it and perpetuated the variety. None of the recognised authorities in the country have ever been able to identify it for me, so it is almost certainly specific to Grove Farm. There were also great varieties of cherries in this area and on Grove Farm these grew on trees which were nearly as tall as the surrounding beech trees. They had to be picked, at considerable risk to the pickers, using enormously long ladders, which were wide at the bottom so that they could stand on uneven ground.

Last of all, there were enormous walnut trees. The walnuts were not picked, but fell off and were gathered every autumn. They were then left on the barn floor until the green husks had all rotted off and by about Christmas time could be sold to the local greengrocers in hundredweights. To my great shame, later on in life when I was hard up, I had to cut all the walnut trees down for the value of the wood. I think there were ten large trees. I subsequently re-planted some young ones, but they will never get to the size that those old ones were in my time nor carry the enormous quantity of nuts that they used to bear.

It is important to realise that the orchards on farms then were not orchards in the modern sense. They were just higgledy-piggledy collections of trees, not even all in one enclosure but dotted around

Dwarf fruit trees which can be picked from the ground in a modern orchard in Kent.

close to the farm. On Grove Farm they were round the rick yard, on the moat banks and in an area of rough ground just near the farm buildings. Gradually this rather haphazard method of fruit growing was entirely replaced by the kind that our neighbours, Messrs Mash, were already operating in 1921; that is, hundreds of trees of the same variety, such as Bramley Seedlings, Lanes' Prince Albert or Worcester Permains, all planted in neat rows, the fruit picked all at the same time, graded and then marketed through Covent Garden. But the trees were all still reasonably big. Now, following the pattern of most forms of agriculture, fruit growing has moved on to an entirely different method of production. Little trees, just a few feet high, have been bred, which can be picked from the ground and which grow fruit of a completely uniform size, exactly what the supermarket buyer wants so that he can provide the same thing for his customers via cold store throughout the season. Fruit farmers now grow very few varieties of cooking and eating apples, and those they do grow are all the same size, all the same colour, free of blemishes, all identical.

Since 1984 I have watched the Mashes' orchards in Grove Lane be cut down because the trees are too tall and the fruit too individual, and thought how much the lifespan of an orchard is shortening. The orchard I first remember around The Grove must have been hundreds of years old. The life of the orchards of large identical trees being cleared around me must have been something between fifty and a hundred years. How long the life of the little trees of modern-day orchards will be, heaven knows.

The Teacher

My mother was very anxious that both my brother and I should finish up in so-called public schools. My brother failed several times to gain entrance to various establishments until finally she sent him to a school on the other side of Chesham called Chartridge Hill House in order to be 'crammed'. It was a small school kept by a Mr Stafford Webber, who might well be described by some people as a crammer in that he specialised in examinations, but I noticed in an old directory of Chesham that he described himself as a 'tutor' which is probably more accurate. I suppose my mother was trying to make sure that I did not go through the same troubles as my brother when she decided to send me to the same school at the age of only nine. I don't think this precaution was actually necessary, but it proved, on the whole, to be an extremely good experience. Apart from Mr Webber there was just one teacher, Miss Shaw. Mr Webber taught Latin, geography and history while Miss Shaw taught mathematics. All the teaching was geared *solely* to passing exams and Mr Webber was very expert at this. I particularly remember Mr Webber's Latin teaching. No effort was made to make you pronounce Latin the way that the Romans are presumed to have done because there was no spoken examination in those days in Latin. We therefore pronounced all the words in a purely English way so that we did not waste time in learning what we did not need to learn. This had the effect in my case that the Latin I knew was absolutely useless when I got to my next school. However, nobody that I know of ever failed an exam at Mr Webber's school and nobody was worked to death. He was, in his way, quite brilliant. We had a lot of time to ourselves and when we were not working or playing games, which were a bit sporadic, we were allowed to go for long walks in the countryside. We were not supposed to go to Chesham but as far as we liked in the other direction. So if you wanted to go and buy sweets with your pocket money you had to walk all the way to Ballenger, which is two or three miles away.

Mr Webber was eccentric in many ways. He had an absolute obsession about the regular functioning of the boys' bodies, so

Chartridge Hill House and tennis courts. For a small preparatory school it had a lot of facilities. (Bottom of the Garden (1) and (2) were behind the bushes to the right of the house.)

G. Stafford Webber – a progressive and enlightened teacher, despite the fact that his main brief was to get his pupils through entrance exams for other schools.

Opposite top: The view from the playing fields in 1926 which diverted me from cricket.

Opposite: This view from the edge of the same playing fields now (but slightly further round to the right) shows how quickly the Chilterns will revert to woodland if you give it half a chance.

much so that pinned on the door at the back of the house was a notice. The notice said: 'Back Door' with a list of names and times, 'Front Door' with another list of names and times, 'Bottom of the Garden (1)' with another list and 'Bottom of the Garden (2)' with another list. This referred to the four available lavatories. Your name appeared on one of these lists and you had to go to that particular lavatory at that particular time in the morning. You just had to go and there was no argument about it. If, subsequently, you needed to leave the classroom to go again, it either meant you were ill or that you had not obeyed the rules earlier in the day. Either way you would probably get some vile purgative or castor oil or God knows what administered to you. This was not inhumanity on Mr Webber's part, just his fixation with the necessity of building up regular bodily functions – his name was on the rota too. The system certainly worked for me as, for a great many years afterwards, my body functioned at exactly the same time of the day as my name used to be on the list. We used the four lavatories in rotation. One term you had one, the next term another. This was to share out the hardship fairly, because Bottom of the Garden (1) and Bottom of the Garden (2) were exceedingly uncomfortable if there was a gale blowing or snow.

The opportunities we had for long walks suited me because I began to get to know the farms all around the Chartridge area and see what the farmers there were doing. In my mind I used to decide what I would do with their land in comparison with them. I also met on the roads one or two people that I met at home. There was a 'higgler', a man who collected eggs from the farms, called Brownsell. He had one day a week in the Whelpley Hill area where I lived and one day a week in the Chartridge area. He drove a pony cart and sold tea in the countryside and bought eggs. When he got back to Chesham presumably he sold eggs and bought tea. There was a rag-and-bone man called Abel Southam, whom I also had previously got to know. And there was a corn merchant who called on us at home with his horse and dray to get orders. He was called Teddy Burgess and he had a shop in Newtown, Chesham.

The cricket and football fields at Chartridge gave a beautiful panoramic view of Pednor Bottom, the village of Pednor itself and Hundridge, and although when playing football or hockey you had to concentrate in case someone came barging into you, when playing cricket my mind was never on the game. My eyes were always wandering over to the fields that I could see where there was always something going on which interested me. Somebody

would be working in the fields or there would be some livestock out grazing. I still have a very clear memory of everything that was going on on the farms that were visible from those playing fields during the whole of the early twenties.

The landscape at Chartridge was different from ours at home even though the two areas were only a few miles apart, the main difference being that it was so much more open. The fields on the west of Chesham have always been bigger than those on the east where we are because the land is poorer, so when the land was originally cleared for cultivation, farmers would have had to have had bigger areas to farm in order to survive. Around Grove Farm, because, I assume, it is better land and slightly flatter, the ground was cleared and divided into fields very early on, and it seems to be a general rule that the earlier the clearance, the smaller the field because each man simply cleared what he needed for himself. One additional factor may have been that the area I could see from the school playing fields was all part of Bury Farm, Chesham, Squire Lowndes' home farm, and it is possible that his family had had the opportunity of enlarging their fields at an earlier date because of their local power and influence.

In 1921, when I first saw it, the landscape around Chartridge Hill House was all arable fields. In my first term, I remember watching crops still being harvested in the late autumn (harvest was much later in those days), and there were big ricks of clover hay, easily identifiable by their dark brown colour, in several fields which had been harvested from a clover break. During the four years that I was at that school the whole of Bury Farm, and nearly all the other farms that you could catch a glimpse of, just fell down to grass. Much of it wasn't properly sown down as ours had been at home, but was just left to become grass of its own accord. Consequently, at the end of that period it had a very low productive and stock-carrying capacity, especially because it is poor, stony, hilly land anyway. That landscape, which is almost unaltered to this day, is much more typical Chiltern countryside than our particular bit. It is entirely made up of steep hills and narrow valleys with no flat land like we have on several parts of Grove Farm. When you walked across to the beech woods in the distance, which I did from time to time, you would find within them large pits where chalk had been dug out and spread on to the fields using horses and carts. But there were none of the little shaft pits dotted all over the fields that were so common only a few miles away on the other side of Chesham where we lived.

The small area which most concerns me – that is, the area bounded by Chesham, Hemel Hempstead, Berkhamsted and Chipperfield, a small quadrangle of a few thousand acres – was quite considerably different from the rest of the Chilterns then and right up to the Second World War. It was different because the small fields and high overgrown hedges made it so extraordinarily closed in. The fields were small not just because they had been cleared and farmed at a very early date, but because the open-field system (also known as 'strip-farming') practised in most of Britain, including North Bucks and the Vale of Aylesbury, in the Middle Ages apparently never appertained in the Chilterns. From the word go land was farmed in individual holdings, and by Tudor times, as you can see from the numbers of births, marriages and deaths in the local parish register, the community at Whelpley Hill was bigger than any other around Chesham. Land ownership here was fragmented, with each owner having just two or three fields, and the pattern of hedges and even the names of the fields remained about the same from the mid-sixteenth century right up until the 1920s.

This is the way it was – small fields, tall trees, high hedges.

When labour was cheap and plentiful the hedges would have been cut and the fields would have looked neat and tidy, but by the early twenties the hedges had all become overgrown through neglect and there were no long views. From the moment you left Chesham until you reached Hemel Hempstead, Berkhamsted or Chipperfield, at only one point could you ever get a view of more than 200 or 300 yards. This would have been across Ley Hill Common, which in the twenties was an open common with no trees or bushes on it, except for a few raspberry canes which everybody used to pick. It would regularly get grazed by sheep and was therefore kept in short grass.

Because the hedges in our area were so old and neglected they were very wide. They also consisted of a great variety of species, unlike modern hedges which tend to be of one type, such as quickthorn. Added to this, the hedges were full of trees, large hedgerow trees, which were usually either elms or oaks, and these were not there by chance but because they had been planted 200 years earlier by the local landowners, who looked after them as a commercial proposition.

Another factor which contributed to the distinctive appearance of the landscape around The Grove was that the chalk pits in the area were unlike those in the rest of the Chilterns. Instead of being large pits dug in the woods or where woods were subsequently created, they were small and were dug out in the middle of fields. Chalk, of course, was supplied to compensate for the acidity of the top-soil and the method in this immediate area was to mine the

Site of a former chalkpit (Hertfordshire shaft-mining method) at the top of First Hangings, Grove Farm.

chalk by hauling it up with a windlass and rope and spreading it on the fields with hand labour and barrows. In 1804 Arthur Young, in his survey of agriculture in Hertfordshire, was of the opinion that this was a good method of spreading chalk because it was not hard on horses in the way that the method used elsewhere in the Chilterns was, where horses dragged the chalk out of large pits. He apparently didn't think that the hard labour it was for the people wheeling the barrows was of any consequence.

The chalk is about 25–30 feet down, so the farmer would have employed a 'chalk drawer' to dig a straight shaft, which then branched out at the bottom. Once the chalk had been removed and distributed, the hole was then pushed in to form an inverted cone. So in the twenties and thirties, before people had started to fill them in, every field had at least one small round hole and around these holes, bushes had grown up which helped to obstruct the view along with the high, thick hedges. Stick Stevens of Whelpley Hill, a local character still working until after the Second World War, could just remember a family from Bovingdon mining the chalk in this way when he was paid a few pence for helping by breaking the larger lumps with a hammer sometime in the 1880s.

In the neighbourhood of Grove Farm there was one almost freakish aspect of this business. To the west of the farm, along the road known as Two Dells Road, there were no less than fourteen large pits dug out of the side of the hill. Since these must have been producing far more than could possibly have been used in the immediate vicinity, this implies that somebody was working them

A modern chalk quarry at Flaunden.

commercially at some stage. Nowadays lime and chalk are mechanically dug in large industrial pits and are transported long distances to the areas that need them.

There is one further factor which was almost unique to my home area in those days, which has now nearly disappeared. This is what was known as a hedge green, a permanent area left around the edge of a field about 5 yards wide for machinery to turn on. It was never ploughed and was mown by hand for hay. Cobbett, in his 'rural ride' through this area, remarked on this system and thought it an extremely good one, but, of course, when hand labour became too dear for these strips to be mown, they were left to become overgrown and formed yet more small spinneys of thorn bushes. They were then known as hedge brows or brews.

This unusual closed-in landscape in this small part of the Chilterns had started to disappear by the early thirties. The first things to go were the hedgerow trees since selling the big oaks and elms was a way in which farmers and landowners could keep themselves going in the depression. They sold them to the local timber industry in Chesham, which was still moderately prosperous, and since they did not replace them either by planting or allowing new ones to grow naturally in their place, the countryside immediately started to open up.

Then the roads, which had remained the same for hundreds of years, ceased to be wide enough for motor transport and the local authority started to implement road-widening schemes. These were fairly small-scale to start with, such as cutting off a corner here and moving a bank there. Needing somewhere to deposit the material they had dug out, they tipped it into the chalkpits. So most of these disappeared during this period as it was convenient for the farmer to fill up the pit and convenient for the council to get rid of their surplus soil. On Grove Farm the vast majority of these pits were filled in in the late twenties and early thirties, but I have kept one or two just by way of an example. They caused great inconvenience for working even in times of horse ploughing, and were almost impossible to cope with with a big tractor. You would have to keep stopping and turning round the corners of the hole, wasting time and wasting ground. It was common sense from a farming point of view to fill them in.

The last feature to go, which really had the biggest effect on the appearance of our countryside, was the hedges. Take Grove Farm as an example. Originally there was one field of 13 acres and all the others were anything from 4½ to 8 acres. Nearly all were about 220 yards (10 chains) in one dimension. This must have related to past agricultural tenures since 10 chain by 1 chain happens to be an acre. These sizes of fields were, of course, hopeless for mechanical agriculture and bad even for non-mechanical agriculture because near the hedges it is very difficult to get crops dry, and in muggy weather they rot because neither sun nor wind can get to them. It really was an unacceptably inefficient pattern of fields. In Arthur Young's time the hedges were all cut and kept trim so that damage to crops was fairly minimal, but the long agricultural slide from around 1850 onward had gradually led to deterioration and they were very overgrown and had to go.

Taking hedges out was an expensive matter. Therefore it was not until the advent of the bulldozer during the last war that they started going really quickly. In 1944 I organised a demonstration for the Ministry of Agriculture of bulldozing out hedges to show what could be done to provide more land and make it easier to farm what little land we had. So I witnessed, and later helped, the opening out of the local countryside around Grove from the 1920s onwards. Now if you travel through the area from Chesham to Hemel Hempstead or Chesham to Berkhamsted it is like any other

This is the way it is now – large fields, short hedges and few trees. This field was originally seven.

area of the Chilterns and you can see across the fields for quite long distances, perhaps a mile or more at times. The old closed-in atmosphere has disappeared for ever. Sometimes I can't help regretting what I've done. The small fields, hedgerows, trees and the rest of it were extremely attractive.

Now the views around my home are very similar to those I gazed at from the cricket fields at Chartridge, but then it was all new to me. I hadn't seen big open fields before, except briefly in Norfolk, and I hadn't seen a large arable farm in operation until I saw Bury Farm at a distance. All in all, my mind was never on cricket. Cricket balls came whizzing towards me and I never even saw them, let alone stopped or caught them. I quite infuriated Mr Webber who simply could not understand a boy not being interested in games and being more interested in a distant agricultural prospect. Eventually, however, he accepted the situation and put me in charge of the considerable collection of lawn mowers which he had. I had to clean the machines and oil them from time to time, and I also had the duty of allocating them to boys when they were directed to do the mowing. I much preferred this work to games. I would have happily mown all day rather than play cricket with balls coming at me from all angles.

The population at Chartridge Hill House was constantly changing. This was because of its total success in getting boys

A Chartridge Hill House cricket XI. Not good enough to be a player, I am the scorer cross-legged at the front.

through exams and the fact that most only went there when they were twelve or thirteen for a year or two to get over these hurdles. I suppose I was the longest inhabitant because I was there four years altogether. I remember I used to sleep with three other boys in a room right at the top of the house. They were all older than I was but, of course, I was the one who had been at the school the longest. One evening, a young Chesham girl, who worked as a maid in the house, came up to the bedroom and lay under the eiderdown of one of the boy's beds talking and laughing. This went on for quite a while and we all thought it was rather naughty, although I am sure nothing improper actually happened. I remember she recited a rhyme which went: 'In the woods where the nuts are brown, Billy comes with his trousers down. I lie down and he on top and see if his key fits my lock.' Just after this, we heard a step on the stairs and Mrs Webber came in to see who had been talking. There was no escape and, of course, the girl was sent packing. Within a few minutes we saw her walking down the drive with her suitcase looking dejected and no doubt feeling a sense of injustice. If something like this had happened at a public school, there would have been an awful business for the boy concerned, but Mr Webber showed his real qualities in the way he dealt with the situation. He had the boy into his study for a very long while the next morning and what he said, I do not know, but the boy never boasted about the incident. It was never mentioned again and I am sure his parents were never told. Nobody else in the house knew anything about it except Mr and Mrs Webber. The situation was dealt with in the most progressive and sensible way because really nothing dire had happened. However, because I had not stopped it, I received a lecture which centred around the biblical quotation: 'Unstable as water – thou shalt not prevail'.

Looking back, although he would hate me to say it if he were alive, Mr Webber was a most progressive man. Within the limits of his job of helping boys pass exams, which is not real education, he did provide all sorts of facilities and quite a wide education outside the purely academic. The lectures that he gave every term were very varied and the fact that we were allowed to go to the cinema, to have freedom to walk about the countryside and always to have questions answered, within the limits of a very small establishment, made school life there extremely enjoyable.

The Preacher

During the holidays, most of my time was spent on the farm which, by this time, was being managed by a man called George Larkin. Benny Wingrove had retired to a house in Whelpley Hill in September 1921 and George Larkin moved in to take over. I think of him as 'the preacher', which is strange as he spent six days of the week working on the farm and only a few hours of one day preaching. But it was fairly obvious that preaching was the most important part of his life. He had worked, I think for all his life, on the Rothschilds' estate at Tring, mostly on fencing work at which he was very expert. As a farm manager, he was a very practical man, who was well aware of the economic necessity of adapting to new times. He was also a very thoughtful man in his work and knowledgeable about trees, which greatly interested me. When, thanks to his efforts, it was decided to establish a milking herd (and he had an awful job to get enough capital out of my mother to do so), he used to take me round buying with him and generally involved me, although I was very young. I think he sensed that I had a genuine interest in agriculture, not just a small boy's instinct for playing around on farms. Therefore he set to work to teach me whatever he knew.

He did almost everything on the farm himself, including veterinary work such as castrating little pigs. In connection with this, he demonstrated to me that there are male pigs, female pigs and what is known in this area as 'willjills', occasionally pronounced 'willjews'. These are hermaphrodites. He showed me how these small pigs differed from both the males and the females, and then went on to explain, 'It's the same with all animals – you get it with calves and you get it with humans as well.' He named various prominent citizens of the county, including at least one peer, who, he claimed, were 'willjills'. 'It's like these little pigs,' he said 'Some of them know they are males and some of them know they are females, but some of them don't know what they are and these are the "willjills".' This stuck very much in my mind, and when I later went to a large boarding school with, of course, lots of talk about homosexuality, I got the two things rather mixed up. On occasion we were all made to take cold showers together and I

'The Preacher', George Larkin.

looked around with great interest to see if I could spot the 'will-jills'. Not surprisingly, all the boys looked the same as I did and it dawned on me that the difference was not a physical one after all. Nevertheless, thanks to Larkin's teaching – oversimplified though it was – I have always kept an open mind about people who do not fit into the normal mould, and I think country people in general are more broadminded about such things.

George Larkin not only taught me everything he could, but would also try to fall in with things in which I was interested. I was a great reader of the farming press and, through my reading, took a liking to Suffolk horses as opposed to the Shires we had. Suffolks had the advantage of clean legs without much hair on them and so would not suffer from 'greasy heel' which seemed to be almost endemic on Grove Farm. Therefore, when it was decided to breed with one of the mares on the farm, George Larkin took up my point and arranged for the mare to go to a Suffolk stallion instead of a Shire. This added to the difficulties involved because there were plenty of Shire stallions in those days which used to travel around the farms, but the nearest Suffolk stallion was at a farm in the Watford area. As it was my suggestion, he said I should take Dolly there while I was on holiday and it took me five and a half hours to get there. Disappointingly, the mating was not a success and the mare did not conceive. They later put her to a Shire stallion and a foal was bred as required.

The Baptist chapel at Buckland Common where Larkin preached.

Like so many working men who had positions of responsibility in those days, Larkin was a lay preacher, as old Newland, the gardener, had been. He used to go in a pony and cart on Sundays round to places like Buckland Common and other local villages to preach. I do not think he was a liberal, good-natured type of preacher like Newland. He was a hell-fire and damnation Baptist and I think he gave his congregation a bit of a time. He was a very strict man and no swearing was allowed in his presence, which was very difficult on a farm where everybody usually uses the most obscene language. On one occasion, his son-in-law went with him in the pony and cart to the service he was taking at the little chapel in Buckland Common, a long way from Whelpley Hill, and as he was getting back into the trap, he slipped and said 'Damn'. He was made to walk all the way home as a penance.

Larkin also seemed to be obsessed with death. From time to time, he would come out with odd statements such as 'Queen Victoria and all them great 'uns, they all had to die like the rest of us', and, 'I never mind killing anything because I always know I be doing it a good turn, taking it away from this wicked world'. We always had the feeling that, if a member of his family became very ill, he might take it upon himself to put them out of their misery. In fact, I think he was a very loving husband and father and probably applied different rules in practice to those he preached. On the other hand, I remember his recounting to me how he had been to see a relation of his who was dying and how he had told the poor chap what a wicked man he had been all his life and how, within a few hours, he would be burning in hell fire for ever more. He seemed very satisfied with the effect he had had for, by the time he had finished, 'there was not a dry eye present'. In spite of this oddness about death, I think he was basically an intelligent man who in a different economic climate could have done very well.

Amongst other things, Larkin appeared to be quite impervious to pain of any kind at all. He was able to scoop out wasps' nests (or 'wapps neesties' as he called them) with his bare hands and dispose of them, taking no more notice of the wasps than anybody else would of house-flies. When he had a broken tooth with a rough edge which hurt him, I saw him simply file it off with the sort of file you used for sharpening small tools. He was quite offended once when somebody would not allow him to pull out a bad tooth they had with an ordinary pair of pliers from the toolkit. He had a little brown terrier dog called Jack, which was very faithful to him but to which he was slightly unkind. He would occasionally make it go home on its own from places miles away from the farm, but it would always find its way back successfully. One day, he even threw a very large stone at it, which missed and hit my sister instead, injuring her arm quite seriously. Larkin did not even appear to notice and when she emerged the following day with her arm in a sling he merely said 'Seems I hit the wrong one'. He was not brutal; it was just that because he did not feel pain himself he did not expect other people to do so.

Larkin managed the farm from the year after my father died until I took over myself; that is to say, from when I was nine years old until I was twenty. Above him in life were upper-class and middle-class people who lived too well and of whom he did not particularly approve. Below him were working-class people on the farm, who blasphemed constantly, drank and gambled occasionally, and who would have worked on Sunday if they had been given half a chance and the rate of pay had been good enough. There were only two or three men working on the farm then, so the farm manager had to work as hard as they did. In fact, Larkin worked much harder. He would tell me that this was because the Lord was with him, he did not drink and he kept himself clean, whatever that might have meant. I suspect that he was so exhausted by Saturday that he needed the Sunday day of rest. Certainly the thought of working on Sunday would have horrified him. To me he seemed a throwback from the Puritan age, a seventeenth-century man newly demobilised from Cromwell's army at odds with the twentieth century. When he retired, I had to manage with just the blasphemers, who at least had the advantage that they would work on Sundays, if required.

Another person who played a very big part in my life at this time was Miss Warrender, our godmother. When the annual Agricultural Show came to Tring Park, which was the big local show in those days, it was Miss Warrender and not my mother who took me there. Very often she used to take us to church. She was a very formidable lady, who appeared to me to be very very old, very ugly, very over-made up and very dogmatic. She was actually extremely kind and a good godmother, but you had to be extremely careful what you said and what you did. For instance, she would often drop off to sleep in church. We were, of course, frightened to wake her up, but we got into terrible trouble if we did not, so we had to try and rouse her as gently as possible. And if people pushed past her at the Tring Show, she would make very loud comments about them, such as 'Have you ever seen such

A portrait of Miss Warrender, my godmother, painted by a local artist.

Tring Show in the 1920s. This event, which took place in Lord Rothschild's Park, was a tremendous get-together for Hertfordshire and Buckinghamshire farmers.

hideous people in your life?', which we found highly embarrassing.

Very gradually, under George Larkin's guidance, the emphasis of the farming system at The Grove was altered from arable to dairy. He slowly built up a herd of dairy cattle, mainly comprising Shorthorns, but with one Ayrshire and two Guernseys which my father had bought in Cornwall. The milk produced was sold to a dairy in Hemel Hempstead, who would collect it once a day. He kept about 40 acres in arable, mainly barley, but with 2 or 3 acres of mangels for cattle fodder, and rented almost 100 acres off to neighbours. So, with the milk we sold and the fairly large number of pigs we still kept, combined with the good supply of hay and roots we produced to feed the livestock, Larkin managed to keep the farm going at a time when many people went bankrupt. Of course, there were others who switched to milk production too, but few in our area were able to adapt as easily as we could, thanks to the good grass my father had sown down, the water he had laid on and the buildings he had provided for the animals.

Gathering and storing the hay was obviously an important job and the traditional method of doing this was very laborious. First it had to be cut with a horse-drawn mower, then picked up by hand with pitchforks and loaded on to carts or wagons, and finally taken back to the farmyard and stacked in small stacks. This had not

A sweep, in this case pushed by a tractor, and a horse-driven elevator. Of the three jobs shown here the best was definitely driving the tractor!

been too much bother when there was only a small acreage of grass but, with the increased acreage sown down by my father, it became a very inefficient way of handling a large amount of hay. One of the first things Larkin did was to introduce a different system – a system which was quite common elsewhere but not used in the immediate area of Whelpley Hill. It involved a 'sweep', which was used in conjunction with an elevator to lift the hay on the rick. The sweep was an enlarged version of what nowadays would be called a buck rake – a large platform of wooden tines about 9 or 10 feet long, which were fixed together and pulled by two horses, one on either side, along a row of hay, gathering the hay on top of the platform. This was then driven up close to the base of the elevator which was set up where the rick was to be made, and the horses were backed out so that the hay was left on the ground to be pitched by hand into the base of the elevator. It was a very quick way of clearing a field – much quicker than the previous way – but it still had several disadvantages. For a start, pitching the hay after it had all been gathered up in a big heap was extremely hard work because if it was not completely dry, it would get doubled up, bind

This thatcher has a wooden peg and a yealm of straw ready for laying on top of the rick. Each yealm is laid rather like a roof tile, tucked over the one below it and under the one next to it.

Corn carting: the sheaves were all loaded and unloaded onto the cart by hand. When you removed the ladders that formed the sides it doubled as a dung cart.

together and was very hard to sort out. It then went up the elevator and descended on the men on the rick in great lumps which they had to pull about and make into a neat, square stack, which then had to be thatched and covered. Also, with this system, all the hay stacks were built out in the field rather than back at the farm, so the hay had to be cut from the rick in the field and carted back to the farm whenever it was needed. Alternatively, if it was to be sold, we would have to get Mr Joiner from Ley Hill to come out to the field and cut it into trusses.

Mr Joiner did little else all year but cut and truss hay for the local farmers, for there were no balers then except for heavy fixed machines into which you could feed hay or straw and get tied bales at the other end, but the vast majority was trussed by hand. Joiner could cut out completely square chunks from a hay stack and tie them almost to an exact weight, which he would just check on a steel yard. His trade completely disappeared with the arrival of improved balers from America during the Second World War.

All the grain we produced was brought back to the farmyard and stacked in small ricks, designed as far as possible to represent about one day's threshing during the winter. Each rick was always started from a bottom made out of faggots, or wood, or hedge trimmings to keep the sheaves off the ground and stop the bottom layer getting wet. On some farms there were Dutch barns in which to store grain, so it was not necessary to thatch the top, but we did not have one and so every rick had to be thatched. It was customary to do a rough thatch first, very quickly, by just spreading straw reasonably straight across the pitch of the top of the rick and pegging it down with string and large wooden pegs. Then later on in the autumn the job would be done properly. First you would select the cleanest and straightest bundles of straw you had retained from the previous year and these were laid in a straight row. They would then be wetted and a heavy weight placed on top. The boy or assistant to the thatcher would then pull straws out from under the weight so as to get them absolutely flat and straight and lay them in neat bundles ready for the thatcher to use. This was known in this area as 'yealming'. It was quite a lengthy and expensive process.

The yealms were tied in bundles and carried up the ladder to the roof of the stack. They were then laid rather like roofing tiles on the stack, starting at the 'eaves' and moving up to finish at the ridge (if it was a square rick) or point (if it was a round one). Each yealm was tucked under the one next to it and over the one below it, and was secured with a peg and twine. Ricks were built in all sorts of shapes and sizes; the ones on The Grove were usually square but Arthur Puddephatt's were round and beautifully neat and tidy.

During the winter, as grain or money was wanted, the thresher would be called in. Very few farmers in the Chiltern area had their own threshing machine, so they almost always relied upon contractors. In Whelpley Hill there were two farmers – Stanbridge and Payne – who ran a threshing machine in partnership and did the job for everybody else around. If you did not want to have

Steam threshing was a dirty, dusty, heavy job needing a lot of men. Lifting and carrying the 2¼ cwt sacks of grain needed a lot of strength.

them, there was also a man called Ned Gomm in Chesham who ran a threshing gang. The whole outfit consisted of a traction engine, the threshing machine itself, a chaff cutter to cut up oat straw for the farm horses and a straw trusser which tied straw in bundles ready for stacking.

The thresher needed somewhere between eight and ten men to operate and no farm in the area had this number of men. Therefore the threshing machine would be accompanied not only by its driver, but by a whole group of casual labourers, some of whom would be tramps who slept rough on the farms where they were working. You needed, besides the engine driver (who supervised the operation as well as looking after his engine), two men on the threshing machine itself – a feeder who dropped the corn down into the top of the machine at a suitable speed and a band cutter to cut through the bands round the sheaves and hand them to the feeder. You also needed probably two men on the corn stack to pass the sheaves over towards the machine or to put it up on to the machine if the rick was getting low, and at least two or three men to deal with the results (one to carry away the grain from the machine and one or two to deal with the chaff, dust and 'cavings' – short bits of straw and weed – that dropped out of the bottom of the machine. The dirty jobs of dealing with the straw and cavings were normally done by the tramp-type labour. The farmer would provide the men to carry away the grain (they had to be reasonably strong), the driver and the feeder were probably retained by the contractor on a regular basis, and the rest were just casual labour. I always found the threshing operation exciting because all these people arrived with all this machinery. The threshing machine made a colossal noise, what with the chuffing of the traction engine which powered it and the humming of the machine itself, and corn, chaff and straw would all stream out in different directions.

As the winter went on, the corn stacks would become very heavily populated with rats; it was a warm, comfortable place for them and they could get in among the sheaves and nest. The longer the rick stayed in position, the more rats you got in it, so when the men were threshing they would put low wire around the rick to make sure of catching and killing as many as possible. In those days there were no municipal rat catchers and so rats and mice on a farm were quite a problem. We had anything up to twenty cats on Grove Farm, which did not get any food – certainly not in the winter time at least – to encourage them to catch the vermin. When she first came to live at Grove Farm, Florence, my wife, was quite staggered to have so many cats coming to beg around the back door for scraps, particularly during the summer when there were fewer rats and mice around.

Storing the corn in ricks meant that you did not need much bin storage for the grain, nor did you have the acute marketing problem for the grain that you have at harvest time nowadays. Now, using combine harvesters, it is all threshed out as it is harvested so you have to have storage for a vast tonnage or sell it immediately. At least the old-fashioned system avoided this, though it was terribly expensive in labour and very wasteful because the loss to vermin must have been quite considerable. You did see on some farms, though not on Grove, special stands to put the ricks on to try to prevent the rats from getting in. Many of the staddle

This beautiful round rick is built on a rick stand mounted on staddle stones to keep the rick dry and to discourage rats.

Top: Rivet - note the long beards.

Bottom: Square Head Master

stones you now see decorating suburban gardens were originally used for supporting these rick stands, which were a permanent feature of farm yards. The staddle stones, or sometimes cast-iron pedestals, supported pieces of timber which were laid across them and the rick was built on top of these. The idea was that the rats would not be able to get in easily, because they would have to climb up the stand. Personally I doubted that it ever stopped them, but at least it probably kept the bottom of the rick dry.

Larkin conducted the arable on the farm in much the same way as it would have been done by Benny Wingrove ten, twenty or even thirty years earlier with the simplest of rotation systems. The seed corn Larkin used, which nowadays one buys from national merchants situated many miles away with all sorts of certificates of origin etc. attached to it, came in those days from a neighbour or from a small seed merchant in Chesham or Hemel Hempstead. Instead of having it chemically dressed against disease by the merchant before he bought it, as happens now, Larkin did this himself. All seed corn, the night before it was sown, used to be made into a heap on the barn floor and soaked with copper sulphate solution, which protected the plant against fungal diseases. It was then allowed to dry off overnight and sown the following day. This was a regular procedure you had to follow if you did not want your crops to be diseased. It seemed to be fairly effective although, no doubt, modern methods of treatment are much better.

Our yield of grain would be considered laughable nowadays. Right until the end of the 1920s, four quarters to the acre (that is to say, 18 cwt) was considered to be a good crop of wheat in this area. If anyone claimed five quarters, which would be 22 cwt to the acre, they would be called a bloody liar. It would be very disappointing nowadays to get twice that amount from the same acreage, which really shows what the plant breeders have done for agriculture in the relatively short period of fifty years. The varieties we grew right through the twenties and thirties were principally Square Head Master and Rivet. These wheats had a long straw and a relatively low yield of grain. Because they had such a long straw they would almost all be knocked flat in a wet or stormy season and be extremely difficult to cut. With a modern combine they would be quite impossible to handle without delays and probably damaging the machinery. The new varieties bred since the Second World War have a much increased grain yield and a straw only about half the length of the old types, which has made harvesting very much easier. The variety known as Rivet was a bearded wheat

which is very seldom seen nowadays. It was awful stuff to handle
because the beards came off and got inside your clothes, making
you itch. But it was considered to be hardier than the other wheats
and so was grown if conditions were difficult and the fields had to
be sown rather late.

In addition to improving the types of grain grown, agricultural
scientists have also tackled another problem facing arable farmers –
weeds. In the twenties and thirties all spring-sown crops were
completely yellow with charlock by early June, and nearly all
winter crops were either black with what was known as 'black
grass', a very troublesome weed, or red with poppies. The poppies
have just about survived – you still see patches of them, but
charlock has nearly been eradicated by modern sprays. (If you see a
yellow field now it will be rape sown by the farmer as an oil seed
crop, something quite new.) Black grass has been greatly reduced
too. This small wiry grass is an annual, like grain, and it flowers
and comes to seed very early. Consequently the seed would fall
onto the ground before harvest-time, lie dormant through the
winter and reappear the following year. Old people used to tell me
that black grass never actually sprouted until it heard you drilling
the corn. Then it would come up with the corn so that you could
never deal with it. If it had sprouted before the corn was drilled,
you would have been able to destroy it by using a cultivator.

Thanks to chemical sprays farming is now much cleaner, but
we can still never relax. As soon as you get rid of one weed,
another seems to gain dominance and so, every year, the chemical
manufacturers bring out new sprays to deal more effectively with a
wider spectrum of weeds, because those which are immune to the
existing sprays seem to multiply to take the place of those which
are destroyed. And, of course, there is a price to pay for all this
spraying. The same sprays which kill the weeds have also reduced
many of the wild flowers in the pastures, as has the cultivation of
land previously kept for grazing. There used to be a number of
meadows around the farm when I was young where hosts of wild
daffodils bloomed in the spring. Since then these meadows have
either been ploughed up or sprayed and the daffodils have
disappeared. There are far fewer cowslips now too.

During hard times farmers make as much as they can from the
fringe benefits of farming and during the twenties these were
particularly important. Apart from selling sporting rights and the
rabbits they shot, local farmers also derived some income from
selling the by-products of hedges. Whenever these were cut back,

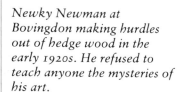

Newky Newman at Bovingdon making hurdles out of hedge wood in the early 1920s. He refused to teach anyone the mysteries of his art.

which was not all that often then, almost everything that was cut from them was used. The predominant species was hazel and, left for a long period of, say, ten to twenty years, hazel would grow big enough to make hurdles for folding sheep. Cut earlier, it made the best pea and bean sticks and was sold to allotment holders in Chesham. It also made, when younger, extremely good rickpegs for use in thatching. Other species, such as maple, made excellent firewood when it was big enough or, when it was young, it was faggotted up and left to dry; the faggots would then be used for firelighting or as fuel for the old-fashioned bakers' ovens. Stick Stevens gained his nick-name because all winter he went hedging and was never seen then without a bundle of faggots or pea sticks. Ash and hornbeam made useful stakes for sheep-pens, although the stakes did not last very long. Only the blackthorn was useless except that it bore sloes for sloe gin, so some people thought it of considerable value!

Another natural resource which used to provide some extra income on farms were the stones on the land. The Chiltern area has particularly stony soil and these are always flints which make very good hard core. So in the days before tarmac surfacing came in, all the roads in the counties of Bucks and Herts were made of flints and these flints were, for the most part, picked up on arable land by women as part of the general farm work. Every ten years or so, a field could be picked. It would be prepared by the farmer by being harrowed to bring the stones to the top. Then the women would come along, pick up all the stones that showed, put them in buckets and tip these into a box one yard square and one yard deep, which had handles on either side but no bottom. When it was full, they would be paid a few pence for the stones and two men, or perhaps stronger women, would pick up the box and move it along. So, in the end, you would have rows of one cubic yard heaps of flints all over the field. These would then be picked up with special stone forks into an ordinary farm cart and carted to the nearest road where they were sold to the county council. It was reckoned that if you did this too often on certain fields, you could ruin them. There was so little soil there that, if you took the stones away, there would be nothing left except bare clay or chalk. On the other hand, if you never picked the stones, they would gradually work to the top making cultivation difficult and resulting in poor crops. So a careful balance had to be achieved, picking the stones often enough to keep the land from being overwhelmed with them and not so often that you made the land unworkable.

By the mid-twenties the increase in the number of motor vehicles on the roads meant that road-making had become bigger business. Stone-picking died out and the materials were quarried in bulk in other parts of Britain. But I have a feeling that, sooner or later, efficient stone-picking machines will bring this practice back. Hard core of all sorts is becoming more and more valuable now that local authorities are increasingly reluctant to give planning permission for new gravel pits to be dug and the old gravel pits are becoming worked out. Vast quantities of flint lying about the countryside could become a valuable asset again.

George Larkin made the best use he could of such side-lines and, I believe, got Grove Farm through a very difficult period through his own good sense and hard work. Nevertheless things were very tough. I remember that a firm of land auctioneers at Tring (Brown's, now Brown and Merry) had responsibility for supervising the farm in a rough sort of way. A manager used to call in from time to time to see that Larkin was keeping proper accounts and on one occasion he called him in and said: 'Now look, Mr Larkin, everything is costing too much and the farm is not making any money. You must be more economical.' Larkin looked earnest. 'I be as 'comical as I can be already,' he declared. 'I just can't be any more 'comical.' I am sure he was telling the truth.

Irrelevant Education

After four years at Mr Webber's school my education had to continue elsewhere and Mr Webber advised my mother to send me to Harrow, where his son had been. Because of the nature of Mr Webber's teaching, I had absolutely no trouble whatsoever with the examination and in January 1926 passed quite high into the school. I suppose I ought to have considered myself very fortunate and very privileged that my mother was spending quite a bit of money on my education. It was, after all, supposed to be one of the best schools in the country. Actually I thought it all rather a waste of time.

Initially I passed into quite a high form, thanks to Mr Webber's extreme competence in getting people through examinations. But I fell ill in my first term and could not keep up with the standard, so I was kept at the same level the following year. One problem was that the Latin taught me by Mr Webber bore no resemblance to the Latin taught at Harrow, in pronunciation or anything else. This was mainly, of course, because the system at Harrow was not designed solely for passing exams but was genuine academic learning.

After this initial setback, however, I settled down and made normal progess in the school. But I was always thinking about the farm at home. I remember thinking what an appalling waste of agricultural land the very large playing fields were. Sport was, of course, a considerable feature of any boarding school in those days and in the wintertime, five days a week if you were any good, you played football (Harrow's own version) out on the enormous area of pitches. Even if you were not any good, you still played two or three days a week. I was not any good. I was not really interested in it. If you were not playing football there was a curious custom of the place that you still had to put on football clothes and, during the period when other people were running about on the field, you wandered about the surrounding suburban area in your kit feeling rather cold. So this is what happened to me two days of the week in the winter. I quite enjoyed it, apart from the cold, because it was at a time when the area around Harrow was being rapidly built up, when Rayners Lane, Kenton, North Harrow, South Harrow - all these outer suburban areas - were being

A pretty picture of harvest in the twenties, but it was hard work and highly uncomfortable when there were thistles in the corn.

developed by the big speculative builders such as Laings and Wimpeys, and I spent a lot of time around building sites. I did not talk to the people much, but I got very interested in building construction and this probably influenced me later on in life.

My four years at Harrow passed without really having any effect on my character whatsoever, in spite of all the vaunted traditions which were supposed to imbue you with all sorts of establishment attitudes. I was perfectly happy but the 'aura' of the place simply passed me by. In the final year, after you had passed your School Certificate, which I did successfully with a large number of credits as I had a natural aptitude for exams, you were allowed to specialise. I went over to mathematics with a certain amount of English, both of which I found quite easy, and school life became much more interesting. But whether there was something wrong with me or whether the whole public school

Bradbys House in 1927. Spot me second from the left in the middle row. Fortunately I was never short enough to have to suffer the indignity of wearing an Eton collar and sit cross-legged at the front.

tradition is phoney, this institution – founded right back in the sixteenth century and steeped in hallowed tradition – left me quite cold. You constantly had shoved at you the traditions and customs of the place and the privileges which, so it was claimed, you accrued from having been there. But I was constantly reminded of the money that was being wasted and was always feeling that I could have done with it back home on the farm. It was probably very ungrateful of me to look at it that way, but there is.

During the whole period I was away at Harrow, I continued to try to farm a little on my own. In partnership with my sister, I still kept poultry and rabbits, which we sold, and as the years went on, this developed into quite a sizeable enterprise. The rabbits had long ceased to be pets and we were multiplying them on quite a reasonable scale but, of course, because we were away at school, we had to pay somebody else to look after them for about half the year. In 1925 Mr Newland retired and was succeeded by Maurice Chapman, who had trained under him as a gardener. He took over the job of looking after our animals and had the advantage of being totally honest, which Newland had not been. I remember he was very unmechanical, as I am. Once, at considerable expense, we bought an incubator so that we could hatch out more eggs, but Maurice could never make this work. He managed to cook the eggs instead of incubating them and always lost his temper with it. So we were never able to use it since no holiday was long enough to hatch a full batch of eggs out and he could not do it for us.

I had nearly half an acre of land on the farm, a small piece of one field very near to the house, and on this I used to grow potatoes quite successfully. It was an extension of what I had originally done as a small boy of trying out different varieties of potatoes. I was able to do all the planting work in the Easter holidays, then hoe and earth them up during the half-term holiday, and in the summertime, of course, I was able to lift and sell them. So, all in all, this worked quite well as a hobby and I kept it up until the time I started farming properly. The strange thing is that, although I had this early obsession with potatoes, it is the one thing I have hardly grown at all in serious farming since, principally because the land is not totally suitable. I grew them during the war and for some time afterwards, but at no other period as the land is too stony and the yield you get is not as good as in the real potato-growing areas, like Lincolnshire.

From a fairly early age, I found trees interesting. When I started clearing out and looking after the woods around The Grove

Our poultry business – several different varieties all mixed up with the family dogs.

The ash trees my mother bought me which I planted at the bottom of Chalk Dell (an old chalk quarry) in Little Grove Wood. They are getting on for sixty years old here but look younger because the lack of water made them grow slowly.

at, I suppose, the age of about ten or eleven, I persuaded my mother to buy me some trees to plant in the open areas which had not got any. She bought me about fifty ash trees as a birthday present, which are there at this moment, and I have been planting trees intermittently ever since. I still find it a very satisfactory activity and really wish I had had the scope to do it on a larger scale. The eighteenth-century landowners living in an area like this must have had a wonderful time; they did not farm just to produce food, but used the waste land to produce timber as well and really did the job properly, which nobody has ever done since.

The woods which exist on almost every farm in the Chilterns have meant that the timber industry has always been an ancillary to farming in Buckinghamshire. In the twenties and thirties the town of Chesham, which now has a great variety of industry, relied very largely on timber working. There were some wonderfully skilled turners in the town, who could make the most beautiful wooden bowls of tremendous size out of local wood. They also made big, wide shovels out of one piece of beech, which were used for shovelling grain or malt. At the other end of the scale, almost every wooden spoon sold in Britain in the inter-war years and every child's wooden seaside spade was made in Chesham out of local beechwood. Chesham specialised in these small wooden things while nearby High Wycombe specialised in furniture. Most of this skill has now gone, destroyed partly by the introduction of plastic.

In the really great days of the local woodware industry, you could not go very far through the Chilterns without meeting somebody carting timber. All the timber was moved then by teams of horses – two or three horses strung out in a line. The men who hauled the logs would go away for a whole day if it was for a few miles, or for several days if it was perhaps right down at Henley in the woods there. It was a highly skilled business because they had no winches or cranes. The logs were merely rolled up on to the wagons with long chains, which were looped under the logs and over on the other side of the wagon and pulled up by the horses. This was a skilled operation and quite dangerous. A number of accidents used to take place where the logs would roll on rough ground and people would get crushed or hurt.

You couldn't travel far in the Chilterns in the 1920s without seeing somebody cutting or hauling timber. These tree trunks are being brought to Chesham for use in the local industries. (From The Missendens in Camera *by Clive Birch/S. H. Freese Collection.)*

The timber felling was all done with a cross-cut saw used by two men. Power saws for felling were not in general use until the thirties, but many farmers had a saw bench which they would drive using, for example, a tractor engine as we did. It was during this period that I remember George Batchelor being very seriously injured by our saw bench. He and George Larkin were cutting up logs out of quite heavy pieces and the bench was not properly protected as it would be nowadays. The two men jointly lifted a heavy log onto the bench and, in lifting it, Batchelor over-balanced and his foot came up under the saw and the front part was totally cut off except for one toe. He was carried into the farmhouse and

Tom Reed started work at less than fourteen years of age as a horseman and finished up as a traction engine driver with Boughtons. He lost a finger in a threshing machine and was back at work within the hour. As with all their injured employees, Boughtons kept him on.

what was left of his boot and sock taken off, and when I saw him he was sitting on a chair with his foot in a bucket of cold water smoking a cigarette relatively calmly. I was sent running over to my mother's house to 'phone for a doctor and I can remember, although I was only, I think, about thirteen at the time, being furiously angry because the doctor was so long in coming, and then when he did arrive he attempted to gossip with me before going into the house to see to George. George was in the local cottage hospital for several months after this and, despite there being no antibiotics then, came out quite fit, although slightly lame.

Anywhere where there are farm people you will see signs of such injuries. Will Barnett, who married George's sister and has worked for me for years, lost a finger; other people, especially during threshing, lost fingers and legs. If you went up to our local threshing machine contractor, Boughton's, in the early morning, you would see people arriving for work on crutches and in wheelchairs. These were people who had worked for many years for the firm and had been injured at work, but who were always kept on afterwards. Nowadays inspection of machinery and tools is more stringent and there are fewer accidents, but they still happen.

Tools have changed a lot in the last fifty years. Nowadays, if people are driving in stakes for a fence, they normally use a heavy sledge hammer. But George Larkin, in the 1920s, would no more

A hedger wielding a bill hook. In the Middle Ages these were listed as weapons and in time of war were liable to be called up along with their owners.

think of using an iron sledge hammer on a wooden stake than he would of flying. He would have considered it positively immoral because the sledge hammer would have damaged the stake. Instead he would use a wooden beetle which he made himself. This beetle was merely a short log with two blacksmith-made iron hoops round it to hold it together and a handle in the middle, so that it made a huge wooden mallet. They are still used a little today, but in those days they were universal. It was an article of belief that you did not hit a wooden post with an iron tool of any sort whatsoever, because it would split and ruin the post.

Hedge-cutting tools, which nowadays have quite long handles to avoid the user getting scratched, were short bagging hooks then. You held a small, crooked stick in your left hand to hold the brambles and bushes away, and used the hook in your right to cut the hedge. Cutting the larger stuff, you used either a short-handled bill hook or a very narrow axe. This was a special axe with a narrow head for splitting pieces of wood so that they could be bent down and layered into the hedge. I've not seen one of these narrow axes for many years, but short-handled bill hooks and bagging hooks do still exist.

At that time many of the small hand tools we used were made by the local blacksmiths – paddles, for example, which were small, straight hoes for cutting the thistles and dock out of corn

One of the many blacksmiths in Chesham at the turn of the century; this one was still in business in the twenties.

with rather the same action as a gardener would use with a Dutch hoe. You walked along the rows of corn and, instead of chopping the weed down, pushed this paddle into the bottom of the thistle or dock and removed it. A slightly heavier version was carried by every ploughman to clean the mud off the board of his plough so that it ran more easily. Chesham supported at least three blacksmiths then, as well as a small agricultural engineer, Mr Sonny Morton, and even a little iron foundry run by a Mr Redding in Frances Street, who could cast plough shares and other plough parts for you more or less to order. He made them out of scrap, so they were not anywhere near as hard or as long-wearing as modern parts, but nevertheless he could make anything that you required. Then, of course, you only had to go to Hemel Hempstead to find a full-scale agricultural engineering firm able to make anything required on a farm. This was a firm called Davis & Bailey, situated in Marlowes (where the new town centre is now). They had a large yard, a foundry and they used to make ploughs right from scratch,

A single-furrow horse-drawn plough – the basis of all agriculture. The function of the plough has remained the same since it was first invented, that is, to turn the soil over. Therefore its design has been remarkably constant, affected only by the materials available with which to make it and the power available to pull it. Until relatively recently the body of the plough and the mould board which turns the soil over were made of wood, with only the colter and share, which make the vertical and horizontal cuts in the soil respectively, made of cast iron. Consequently the people described as 'plough makers' in early church registers would have been mainly carpenters or even wood carvers, since some parts of the plough would have had to be carved to the right shape.

making their own castings; their ploughs were particularly suitable for the stony ground of the Chilterns.

In the twenties, most farmers in the area were still using a single-furrow horse-drawn plough, although two- and three-furrow ploughs had earlier been developed for use with the tractors that were available from just before the First World War. Some of the latter needed two men, one on the tractor and one on the plough, and all had to be lifted and turned by hand. The basic single-furrow plough had barely changed in design since the Middle Ages.

Davis & Bailey reflected the long-term static situation in agricultural practice up until the Second World War for they made nothing new for a very long period. In the 1930s, they were still making what they called their Jubilee Hay Mower, originally designed to celebrate Queen Victoria's Jubilee. It was a good machine but only suitable for horse-power. As soon as tractors came back into widespread use, one had to look for something which was made for higher speeds and would have a bigger output.

Ploughing in Turville at the southern end of the Chilterns in the 1920s.

This type of binder was in general use in our area in the 1920s. It had to be drawn by three horses because the machinery was driven by a ground wheel which made it very heavy to pull.

'Shocking' in Bucks, 'stooking' elsewhere. Whatever it was called, it was an uncomfortable job.

Still, the original horse machinery made by firms like Davis &
Bailey lasted a long time. On Grove Farm we had a corn drill made
by a firm called Knapp, which had been bought second-hand in
1916 and this was still running in 1940. Of course, it was never run
at high speeds, so it was never shaken to pieces as machines are
nowadays. It was pulled behind horses and taken over to Ley Hill
for repairs or new parts. The blacksmith at Ley Hill, a Mr
Saunders, could do far more than just shoe horses. He completely
repaired harrows and cultivators of all sorts and made new tines
for them, or anything else that might be required. There was also a
wheelwright in Ley Hill who could build carts and make wheels
right from sawing the tree trunk to building a wooden wheel and
putting the steel tyre on it. Of course, this business was put out of
operation completely by the arrival of rubber tyres in the 1930s,
but in the twenties everybody had wooden farm carts with wooden
wheels.

One machine which had been introduced before the First
World War and was universally used by the twenties was the
binder (actually a combined reaper and binder). Almost all
American or Canadian in origin, these machines were cutting all
the corn in the country by 1920. The machine which immediately
preceded the binder was a type of reaper called a sailer, which did
not tie the sheaves of corn but just pulled them off a cutting
platform with revolving rakes. I did see some in use in Norfolk but
never at home. The binder, on the other hand, not only gathered
the corn but also bound it in sheaves. It was really quite a
complicated machine. Properly set, it would make even sheaves,
neatly tied together, and the knotter itself was a neat mechanism.
Exactly the same sort of thing is used on modern balers and little
alteration seems to have taken place since.

No doubt the binder was an improvement on the previous
method of harvesting where the corn had to be bound by hand,
but, nevertheless, it still involved a tremendous amount of hard
work. The bound sheaves had to be stooked, or what was known
in our part of the world as 'shocked', in the field into sixes or
eights or whatever. They were left out for a week or two to dry
and then picked up with a pitchfork on to a cart, taken back to the
farmyard and put in ricks to be threshed out later on. The
stooking, I remember, was a painful business when you were not
used to it because, in those days, the corn was absolutely full of
weeds and thistles. You took two sheaves, one under each arm and
you slid them down your arms and stuck the butts on the ground

so that the ears of corn were against each other at the top. This was so that they would stand up and, if it rained, the water would be thrown off the grain. As you slid them down your arms, they scratched you dreadfully unless you kept your sleeves done up. Every sheaf of corn in the country had to be handled in this way until combine harvesters came along towards the end of the Second World War.

For spare parts for our machines, we relied largely upon Davis & Bailey in Hemel Hempstead and, with the frequent breakdowns in harvest time, I remember Larkin was always going there to get parts. The firm at that time was in the hands of two old brothers Bailey. They were elderly and eccentric gentlemen, who kept the business going until the new town of Hemel Hempstead took over their premises. The younger of the two brothers, Ben Bailey, used to amuse me because if he was asked for a part and it was not in the stores, he would say he thought he had one on an old machine somewhere in the yard. He would stand there tapping his head with his clenched fist and gradually this would cause him to remember whereabouts in the vast yard full of junk the part he was looking for was. He would have to tap the information out of his head.

The other machines on the farm were all quite simple and crude: harrows, cultivators, and so on. They were basically the same as nowadays but made of low-quality soft steel or cast iron which could be repaired and even made by local craftsmen, so the system was moderately self-supporting. You did not run out of spare parts as can happen now. At the end of each sowing season, you would take your harrows into Saunders at Ley Hill and have them repaired for the start of the next season. Sonny Morton in Chesham would repair your mower or binder and set these up for next year. A lot of these people were extremely competent craftsmen and, although the machines are much better now, I do not think there is quite the same standard of excellence among the people who are servicing them. I suppose the blacksmiths and engineers in those days served long apprenticeships and did not have so many different machines to deal with. They took a long time learning about them and so understood them very well.

There was a whole network of ancillary trades which served local farmers then, not just to look after the machinery but to care for the livestock too. With the increase in dairy cattle during the twenties, new skills became necessary and the influence of vets became more important on the farm. Captain Wilson, the stone-deaf vet from Berkhamsted retired and was replaced by a younger man, and vets also used to come out into the district from Watford. But far more important than the vets, or even the legions of patent medicine vendors who used to besiege the farmers selling remedies for every known complaint (none of which had any great value), was the local knacker.

I suppose there was a knacker in every district – somebody who was prepared to come and remove dead animals at short notice and dispose of them. Since the livestock was very unhealthy, there was a lot of this sort of work to do. Tuberculosis was rife amongst cattle and frequently spread from them to human beings. Johnes disease, brucellosis, you name it, all of them occurred very frequently and they were all things about which the vet could do absolutely nothing and against which the patent medicines too were completely ineffective.

The local knacker in Chesham was Harry Wing, and he would come, in the early days with a horse and cart, later on with a lorry, at only an hour or two's notice and remove dead bodies or put down animals which were too sick to recover. Originally, his trade had mostly been in horses. He kept the *Golden Ball* public house in Church Street, Chesham, and behind it had some sheds and stables where he carried on his trade. Such a gory business would not be allowed in the middle of the town these days and certainly would not be acceptable immediately behind a pub. Somehow or other, he managed to keep it fairly clean and tidy and he had some farmland of his own where he could dispose of some of the waste products. In Church Street, he would sell some of the more healthy parts of the animals to local dog and cat owners, and occasionally people would buy it to cook up for their pigs or poultry. In those days, there were no patent tinned pet foods; no doubt those that exist now are made of about the same things that Mr Wing used to sell.

Mr Wing seemed to conduct his business on the lines of a charity, which he completely controlled himself. What he paid you for the animals he collected would vary considerably from visit to visit. The factors he took into account were how easy the animal was to collect, how much meat it had on it and how much sympathy he had for you. If you had a lot of losses, it was very noticeable that the amount he paid you for carcasses gradually went up.

Because he had dealt with thousands of sick animals, he knew a lot about the job. He would do autopsies on your animal and report to you what had been wrong with them which, just occasionally, gave you some lead as to how to avoid further trouble. Also, if he came up to see an animal and he did not think it was necessary to slaughter it, he would tell you so and maybe suggest some form of treatment, in particular with regard to horses about which he was a real expert. He gained a tremendous reputation among the farming community and they had great faith in him. On occasion, this faith was taken to somewhat bizarre limits. He told me himself of an occasion when, one Sunday afternoon, after the pub had closed and he and Mrs Wing were sitting quietly in their parlour dozing, there was a tremendous clatter up Chesham High Street and he heard a horse and cart turning into his yard, rattling on the cobbles. He looked out of the window and recognised a farmer from some six miles away, driving what he knew to be a very young and quite frisky horse, who was in the most terrible sweat, having been driven very fast. There in the back of the pony cart was something else, wrapped up in rugs. The young farmer jumped out of the cart and came running into the parlour saying, 'Mr Wing, you've got to help me – my wife's going to have a baby!' She had gone into premature labour and, instead of calling the local doctor, her husband had panicked and

Harry Wing, the knacker. Farmers trusted him more than the local veterinary surgeon.

had come five or six miles to see the one person he had faith in –
Wing, the knacker.

To this day, the knacker performs a marvellous service to
farmers, though now, of course, there are fewer deaths among our
animals. We know more about mineral deficiencies. The vets are
better-trained. We have eliminated TB and brucellosis. We have
nearly eliminated Johnes disease. But still they die for one reason
or another and still, anywhere in the country, there is a knacker
who will come out any day of the week to remove the animal and
dispose of it. Still, I believe, they give you, not necessarily what the
animal is worth, but what their sympathy for you dictates.

I suppose, inevitably, the atmosphere at home during the latter
half of the twenties altered quite a lot. My brother, who had gone
to America when he was quite young to stay with relatives, had
come back to England. He did not like the idea of an office life at
all and was working in the film business, helping to produce short
films – silent films, of course. Through him, an actor called
Maurice Braddell turned up at the house and formed an attachment
to my mother, which was to last for very many years and she
subsequently married him. Almost immediately, he started spending
a lot of time with us. He used to play chess endlessly with me and,
although he was not exactly like a stepfather, he provided me with
very entertaining company during the holidays. In a way, he was a
very clever and knowledgeable man. (He still is, for that matter,
being still alive in 1986.) But he was too erratic and could not stick
to anything for long.

At the same time, my sister, then a teenager, after various
slightly emotional episodes where problems arose, became engaged
to a man who was also working in the film business. So, quite out
of the blue, I got to see quite a different side of life. The talk was
all about films and film studios and, on one occasion, our house
and grounds were borrowed for making a film. This was *School for
Scandal*, directed by a man called Victor Saville, who became very
well known, and starring a beautiful girl called Madeleine Carrol.
The location work was shot in and around our house and at Ley
Hill Common. In one scene a coach and four was driven across the
common with various people in it dressed in eighteenth-century
costume. Unfortunately somebody forgot about the telephone lines
overhead and they all had to come back a few days later to re-
shoot it on a different part of the common.

I suppose that among the people who were friends of my
mother's and the people who came down to stay with us, there

Here is a quote taken from an interview with my step-father published in The New Yorker *quite recently. Obviously there were a lot of 'goings on' at Little Grove to which I was quite oblivious:*

'Jean, my wife, . . . was a very good hostess. Our apartment in London became a sort of centre of theatre. . . . We had drinks and parties all the time, and there were all sorts of political things going on . . . We were very close to Hyde Park Corner. I used to go and listen to the speeches and see if I could find anybody worthwhile, and then drag them back with me. And Jean had a lovely house in the country, so we'd all go in our cars and have weekend parties and half the West End would be there.'

were probably some very interesting characters, but I was not really very interested in them so I probably missed quite a lot. Sometimes I wish I had not been quite so much of a philistine and had paid more attention to what was going on indoors as well as outdoors.

Some people look on the whole of the period of the 1920s as a happy period, as a period of gaiety and fun. It did not seem like that to me. It seemed to me a period of anxiety, when most of the world was in trouble and those that were not tried to pretend that the others were not either. The people in the South East of England, who were mostly in work, talking amongst themselves, would try to pretend that it was the fault of the Welsh miners and Northumbrian miners themselves that they had not got any work to do and we were all right here because we worked hard. Of course, this was a load of rubbish. It was a divided country and a divided society, where people could still turn their backs on other people's problems. I felt that this situation couldn't last and also that, for us in particular, things were already going wrong. My mother was spending very freely and not just on my education, and this could not continue. At the end of the twenties, the whole thing collapsed – the economy nationally, and the Harmans!

I was a little confused about exactly how I was going to make a living, but my intention was always to farm. I do not think though that that was my mother's intention; she would have much rather I had tried to get into some other form of business because, at that time, farming was not at all prosperous and was a very difficult way of earning money. Agriculture in our district at the end of the twenties had settled down after the disastrous price slump of 1921 to some sort of stability though at a very low level. Farms like Cowcroft Farm or the farms around the village of Latimer that are not on very good soil had gone out of cultivation altogether. Cowcroft Farm had no tenant for several years, and for five or six years no rent whatever was collected on White End Farm and Hockley Farm on the Latimer Estate. Bury Farm in Chesham, which was one of the biggest farms in the whole area, was being more or less ranched. In other words, it had fallen down to grass, purely natural grass, and the tenant was herding sheep and cattle on it all year round rather like an American cattle ranch. Another phrase for this was 'dog-and-stick farming' because all you needed was a dog and a stick. The better farms had mostly gone over to producing milk and were just about viable but at a very low standard. Grove Farm, under Larkin's guidance, had also gone right over to milk production but part of it had been let off to our neighbours, the Mashes, and another small part of the far end of the farm had been let as a separate farm to some people called Miles, who produced milk on that as well.

I suppose there was not any actual decline in agriculture in the second half of the 1920s, just a stable depressed state. At the end of that period, there were many hundreds of acres all over the Chilterns which had been completely abandoned, and which became overgrown with bushes and trees of different sorts. Only the best farms were still being cultivated properly, those with really good occupiers, who knew their job and managed to keep up their standards. But these were the exceptions rather than the rule and, on the whole, it was a period of very low productivity which did not start to alter until well on into the thirties.

It was in this atmosphere that, all the while, I was having to think how I would start farming in due course and how I would survive at it. At Harrow I passed the entrance examinations to Cambridge, originally to read Economics, but once there I changed to Agriculture in the hope that I might get some other ideas apart from the ones I had already collected on my own. So, in the autumn of 1930 when I was eighteen and a half I started my degree course at Cambridge, which should have lasted three years but which, in my case, got cut short.

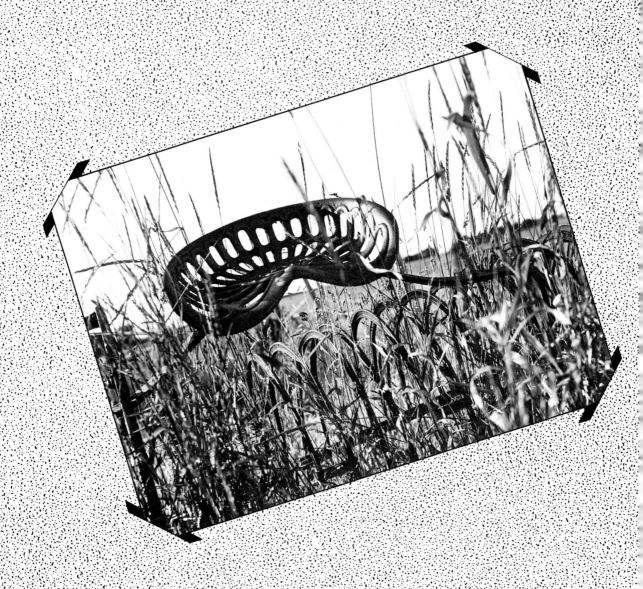

Cambridge Cut Short

The Chiltern countryside in 1931 must have looked as beautiful to the outsider as it had at any time since the original clearance of the forests. I say to the outsider but not, of course, to the farmer. Eleven years of agricultural depression – deep agricultural depression – had led to a panorama of overgrown farmland. To the outsider overgrown hedges look more attractive than neatly trimmed ones. They provide more living space for small mammals and birds and, indeed, the bird population was probably very high then. But to a farmer they signify neglect. In addition to the farms that were neglected there were, in our immediate area, at least 500 acres that had been completely abandoned. Abandoned Chiltern land is soon taken over by bushes and shrubs of all sorts and also a certain number of oak trees. Most of the growth was thorn scrub but there were also great quantities of briars – that is to say, wild roses. One 16-acre field on part of nearby Shepherds Farm became almost entirely overgrown with wild roses, and when they were in flower, it was a scene of indescribable beauty. But in farming terms it was a field that was completely wasted.

Almost half the land that had not actually been abandoned had just been allowed by the farmers to slip down to grass of its own accord, instead of being properly sown down for grazing. For this reason, the wild flower population – weeds to farmers – was very high; all the different types had multiplied endlessly and so had the insects which lived on them and the birds which lived on them.

In 1930 legislation had been introduced in an attempt to raise the price of grain and bring more land back into cultivation. Called the Wheat Act, this law did not offer a guaranteed price to farmers, but instead imposed quotas on the milling industry so that firms had to use a percentage of British-grown wheat in all the flour that they produced. However, the percentage set was so small that the price of grain remained very low and most farmers in our area concentrated on livestock – particularly dairy farming – aided by a general improvement in the services, such as piped water and roads, that were by then available. As a result, this district produced a really large amount of milk for a short period in the early thirties.

A horse rake, not used for years and left to rust in the hedge. Such sights were common in the late twenties and early thirties.

Even the tiniest farms – smallholdings of just 4 or 5 acres – were proving unviable and being abandoned by 1931. These had usually been started by ex-servicemen after the First World War and were distinguished by ugly asbestos bungalows that mercifully soon became invisible behind overgrown gardens. The owners attempted to make a living by growing fruit and vegetables or, more often, raising poultry, but eventually they gave up the fight against the larger producers and drifted back to the towns where industry was slowly beginning to turn up jobs.

To the urban worker from Chesham and the other towns, this abandoned countryside offered an endless supply of nuts to pick, of blackberries to gather, of rabbits to poach, of sloes, of firewood and of peasticks for the allotment. It was a beautiful place to look at and to walk in. To the countryman, it was a picture of complete neglect and dereliction which he was powerless to remedy.

Despite the depression, for me 1931 started well enough. I was very happy at Cambridge and the work came quite easily to me. The agricultural course I was doing was partly science, which I had never done before but which I enjoyed, and the actual agricultural work that we had to do was child's play because I had seen it all happening. At least once a week, we used to visit the university farm and all walk round it together. As the majority of students were townsmen, it was all new to them but very familiar to me. The only trouble occurred when I was asked to identify a crop. I knew what it was but could not always explain *how* I knew what it was.

The management of the university farm at that time was in the hands of a man called Mansfield, who was an old-fashioned type of East Anglian farmer in his attitude. The principal lecturers on agriculture were Dr Sanders and Frank Garner, both of whom became very influential figures in the agricultural world. Mr Mansfield, in his lectures liked to keep us all in touch with what was going on at the farm at that particular time and what was happening in all farms in that particular season. I remember one day going into a lecture and each one of us found in front of our place a saucer full of warble larvae, which are large, rather unpleasant-looking maggots. It was the time of year when these had to be dealt with in cattle so Mr Mansfield thought it was right to draw our attention to them!

Cambridge University in the early 1930s was a far less pressurised place than any university is nowadays. Some people were working very hard and there were certainly many highly qualified academic people there but, on the whole, the atmosphere was very relaxed. The vast majority of undergraduates had come from public schools, from comparatively well-off families, and did not seem to worry much about their courses, preferring to spend a lot of their time on sport. I was never particularly interested in sport. I made one attempt to take up rowing, and indeed when the rowing club looked at me they thought I could be very useful to them, being big and strong-looking. But I was so badly co-ordinated, I turned out to be quite useless and, having broken one oar, they decided that rowing was not for me.

I did not live in my college, Trinity, the year I was there. Freshers spent their first year in lodgings and I lived in a little

Trinity, my college at Cambridge. Because I was only there for one year I never lived in.

house, No. 16 Maid's Causeway, on the Newmarket Road, along with two other undergraduates. One of these had been to a public school and was full of self confidence and did absolutely no work at all; the other was more like a modern undergraduate. He had come from a grammar school in Kent, was intending to be a doctor and worked very hard. He would often study in his room until two or three o'clock in the morning.

We had most of our meals in college. The college itself, of course, is a most beautiful building and there was quite a high standard of catering with reasonably priced beer and things of that sort that young men appreciate. My landlady's idea of catering for her lodgers was most peculiar. She would provide us with a very large, rather greasy breakfast and we reckoned the teapot, a huge brown one, was only emptied once a term. She would just add a little tea each morning with extra hot water. After the first few weeks, the tea leaves, by rotting away, started to stain the water without her having to add any more tea at all. For some unaccountable reason, the resulting beverage started to taste more of onions than it did of tea.

I had private tutorials on botany from Dr Lines, who subsequently became Professor Lines, one of the leading botanists of that period. Attached to the School of Agriculture were Professor Engledow and Professor Biffen and all the other originators of the plant breeding programme which has dominated cereal production in Britain ever since. Highly qualified academic people do not talk down to undergraduates like older people in other occupations do, and I enjoyed talking to them and being treated as an equal.

It must say something odd about my character that, although there were quite a number of undergraduates there who had been at the same school as I had, I do not believe I ever spoke to any of them all the time I was at Cambridge. It was almost as though my whole period at public school had never taken place at all. I had a very fortunate working relationship with one other undergraduate called John Weiler, whose experience previously was exactly the opposite to mine. He had had a good scientific education whereas I had practically none, and he knew nothing about agriculture while I had first-hand experience. So I could explain the agricultural side of the course we were doing to him and he could work with me in the laboratory work we had to do. I think we were very helpful to each other. Although he was doing the agricultural course, John had no intention of farming but planned to become a land agent.

The country at that time was in the deepest of depressions economically as well as agriculturally. I suppose, in a way, although I associated myself in my mind with the people who were suffering from widespread unemployment, it did not really come home to me because at that point it had still not affected me personally in the slightest degree. Therefore, though I went to union debates and Labour Party meetings, I did not take any active part; in any case, I was still desperately shy about opening my mouth in public. I was so shy that when it came round to the May Ball season at Cambridge, when most people went to college dances and that sort of thing, I did not. I did not attend any of them, either in my own college or in any other. I did go to one at Balliol College, Oxford, at the invitation of an old friend of mine, but my lack of social graces depressed me so much during the course of the evening that I drowned my sorrows in drink and don't even remember how I got back to my hotel. I do, however, remember waking up next morning feeling perfectly all right, thus proving to myself what I have known ever since, that I have a remarkably good liver.

At the end of the academic year I received the results of my first year's work. Agriculture in those days was not an honours degree, so they just gave you gradings at the end of each year depending on how you had done. I was one of three people who were awarded first-classes in their first year and I felt very pleased with myself. My tutor congratulated me and said if I wished to change over to another subject and do an honours degree, it would present no problem. I went home for the long vacation.

I had had an inkling previously that things were going wrong and, sure enough, I arrived home to a crisis atmosphere. My mother's income had been greatly diminished because it came from my father's old business in London, which had not been well managed and which, in any case, was hit by the general slump. What's more, she was extremely extravagant, living right up to and beyond her means, and her final man friend, Maurice Braddell, was also extremely impractical. In some ways, he was quite a brilliant person and, if he took anything up, for a short while, he could do it very, very well. He got some good jobs acting in films and the theatre, but he had a habit of not turning up when he was required so the producers did not engage him again. He had also written one or two plays which had been performed, including one called *The Best of Families* which was extremely successful, running in London and Paris at the same time, but, again, he did not stick at

Maurice Braddell with Merle Oberon. This must have been one of his top moments.

it. By 1931 he was getting very little acting work and was largely supported by my mother. He felt they were living too far away from London for the good of his career and that they should go and live there, and my mother eventually agreed to this. It was probably necessary anyway by this stage for her to give up the house we had always lived in.

The financial stringencies made it necessary for me to leave Cambridge right then at the end of only one year of the three-year course I had started. I was sad about this, of course, but accepted it as being quite inevitable. My tutor, however, when he was notified, was very upset. He offered to get me on any other course I wanted and to see if there was any financial help available, but, of course, there was not much in those days. Anyway, I just accepted the situation and worked towards my new objective: obtaining the tenancy of the farm which the trustees of my father's estate wanted to sell to meet my mother's debts. I planned that, some time in my middle age, I would try to go back to Cambridge and finish my degree course, which would theoretically have been possible. When it came down to it, however, I adopted too many other activities and I never went back. One small legacy of my year at university came to fruition quite recently. During one vacation I had brought home from the School of Forestry a large number of poplar cuttings, with which they were then experimenting and in which I was taking an interest. I planted these on the farm and a few years ago sold the resulting trees, so that was one very practical benefit I gained from my brief period of higher education.

The farm was still being managed by George Larkin at this time, but he was now getting on and ready to retire. My sister was still at home, but my brother had gone abroad again to work and I was the only member of the family to express any interest in taking over. However, I was still a minor and the two men who controlled the estate, Harold Walters and Alistair Urquhart (successors of the original trustees), were both completely hostile to the idea.

Harold Walters was a very well known accountant and an auditor of one of the biggest building societies, the Abbey Road Building Society, which later became the Abbey National. He was a hard, dry man who dealt with nothing but financial facts, and who would have closed down everything if he could have done. He wanted to sell the business in London and the farm and provide a small, but reliable income for my mother out of it. Urquhart, the other trustee, was an insurance broker who lived at Latimer, a village about three miles away. He was rather vague, but, I think, a sensitive, sensible man who said I should try to get a better job because he felt it was impossible to make a living out of farming. In fact, nobody at that time thought that becoming a farmer was a sensible proposition. Working in the family business in London was not possible either because this was doing badly and the manager, Mr Evans, would have opposed taking on extra people.

So I had to go through the motions of trying to find a job. For a nineteen-year-old boy in 1931, even with what was deemed in those days to be a fairly good education, this was not easy, especially as I had not finished my course at Cambridge. I wrote off for a whole lot of jobs but nobody was remotely interested in employing me, except, I remember, someone I wrote to in the entertainment industry. Since my mother's friend, my sister's fiancé and my brother were all working in the entertainment business, this had seemed a good place to start looking, and I applied for quite a lot of the jobs advertised in the film and theatre magazines which were always strewn round our house. The only one I was ever offered involved selling flexible gramophone records. In those days, gramophone records were stiff, brittle things that were very easily broken and this one small company in Soho, run by a Mr Green, had brought out a patent for a flexible gramophone record, which he was trying to push. The quality of the sound it produced was nowhere near as good as the normal HMV-type records, but Mr Green assured me that it was the coming thing and offered me a job selling   but on commission only. This I knew was not on so I did not take it. I do not know how his particular business developed but it is interesting that modern discs are very similar to the type he was then trying to market.

After some weeks of job hunting, the two trustees finally accepted that, in the prevailing economic atmosphere, it would be impossible or, at least, very difficult for me to get a job. So it was agreed that I would be granted a lease on the farm. Harold Walters, being a hard money man, insisted that a valuer be brought in, that I paid the full market value of the rent and paid for all the stock that was on it – about £1200. The one concession he made was that I should have two years to pay for all this. It was, of course, the personal property of my mother and not the Trust but, never mind, he made the terms. A rent of 15 shillings an acre was fixed and I acquired the farm, or part of it, because quite a lot of land had been let off. George Larkin moved out of Grove Farm House, my mother, my sister and I moved in and some improvements were made. My mother also got herself a flat in

London where she often stayed and helped Maurice Braddell with his career.

The farm was not particularly well equipped and there was not enough stock, especially as I intended to take back the acreages which had been let off to our neighbours, Mr Miles and Mr Mash. The only capital I had arose from the fact that my father had given each of his children a £1000 debenture in his company in London. As this had not been well managed, however, the debentures were not deemed at this time to be worth the £1000. I sold mine for £850. It had been given to me without my knowledge when I was six years old, two years before my father died, and the solicitor who had dealt with his estate after his death had not declared it for estate duty. As soon as I transferred my debenture to another person, the estate duty authorities became aware of the fact that I had owned it and came to me for estate duty at the 1918 rate plus eleven years' interest. This seemed tremendously unfair but could not be avoided. All I could do was, again, get time to pay and it was agreed that I should pay £1 per month for twenty years.

It was essential for me to retrieve the land that had been let off as not enough had been kept for anybody to be able to make a living. About 47-50 acres of land had been let to Mr Mash, who was one of the few people who had made a success of farming in the Depression. He was a very energetic man, who grew a very large acreage of vegetables, trading as the firm of Mash & Austin.

Grove Farm House when we moved in. I slept in what had been the harness room (far left) and had my own outside door.

They had large orchards and contracts with businesses such as the Cunard Line. All through the twenties and thirties, when everybody else was failing, the Mashes had been doing very well, mainly because they had these well established wholesale and retail outlets. This particular member of the Mash family who ran the Chesham end of the business and was our neighbour was very helpful to me although extremely aggressive and rather boastful. He agreed to give up the tenancy of the land he had and also gave me lots of advice, though he never forgot to tell me what a good turn he was doing me.

About 50 acres had been let to the Miles family, who occupied Sales Farm and were dairy farmers. This took rather longer to get back, partly because Mr Miles depended more upon having the extra land than Mr Mash did, and I did not retrieve it for nearly two years – one field not for three years. I was dealing, therefore, to start with, with a total acreage of only about 120 acres and employed two farmhands, which would be considered grossly excessive labour these days. We had eighteen cows which had to be milked by hand, quite a lot of poultry, a relatively small arable acreage and very little equipment.

Looking back, I don't think that when I went into Grove Farm I planned ahead as well as my father had done twelve years before. I was so obsessed with the idea of getting the tenancy that I don't think I thought all that much about precisely what I was going to do with it. It was still being farmed immediately before I took it over in a way that did not differ in most respects from the way Benny Wingrove had farmed it before my father took over. It is true that George Larkin had introduced a small dairy herd and that the other types of stock had largely disappeared, but the arable farming, which had been reduced to only about 30 or 40 acres, was cultivated on a simple three-course rotation exactly as Benny Wingrove had done. The only exception was that the fallow break involved rather more roots and rather less bare fallow than in his time, in order to feed the larger number of cows.

Once I had actually got the tenancy of the farm I did wonder whether I should have formed a definite strategy instead of just dreaming about farming on the playing fields of Chartridge Hill House and Harrow. I therefore wrote to one of the lecturers at Cambridge who had taught me on the university farm – Frank Garner, who subsequently became Professor Garner, Head of the Royal Agricultural College. I wrote to him because he had relations and roots in the Chiltern area around Princes Risborough where

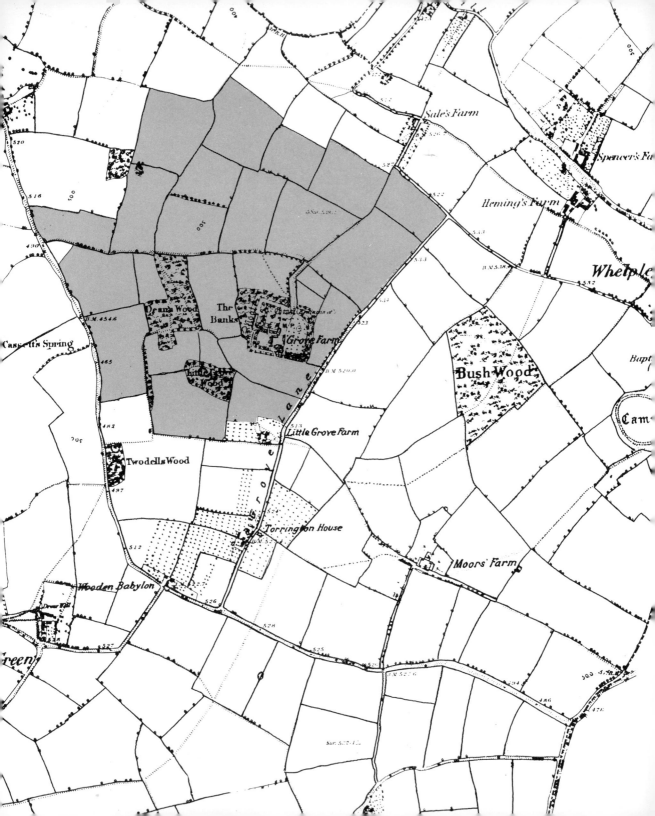

conditions were not greatly different from ours, and he gave some outline advice and a few suggestions, but nothing very drastic.

In my first few years I was hit, as farmers tend to be, by a number of financial crises and my energies and spare cash were all devoted to overcoming these rather than to planning any particular long-term strategy. The one area where I did try to apply some forward thinking and scientific know-how was in increasing our milk yields and, later, in building up a herd of Ayrshire cows to replace the bunch of mixed breeds that I had 'inherited' from George Larkin. This was the period when the theories of the late Professor Robert Boutflour dominated dairy farming. His teaching about what to feed cows to balance the milk that you presumed you were going to get from them really worked. You gave them your own home-grown hay or roots to maintain their bodies and then bought in concentrated food to balance the milk they were producing exactly so that they kept producing it. That one man dominated the entire dairy industry for a generation. He certainly dominated me, with some success.

On the whole, however, I can't claim to be anywhere near as far-sighted as my father had been when he started. If I had I would have got in a combine harvester from America, switched back to arable farming, and gone in for mechanised grain growing like everybody did ten years later. But at that time farming was at such a low ebb that no-one would have dreamt of lending me the money even if I had thought of the scheme. Planning didn't really come into it. I had Grove Farm – that was all that mattered.

Opposite: this map shows the reduced acreage I took over in autumn 1931. The rest of the land my father had bought in 1919 had been let off to neighbours.

Part of the cross-bred Shorthorn herd at The Grove in 1931.

Farming in Earnest

I actually took over the tenancy of the farm in the October of 1931 when grain fetched under £6 a ton, milk was just under a shilling a gallon wholesale and farm wages about 30 shillings a week, give or take an odd shilling depending on the skill of the worker. The records of cows that I bought and sold in the first few months show that I bought cows in milk at about £20 apiece (now they would cost around £550) and sold barren cows or cows that were too old to keep for as little as £10 or £12 a piece. For instance, on 14th December of that year I sold two cows to a Mr Alfred Gee for £32 (they must have been old cows) and bought a heifer from Mr Mash for £25. Old man Gee lived at Hill Farm, which is still there at the south east end of Chesham, and he also ran a corn merchant's business and mill nearby. In addition, he provided loans to local farmers and had rather a bad reputation for demanding the money back just before harvest-time, when they were in a weak state financially. If they could not pay up he would buy their wheat from them at a specially reduced price. Whether this reputation was justified I really don't know because I never got into his clutches.

I only had one man in my employ when I first took over – George Batchelor – but soon I also took on his brother-in-law, a very skilled arable man originally from Lincolnshire. His name was Will Barnett and he concentrated on the cultivations. With one short break, he stayed with me for the next fifty years.

Every morning, starting at 5.30 a.m., George Batchelor and I milked the eighteen cows in the cold, leaky, dilapidated cowshed lit only by a flickering oil lamp. Nowadays one would not be allowed to produce milk in such a place. The roof was collapsing and at one stage had to be tied up with wire to prevent it from falling into the moat.

I don't think I can have started with any illusions at all about milking being in any way enjoyable because I had seen it going on for a good many years during school holidays. It is quite surprising how many people from outside agriculture imagine that milking by hand is enjoyable and clean. They carry an image of fresh-faced milk maids in the open air sitting on three-legged stools or perhaps

One of my competitors, Mr White, with his milk barrow. (Reproduced with permission from The Book of Chesham *Barracuda Press.)*

Will Barnett.

A list of the cows I took over plus the first two I bought, with their dates of birth and when they came into the herd. On the left is the figure put against each cow in the annual valuation. The different colours show what a mixed bunch they were.

jolly West Country men in smocks. It was not like that at all. Cows are just about the most filthy animals you can imagine and, when you were milking by hand, within minutes of commencing work, you too were filthy. Cows brought in from the fields in winter are plastered with mud. You had to do your best to get this off them and particularly off their udders to try to keep the milk reasonably clean. That immediately made the cowshed absolutely filthy and you sat in the filth, milking by hand, while they fidgeted and flipped you in the face with their tails, which were also soon dirty. They occasionally kicked you quite hard with their filthy feet and maybe even knocked you over into the muck. In fact, there was no job more conducive to ill temper and misery in the early morning than fetching in a lot of cows in cold weather when, maybe, you had to go quite a distance in the mud to fetch them

and then had to sit down under them to milk by hand.

As a result of these conditions, the milk was not really very clean. (I assume the people who drank it did not realise this.) Even if you did try to set standards and keep your hands and the cows clean, these soon slipped, I'm afraid, under the pressure of having to get the work done. When milking was over, the milk was poured through a filter – first of all just a muslin cloth, then, in later years, a disposable cotton wool filter – and the most amazing collection of straw and pieces of dirt were caught in it. But, of course, you knew in your heart that much worse things had already become dissolved in the milk that the filter could not trap. So I do not think many dairy farmers at that time – myself included – could live up to the sort of picture people had of how milk was produced. It was therefore an extremely good thing that the

It was very difficult to keep milk clean in conditions such as these.

government began to introduce measures in the thirties to help us improve the health of our cows and generally raise the standard of the milk produced. Not only did pasteurisation become compulsory, but inspection by the sanitary authorities became much stricter too, encouraging us all to introduce improved milking facilities.

Like everybody else, we moved quite soon from milking by hand to milking with a machine, though the cows stood in the same dirty shed as they had previously stood to be milked by hand. You simply moved the machine along to them and it was operated by an overhead pipe and pump creating a vacuum. This was an improvement, but you still got kicked quite often when you tried to put the machine on, and it still dropped off into the muck and you had to be very disciplined about always washing it clean, dipping it in disinfectant and so on before it was put on the cow again. I do not think, even then, that there was an enormous advance in the cleanliness of milking in a cowshed.

Nowadays, milk is largely produced in milking parlours where the cows are brought in to a special place to be milked and the milk is pumped straight off from the cow into a big holding tank or refrigerated tank and goes straight from this to the dairy to be pasteurised. No doubt it is a great deal cleaner and better than it used to be, but whether it is really as clinical as it is represented to be, I do not know because I have not done any milking for some years. I do know from the farming journals and from the vast experience I did have, that the major problem with milk production is not in the milking of the cows, but in disposing of the slurry and we all know what that is. Even now, if I visit dairy farms in the winter they are still pretty dirty places, apart from the parlour itself. I have no happy memories whatsoever of being involved in milk production. I only remember five o'clock in the morning, cold, wet and miserable, dealing with a lot of hostile cows which generally obstructed you as much as they were able. Of course, the one fatal thing to do in this situation was to lose your temper. Then all was lost: the cows got excited, they kicked you, or knocked you off your stool or, later, knocked the milking machine off their udders and everything became filthier and filthier.

The yields of the cows in those days were very much lower than now. I have a record of them and I would hate to quote them to a modern farmer because they were so low. Plenty of cows were not giving more than 2 or 3 gallons a day, when now one would expect 5 or 6 gallons at least to feel that the cow was worth

keeping. The cows I had were mostly Shorthorns, but one was an Ayrshire and because, I suppose, it happened by chance to be the best cow in the herd, I made up my mind that I would eventually establish a herd of Ayrshires. For the time being though I had to make do with what I had.

I did add four new cows to the herd that autumn. The first one I bought was at a farm sale nearly in the middle of Old Amersham. I remember the vendor's name was Mr Lofty and the tenancy of the farm was changing hands. I bought a Shorthorn cow there which, inevitably, was known as Lofty for the rest of her life. A local cattle haulier who was present on that occasion took it back to Grove Farm and charged me £2 for doing so, which I immediately realised was quite a lot compared with the cow's value of £25 and that in future I would have to try to find a cheaper way of transporting my purchases. I then went to a sale at Moonshines

An early milking machine like the first one we had in use on Shorthorn cows.

A modern herring-bone parlour. Taking the cows to the machine instead of the machine to the cows made milking a great deal cleaner and easier. The Shorthorns of my early milking days have now given way to Friesians.

Farm, Flaunden, where I bought a heifer just coming up to calving and had the miserable job of taking her home on foot. She was rather wild, but fortunately there were not many people about so I managed it entirely on my own. When she finally calved down she turned out to have six teats with milk which is unusual – usually cows have only four with milk. The fact that she had six with milk made it extremely inconvenient for milking. She was also a terrible kicker. She was known, predictably, as Moonshine and did not last very long.

I was not being very successful so far. The third cow I bought – looking back I cannot imagine why I was buying them one at a time and not buying a group (probably because I was frightened to spend the money) – was a big Friesian bought from Milk Hall Farm, Chesham. She was called Hope and looked magnificent. She was obviously giving a lot of milk and I proudly drove her up the narrow lanes from Milk Hall Farm, through Botley and Jasons Hill back to Grove. She walked peacefully in front of me as if she knew exactly where she was going, and I was full of hope at the prospect of the good she was going to do me. But, alas, near Christmas she caught pneumonia and died. This put me off Friesian cattle for the rest of my life – rather unfairly since there is certainly no evidence that they suffer from pneumonia any more than any other breed. At the time she died she was giving 6 gallons of milk a day, which seemed an enormous quantity in those days.

The fourth cow I bought that first autumn was a big Shorthorn called Ruth from Hammond Hall Farm, Ballinger, right the other side of Chesham. She seemed very quiet and I successfully drove her about three and a half miles from Ballinger to Chesham with no difficulty at all. In those days it was still possible to drive a cow along public roads as there were very few cars around and, if any came, they approached you with caution and consideration. Not so the children. The children who were out from school all rushed after poor old Ruth, shouting at her, and she set off up the road much faster than I could follow. Fortunately she ran in the right direction. A sensible old man managed to stop her and drove the children off with curses, but by this time she was panting and her poor old udder, which was very big and heavy and swinging from side to side, looked quite sore. By the time we were out through the town, up Nashleigh Hill and home she could only just drag herself along. It was she that I expected would die, not Hope, but Ruth lived for years after and, apart from being a little bit difficult to milk because her udder was so close to the ground, gave us no trouble. She was a hardy old girl and did not seem to suffer from her unpleasant experience.

Before the advent of the Milk Marketing Board, the price of milk used to be agreed annually in the different districts between the milk distributors and the farmers. In Chesham, there was a private agreement between all the dairymen who delivered milk in Chesham and the farmers who supplied them. Because of the change of pattern in farming by the early thirties with so many people going in for milk production locally, the farmers were in a very weak bargaining position. When it came to an agreement about prices in the January of 1932, the milk buyers in Chesham got together to keep the price down that they would pay to the farmers and there was a bit of an uproar about it. I remember, although I supplied Hemel Hempstead not Chesham, going to a meeting which the National Farmers' Union called in Chesham to

An advertisement in the Bucks Examiner *for the sale of Moonshines Farm.*

decide how to fight the distributors over this matter. The main speaker at the meeting was a man called Hodson, who was, I think, the County Chairman or County London delegate of the National Farmers' Union at that time, and he and the county secretary, Tom Biggs, came to encourage the farmers in the Chesham area to stand up for their rights and to obtain a reasonable price for their milk.

The meeting was held in the old town hall in Chesham and was really quite a lively affair. Mr Hodson was a bit of a rabble-rouser and he issued threats about turning over milk lorries and boycotting farmers who signed up with the distributors and was generally going to play it in a very tough way. Lots of people in the audience cheered him on and said that no way would they sign contracts with the distributors at the pitiful price they were being offered and everybody talked very toughly. I was quite impressed at the time. Then, the next morning, in the cold light of dawn, all the farmers could be seen trooping into the local milk distributors' office and signing up for another year. It taught me the lesson that farmers in Britain do not stand together in any difficulty. All the talk of boycotts and stopping milk lorries and tipping milk out of the churns all melted away in cold daylight when people started doing their sums. Later on, in other controversies, the same thing has happened. It is very obvious to me that farmers in Britain will not put up a strong fight for what they believe are their rights in the way that workers in other industries will, or in the way that farmers do in other countries, particularly France. We take it all lying down.

In the spring of 1932, when milk became very plentiful in this area, a terrible blow fell on me and on several neighbours as well. The local dairy in Hemel Hempstead, which had collected our milk for some years, gave me one week's notice that they could not take it any more. With no Milk Board in operation there was no way that I could get rid of the milk. It was a hair-raising time because milk was the main thing we were producing from our paltry eighteen cows. So I took the decision to retail the milk in Chesham. I started by going round to all our friends and acquaintances in Chesham to ask them to buy our milk and told them I would personally deliver it. The customers I got were very scattered, so it was not an entirely economic operation but at least I managed to sell our own production quite soon. Within two years I was actually selling more than I produced and had to buy in milk to sell.

It was hard-going starting a milk round from nothing. This is an advert I placed in the Bucks Examiner *to try to attract custom.*

If you want the
BEST MILK
order at once from
A. S. HARMAN
GROVE FARM, CHESHAM.

For their health's sake—give your children
GRADE A "TT"
we supply it.

FRESH CREAM DAILY
also
BUTTER from 11d. to 1/1 per lb. **AND EGGS**
delivered **TWICE DAILY** anywhere in
Chesham, Chesham Bois and Ley Hill.

People who are not Milk customers supplied
::   ::   just as regularly.   ::   ::

After we had moved out of Little Grove it had been let to a Colonel Miles, a full-time serving Army officer then stationed at the War Office, and his wife had a daughter by a previous marriage called Valda. I had never had any sort of girlfriend before, but Valda was a determined sort of girl and, in no time at all, we were getting on extremely well. She would help me with my milk delivery and all the other tasks around the farm and was, for the following two years, a great help to me. This, in some ways, makes me somewhat ashamed of my subsequent conduct.

We got down to delivering the milk in an old bull-nosed Morris car. I suppose it would be worth quite a lot of money if I still had it now – then I bought it for £10. I didn't have a driving licence but Valda did, so she drove and I would run up and down the paths delivering the milk. Although this milk distribution venture got me over the immediate crisis surprisingly quickly, it was not a wholly practical solution because of the amount of travelling we had to do. So, before long, I employed a man called Ted Wallis to help. He lived in Lye Green and was a carpenter by trade but, being out of work at the time, agreed to deliver the milk by bicycle with a large carrier on the front and back. He delivered milk to customers around Latimer and down as far as Latimer Road in Chesham. In those days there were masses of pheasants in that area, preserved and reared by Lord Chesham's gamekeepers. Ted had been a wonderful cricketer in his time and had played for Essex although a Buckinghamshire man and he used this ability to knock pheasants over with a stone. He would often come back from his milk round with a couple stuck in his pockets to feed his family. I used to worry that he would be caught by the gamekeepers but he never was.

In the 1930s, most milk was delivered straight from the churn, which was either carried around on a horse-drawn milk float or, in the case of smaller distributors, on a three-wheeled barrow pushed by hand. The milkman had a scoop which held a pint or maybe a quart, which he would dip into the churn and then fill the jugs of housewives who came out to him. Sometimes the jugs were filled from the tap at the bottom of the churn, a method popular with housewives as they were given the impression that they were getting slightly more than they had paid for. The churns were often beautifully polished on the outside, many with brass plates bearing the name of the milkman, but the inside was very difficult to clean without steam sterilisation – not then generally available – and so they were pretty unhygienic. It was also a method which was

Valda, who helped me start my milking business.

subject to abuse because a dishonest milkman could make up the quantity in his churn by surreptitiously adding water, and it was not all that easy for the authorities to catch him at this.

The Weights and Measures Department of the County Council were in charge of seeing that the milk sold was of a proper standard and they used to send people round in the early morning to check it. They would buy a pint of milk from each milkman and test it, but the test they did to see if it had been diluted was not a very sophisticated one. They merely tested the amount of butterfat present and, provided it was above the presumed standard of 3%, it was deemed perfectly all right. So if the milkman knew that the farmer who was supplying him with milk had a large number of Jersey cows producing milk with a high butterfat content, he knew it would be safe to add a certain amount of water, and some of them did and got away with it. Conversely an innocent but incompetent milkman could be prosecuted for something he had never done for the simple reason that butterfat rises. If he did not keep the churn well mixed and kept scooping off the top for his customers, what was left at the bottom would contain a lower percentage of butterfat, which might well be less than 3%.

There were more sophisticated tests available but they were not used in Bucks and this method always seemed to me to be rather haphazard. If a sample was found to be too low in butterfat, the next morning, very early, officials from the county would turn up on the farm which had supplied the milk and would test the milk as it came from the cows. If all the milk from the cows on the farm when it was mixed together was above 3% and it had been sold by the milkman at below 3%, an offence was deemed to have been proved. But even that was not quite right because one might not necessarily mix the produce from the whole herd together before selling it to the distributor, but might start selling it off as soon as the first few cows had been milked. Anyway, I never got involved in any problems of that sort, I'm glad to say.

At that time, there were approaching thirty people delivering milk in the Chesham and Amersham area, so it was quite plain that it would not be possible to build up an economic round in a fairly compact area merely by getting new customers. We found ourselves delivering 30 or 35 gallons of milk a day to people who were spread all the way from Grove Farm to Chalfont Station – a distance of 6 miles – and the distributing costs were enormous. So I started to look around to see what possibilities there were for taking over other small businesses. In those days, the goodwill of a milkround was a tradeable item even though you could not be absolutely sure that the customers you bought would stay with you. It was considered to be worth about £10 a gallon for both the goodwill and the cans or bottles or whatever was used to carry the milk, but this did not include vehicles or ponies. A fair amount of pressure began to be applied by the Public Health authorities and the Milk Marketing Board, then coming into operation, to improve the methods of distribution, and some of the very small milkmen became fed up with the business and wanted to get out. So, before long, one or two rounds came on the market in Chesham, and I went to the bank and got enough capital to take some over and improve our distribution.

The first business to come on the market was at Bury Farm, Chesham. The farmer concerned used to advertise widely his hygienic milk direct from the farm, which was delivered with a mule and float by a man called Harry Joiner. I think they sold about the same amount as we did – about 30 gallons a day. I went one early morning to see him about acquiring his round. He was a drinking man, who had obviously had a terrible night and he was sitting under a cow nursing a hangover and producing this highly advertised hygienic milk. He was as dirty as you can only get working with cows without protective clothing in wet weather and he had a dirty old pipe in his mouth, which, during the course of our conversation, dropped from his mouth and fell in the milk! He just dipped his filthy hand into the milk, pulled out the pipe, knocked it out, dried it, lit up and continued milking! I reflected that if the people who bought his hygienic milk knew what was going on, they would not have been all that happy about it. Anyway, I went ahead and bought the goodwill and the majority of customers stayed with us, which nearly doubled our throughput in one go. To be honest the goodwill in the business had not really resided with the farmer, but with either Harry Joiner, who came to work for us, or more probably, the mule, who could do the round by itself so long as somebody took the milk off. Harry Joiner was rather hurt that we did not also take this beloved mule who reminded him of where he had to stop.

The business continued to grow. I took on two more small rounds and it began to look as though we had something near an economic unit of distribution. There were problems though. Quite a number of the new customers were ones who did not pay and so immediately one got into a bad debt problem, especially since Harry Joiner was a very good-natured man and could never bring himself to cut off the supply of anybody who did not pay, particularly if they had young children.

One of the businesses I purchased had given us a foothold in Chesham Bois, where there was a constantly changing population. Every time a new person moved into the area, one had a chance of getting another customer and, in common with other tradesmen, I used to give a clerk in each of the two local estate agents' offices ten shillings a time for the names and addresses of people moving into the area. I suppose this was an accepted perk for people working in estate agents. Then, before these people came to Chesham or Chesham Bois, I would write to canvass their custom and try to get it before anybody else did. Occasionally, if they were within reach, I would even go and see them before they moved to Chesham to persuade them that they should buy milk from me. All this made the distribution altogether more complicated and eventually I had to buy a van, which immediately set me one notch above my competitors who were still using horse-drawn floats. I used to leave the farm at five o'clock in the morning, take the milk to Chesham for Harry Joiner to deliver and then carry on and deliver the rest myself in the Amersham and Chalfont area. This period filled me with a rather hostile attitude to the middle-class people living in Amersham, who were very demanding in the service they expected from you. They insisted on more than one delivery a day, which was quite unnecessary, yet they were often quite reluctant to pay promptly. In Chesham, on the other hand, where most of my working-class customers lived, people did not buy what they could not pay for and were not over-demanding as to service.

Competition in the retail milk business was extremely tough because there were so many people selling in the area. The slightest thing that went wrong with your delivery gave the customer plenty of opportunity to leave you for somebody else, so there was a constant interchange of customers. In those days, milk did not keep very well. Only the local Co-operative Society were pasteurising their milk; the rest of us were selling fresh milk straight off the farm. I think the majority of people still preferred the taste of fresh milk but in hot weather it simply did not keep. However careful you were, if the housewife did not keep the milk carefully it would go off and she would complain.

The milk taken from the cows in the afternoon had to be used up and that would be delivered first thing in the morning. Some of the absurd middle-class people in Amersham thought that they

Loading my first van.

were getting milk that had come straight from the cow immediately beforehand, but since delivery in Amersham commenced before six o'clock this was quite impractical. We would have had to be up all night milking to achieve that. The fact that we had to do two deliveries a day to satisfy people's requirements, made the whole thing extremely expensive, and if anything went wrong – for instance, if you did not deliver on time – there was always somebody else waiting to take over. In the same way other people had their troubles, and when customers transferred to us we had to try to hang on to the new clients as well as the old ones.

Quite soon I had two men delivering milk, Harry Joiner and another, and I used to give them commission for new customers. They would listen out and watch around the district for people who were having trouble and step in to get their business – it was very much a cut-throat affair. Indeed, on one occasion, I reckon I caught one of our people interfering with a competitor's milk, lifting the cardboard tops off the bottles and dropping bits of dirt in, which the customer would find and so turn to us. I had to sit very heavily on this and hope nobody was doing it to us. The man in question was quite hurt, 'I could have got you a lot of customers that way,' he said 'and nobody would ever have caught me'. It is hard now to believe that something as apparently innocuous as delivering milk should have involved so much skulduggery.

Farming In All Directions

The milk distribution business now took up all the morning, with me starting at five o'clock, coming back for breakfast, going out again and normally finishing for an early lunch. At the same time, I was trying to build up the farm's milk production so that I would not have to rely on other people, and the arable production. I had at that time about 50 acres of arable on not quite as rigid a rotation as previously. About a quarter of it was in wheat, which was the only crop I sold (10 to 12 tons a year), followed by winter oats, which were all used for the horses and cattle and which were ground up with the machinery my father had had installed. After that I grew either kale on which the cattle were grazed in the early part of the winter, or an experimental acreage of vegetable crops which I tried to develop but failed. After them came spring barley, also used for the stock, undersown with clover and rye grass for a hay break. So it was roughly a five-year rotation.

It seemed an obvious thing to try to emulate my successful neighbour, Mr Mash, and grow vegetables, for he had proved it could be successfully done in this district. So in the early months of 1933 we put in several acres of peas, beans and early cabbage without really enough thought about how we were going to market them. Within a short space of time we were faced with vegetables ready for sale but nowhere to sell them. I tried to sell them through wholesale merchants, but all of them had long-term contracts and Mr Mash, although usually free with advice and help, could not help me about this because he had plenty of vegetables of his own to get rid of. Only when there was an extremely hard frost and nobody else would pick their Brussels sprouts, would merchants ring me up and say they would buy some of mine. So then I and the two men and anybody else we could round up to help would have to go out picking Brussels frozen as hard as bullets.

In the end I decided to take a lease on a shop in the Broadway, Chesham, now occupied by a travel agent, and started with the idea of selling all of the produce from the farm that I could; it was to be run by Harry Joiner's wife and a girl called Ida Sills. But people do not just come into a shop to buy home-grown peas and cabbage, so we were immediately in the position of

Ploughing land similar to ours in the thirties. Will Barnett did our ploughing in the same way as it had been done for hundreds of years.

having to buy all sorts of fruit and other vegetables from lorries that came round from wholesalers to sell in the shop. I did not really know enough about that job either to do it well, although Mrs Joiner and Ida Sills were very competent. We just about managed to meet our rent and cost, but there was no profit. And why should there have been? I barely knew what I was doing. With more confidence than commonsense, I started getting somebody else to do my milk delivery work on one morning a week. I would then take the van I had up to London, stay the night with my mother and buy the other fruit and vegetables we needed at Brentford Market. This was an interesting experience, but really one needs to be brought up with it to understand the workings of fruit and vegetable markets and to be able to buy to the best advantage. I am sure I did not, though it did at least enable me to check on what we had been charged for the produce we had bought from lorries outside the shop in Chesham.

The farm on the other side of Grove Farm from the Mashes is called Harriotts End Farm and the tenant at that time was a Mr Arthur Puddephatt. He was a farmer of the real old-fashioned type. Right through the twenties and the first few years of the thirties, when everybody else around him had let their standards fall, had not kept their hedges cut or carried out their cultivations properly, he had done everything as it should have been done. The farm still looked clean and well cultivated. He had a large flock of sheep which he used to fold on turnips and kale in the old-fashioned way and he also used to grow mangel-wurzels, which he fed to the sheep in the middle of the winter and early spring. He was absolutely obsessed with doing everything properly.

The Mashes' first planting machine, which put them well ahead of the rest of us. The woman are feeding the machine with cabbage seedlings which were then pressed into the prepared holes. The tractor driver is Stick Stevens.

Fifty years on, the Mashes are still growing vegetables. On the left here a Puddephatt, whose father worked for them in the thirties, prepares swedes for sale.

Unfortunately, in 1933 Arthur Puddephatt had a stroke of some sort and was completely bed-ridden. He could still talk, but he could not move any muscle in his body. I did not know him well but he had, I suppose, known me by sight all my life, as I had him. He sent a message that he wanted to see me. I could not think why. When I got there and was shown into his bedroom the poor fellow was lying in the most terrifying fashion, absolutely motionless apart from his face, with his daughter having to sit by him to knock flies away. It was really upsetting. He said to me, 'You are young, too young to tell lies. Are my men doing the job right on the farm?' I was slightly taken aback. 'Well,' I replied, 'I'm not all that experienced but, as far as I can see, they are doing everything as you would always have done'. He was relieved, but obviously still doubting. It was the middle of May and time that his mangels, which he took such pride in and grew such a good crop of, should have been planted. Suddenly he asked, 'Have they got they mangels in?' I knew they had not and was in a quandary as to whether to lie to him or not. Then I thought what on earth can he do about it to get it put right? He would only worry himself to death. So I lied to him and told him the mangels were in and everything had been done properly. I then went outside to the men on the farm and more or less said, 'You bloody well do it as he would have wanted you to and get on with those mangels now, before it's too late'. They looked a bit askance at a neighbour who they did not know all that well and who was very young, telling them what to do, but they got the message about it worrying him to death and proceeded to put the mangels in. Arthur Puddephat lay there for a year or two longer, in a state of complete paralysis, worrying the whole time about the farm. It was one of the most upsetting episodes in the whole of my life, especially as I was not really able to help him. I toyed with the idea of telling him I would see to the farm for him, but why should he believe that I was any more capable of doing things properly than his own employees?

Our neighbour, Arthur Puddephatt (centre), kept on farming in the traditional manner throughout the Depression. He had a large family but unfortunately his only son (top left) died of TB at twenty.

During this period I worked up a sideline which proved quite profitable. My sister's husband worked in the film business as an assistant art director for various film companies in London, mostly for Gainsborough Pictures in Islington. His job was to find anything that his boss, the chief art director, required, so if there was any sort of country scene needed with animals, or trees and so on, I used to supply them. The company would often only use these for a couple of days, but they were prepared to pay quite readily. We had one or two quiet old cows who were hired out on a number of occasions and I also provided 'country crafts'. I had a man who used to do odd job work for us and he was a very good thatcher. When they wanted a thatched cottage on the set he went up and spent several days in Islington doing the thatching for it with thatch I supplied. I received a profit on his work there while he, of course, found the experience very interesting.

This particular venture only got me into one problem. This was not in Islington but in a small studio somewhere in Soho that my brother-in-law also provided material for. They needed some ducks, so we caught up some old brown ducks we had and sent them up to London to appear in this film. The film people had them tethered by their legs to keep them in position, and as the birds were very tame they were not in the least bit unhappy about this. But the studio was in a fairly public place and some old busybody of a lady looked in, saw the ducks under bright lights and thought they were being cruelly treated. She reported it to the RSPCA, who came along and, unfortunately, found that one of the ducks had a big corn on its foot which was next to where the rope had been. So, the film company was prosecuted for causing the corn on the duck's foot by tethering it. This was actually absolute rubbish because it had had the corn for months, if not years, and certainly long before it had gone on its visit to London. However, proceedings were started and I had to produce the ducks at Marlborough Street Police Court on no less than three occasions (on the first two, key witnesses were not present). On the first occasion, the ducks started quacking loudly and the sound echoed all around the steel and concrete cells. All the prisoners' heads popped up to try to see what on earth was going on. There were looks of amazement when they saw they were sharing the cells with ducks. On the third occasion the case was finally heard and, of course, dismissed.

The arable work on the farm was still being carried on the hard way - ploughing using a horse-drawn plough and harvesting

The ducks that went to London.

Farm sales were the place to collect the local gossip.

the corn with a binder which delivered the corn in sheaves that then had to be stooked and carted. It was a lot of back-breaking work. The machinery that had come with the farm when I took over was quite old and I often needed replacements which I bought second-hand. In those days the average farmer would never have contemplated buying anything new. Instead he tried to get what he needed from a local auction sale, of which there were a great number, especially in the spring and autumn. If I had taken a photograph at an ordinary auction sale on a farm in 1933, the people there would have looked much as they do today, only perhaps less well dressed. The difference would be that there would have been very few cars parked and very few cattle wagons to transport the animals, but a great number of horses and traps.

On the whole I enjoyed the sales. They were an opportunity to get out, to see what other people had done, to listen to the local gossip and meet all sorts of people doing the same job as I was doing, that I would not otherwise have met. If you listened, you could sometimes learn quite a lot. There was always a bar which formed the focal point of a lot of talk about why old so-and-so had had to move – how he had gone wrong, if he had gone wrong, or how well he had done if he was moving up the farming scale by taking a bigger farm (this was fairly rare). The vast majority of farmers were only too anxious to give advice about how I should go on and it was almost always disinterested advice, unless they had something immediately to sell, and honest, although not by any means always good. Many of them were very stuck in their ways and not yet ready to learn any new methods. I have a feeling that the only people who were buying new machinery, as most farmers do now, were businessmen farming for a hobby. Even in those days, they would build their farms up with excessive capital and then either tire of the job or decide it was too expensive a hobby and sell up. It was a notorious fact that if you wanted to farm successfully in those difficult times it was very good to follow a businessman who had farmed unsuccessfully, because he would have left a lot of fertility behind and you could buy his equipment cheaply. Nowadays there are far fewer auction sales on farms, principally because there are far fewer farms. So the existence of larger and more prosperous farms has changed this aspect of farming as well as many others.

I remember that one of the things we all used to say as we stood round the bar was that you could not use the combine harvesters and modern machinery that was being used in places like the USA in this country. We were all talking rubbish. They were available and we could have used them perfectly easily, but we went around claiming that they were not adaptable to British climatic conditions, that our fields were too small, that it was too wet and goodness knows what else. It was all nonsense – it could have been done. Indeed, it could have been done more easily then than it was a good many years later because land was cheap – you could buy land for £20 an acre or rent it for 10 shillings. Money at the bank was relatively cheap too. The only thing missing was confidence to go in for these things. A very few people did go in for modern mechanisation and got on very well, but for most of us our confidence had been destroyed by the very long period of depression. It is no good having land available for £20 an acre if you have not got £20 to buy it with or the bank has not got enough confidence in you to lend you the money. That is roughly what the situation was.

Although I had no particular foresight as far as my arable production was concerned, I was planning ahead during this period with regard to my livestock. I had decided to build up a pedigree herd of Ayrshires and I bought my first pedigree bull at Reading for 18 guineas. He had been born in Scotland and was called Red

In the thirties farms were changing hands all the time. Lots of people were in difficulties.

Light, which proved to be a very suitable name because he was quite dangerous – very quick with his horns and very difficult to handle. Buying a pedigree bull for 18 guineas rather puts prices at that time in their proper perspective. It was equal to twelve weeks' wages for a farmworker, equivalent in 1986 therefore to more than £1000.

Valda's mother and stepfather, although not the sort of people I would normally have become very friendly with, were very kind to me. Colonel Miles himself was a typical Army man, intolerant of new ideas, as Army people often were in those days, still in his War Office job fighting the next war in terms of the last war. However, at home he was kind and hospitable and did not really seem to be all that intolerant of my views, which were certainly different from his. Valda's mother was a little plump lady, shaped like a cottage loaf, who bred dogs as a hobby and showed all over the country.

On one occasion Red Light got in with the herd of pedigree Guernsey cows that Valda's mother kept on the 20 acres of land that had been let off with Little Grove, and there were panicky telephone calls from the family for me to go and remove him instantly. I went over armed with a pitchfork. I knew he would always try to back up to get a run at whoever was annoying him, so the only thing to do was to keep advancing on him with the pitchfork and he would keep drawing back. This he did, making nasty noises and digging holes with his feet to try to get enough room to charge, and I successfully backed him the three or four hundred yards to my own land. Colonel Miles was immensely impressed. I heard him telling his friends afterwards that I had fixed the bull with my eye and had forced him back, that it was great credit to my willpower and courage, etcetera, etcetera. In reality I was frightened out of my wits and knew perfectly well the only way to prevent him charging me was to keep walking forwards so that he would keep walking backwards.

During the whole of my first three years as a farmer, Valda helped me with the cattle, the farmwork and the milk business and her family were very kind to me. I suppose I did not have any serious thoughts about how it would all end. Then one day in 1934 I was invited to go to London with her to meet her real father, who was a Mr Black. I remember him as a rather indeterminate, grey, shadowy figure, who we met over a cup of tea in a London hotel. What he said made me feel that Valda's family were very serious about the whole business. He told me (and this is remarkable when you think about it) in an almost apologetic tone, that all the money of her own that Valda would ever have would be £900 a year. This was quite twice what I was earning at the time and, in those years, was quite a substantial income for a girl to have in her own right. It had the effect of making me think, 'These people are good people and very serious – are you?' I began to have doubts because I realised that Valda was much better to me and kinder to me than I was to her. Indeed, I often used to lose my temper with her and could not really see that there was any future in our relationship.

In Chesham at this time, as, I suppose, in other similar towns all over Britain, after chapel on Sunday nights all the girls in the town used to go out for walks together in Chesham High Street and Broadway. This was quite a sight because they seemed to take great trouble to look good and to me, in that summer of 1934, they all looked absolutely wonderful. Perhaps this was because I was twenty-two years old and that is the way you feel when you are that age, but I actually have outside evidence that the girls in Chesham that year were a bit special. Forty years later at a police dinner, I was talking to a superintendent who had married a Chesham girl. I mentioned the matter to him and he said, 'You are absolutely right. In those years of the early thirties all the young policemen in Bucks used to try to get posted to Chesham because of the girls and they used to like Sunday night duty so that they could go out and see the girls on parade'.

Amongst all the girls I saw as I was going by, one stuck

The girls would parade up and down Chesham High Street on Sunday evenings for the men to admire.

immediately in my mind. I did not know who she was, but I simply could not get her out of my thoughts. She just seemed different from all the others. Apart from the fact that she had a wonderful figure and you could see her blue eyes from the other side of the street, I do not really know what it was, but she had such an effect on me and my guilty conscience concerning my relationship with Valda that I felt I had to end it. It was a bit traumatic when I did so but I felt bound to do it to leave myself free.

At that time, I was delivering milk in Chesham Bois in the very early morning and I had a habit of singing loudly – for my own benefit and nobody else's. I used to sing hymns or psalms, not from a religious point of view but because, for somebody who is not a good singer, they are the easiest thing to sing. I remember receiving a note from a man living in Green Lane, Chesham Bois. It said, 'Dear Milkman – I am a deeply religious man. I am particularly fond of the 23rd Psalm but, sung very loudly at six o'clock in the morning, it brings out my very worst instincts. Will you please stop.' This toned me down but it did not stop me. I realised one morning that, instead of hymns, I was singing an old ballad which went, 'I did but see her passing by . . .' I decided I simply had to do something about the girl I kept seeing in Chesham.

I had to find out who she was for a start. Mrs Joiner, who helped in my shop, knew her name was Florence Plested but looked somewhat horrified that I wanted to know and made appropriate disapproving noises. I also found out where she worked. Although she was only twenty, she had worked since leaving school in various greengrocery shops. At this time she was working for the International Stores at the greengrocery counter of their Chesham shop, also in their Amersham shop, and in their shop at Northwood. In spite of the fact that she was only twenty, they had enough confidence in her to send her to manage these counters, so she was not always in the same place. For some days (it may have been weeks), I arranged that whenever she came out from work I was there. Whenever she came off the train from Northwood I was there too. And whenever she worked in Amersham there I was again. So gradually she got used to seeing me. Then, one Sunday evening, when she was walking along with her friend outside the Post Office, I manoeuvred my van into a position opposite the letterbox as she was walking by. I made some excuse and asked her if she would post my letters for me. She looked absolutely staggered that I had spoken to her when we hadn't been formally introduced, but by that stage I was hardly an unfamiliar face.

Florence Plested, just before we met.

Fortunately she did not call the police as, I suppose, some people might have done and we were able to start talking.

This happened on the Sunday before the August bank holiday, 1934, and, from that moment on, through the rest of that August, we saw each other on every possible occasion. It was the most beautiful month – sunny all the time, or so it seemed to me, but this was perhaps just a reflection of the way I felt. I found out everything I could about her that I hadn't discovered already. I happened to know the headmistress of the school she had been to, who remembered her as being one of the cleverest girls they had ever had at the school and who thought it a tragedy that she had not been able to go on to the grammar school because her widowed mother was hard up. I discovered that she lived in Berkhamsted Road with her mother who had had quite a hard time as a widow, also that she had a number of brothers and one sister. The brothers had all left home and were living in and around Chesham, apart from one, who lived in London. I did not know any of them and they did not know me. I think they were really rather surprised by the fact that Florence and I had got to know each other.

I realised as time went on that I, at least, was certain that I wanted to get married and as quickly as possible. I did not believe in elaborate religious ceremonial marriages and was against having a church wedding. Possibly Florence would have liked one. She sometimes reminded me in later years that I had promised her she would get £5 a week and a maid to help in the house. It was some years before I was able to deliver either, but I did in the end. She agreed to marry me and the arrangements were made for the wedding on 5th November – a good day because you remember it for the rest of your life by the bonfires. It was a bit of an anticlimax as we were married at the Registry Office in Amersham with nobody present except my sister and Florence's youngest brother – added to which I was late. My sister had been living at Grove Farm House up until this point, along with her husband whom she had married the previous year. On the day of our marriage they had moved out to a new house they had had built at the end of the farm drive, taking the maid with them. In all the excitement, I had forgotten to organise myself some hot water and consequently could not get shaved in time. So I was late for my own wedding and in about another ten minutes I believe it would have all been off. We were married by the registrar, Archie Ferguson, a local solicitor, who tried to make something of it, telling us of the importance of the step we were about to take but it did not really impress either of us very much. We then went off in my sister's car, which I had borrowed, to honeymoon for one week in Bournemouth.

Bournemouth in November is a pretty terrible place. We went down through the New Forest, which was dripping wet with leaves falling and a slight fog. All the while, Florence kept saying, 'I don't feel married'. I did not feel married either but it did not seem to bother me. We had made no hotel booking because it had not seemed necessary and so when we arrived I walked into what seemed to be a quite modest hotel. It turned out that I had chosen the side entrance of the Carlton, one of the biggest hotels in

Bournemouth. However, once there with my bride I could not retreat so we booked for the week. I caused Florence a considerable amount of embarrassment because of my huge appetite. The Carlton had a large menu and instead of, for instance, choosing either porridge or cornflakes, and either bacon and eggs or haddock, I would order the lot. After a moment's hesitation, the staff would serve it up. I suppose off-season they were particularly anxious to please their customers. The only other people in the hotel were elderly ladies or elderly couples who realised we were on honeymoon and would put their heads together and titter all the while, which was also embarrassing. When I finally came to settle the bill for the hotel there was one final embarrassment in store for Florence. To her horror, I brought out one day's takings from the milk round in a blue canvas bank bag and counted out to the cashier the entire week's bill in small silver and coppers, including a large number of farthings. Milk in those days was threepence halfpenny a pint and quite a lot of people had half pints.

After the week's honeymoon, we came back to find considerable chaos in the milk business and I had to go to work immediately sorting everything out. We were faced with complaints that people had found broken glass in the milk because the bottle washing had not been done properly, people had not collected money they should have collected – all sorts of pressure that afflict a small but rapidly expanding business. If she resented it Florence did not show it and set to helping me with a tremendous will so that we had things straightened out in next to no time.

The total time between meeting Florence and getting married was almost exactly three months. I have since read in my stepfather's diary the following entry: 'Tony married very suddenly a small girl from Chesham. They are very happy and they are making the farm pay'. He was absolutely right. Until then, I had never more than broken even. We both used to say, 'This is not really for ever' – but it was.

Countdown to War

Florence and I carried on for almost two years trying night and day to build up the milk business, the farm and the greengrocery business in Chesham. During the course of those two years, we also took another shop in Amersham, which Florence's youngest brother, who had experience in the retail trade, took over for us. He ran it really rather well, building it up from scratch, and simultaneously delivering our milk and selling from the shop.

Life was extremely competitive. Although the depression which had gripped the country since the First World War was supposed to be over, the country's economy was said to be improving and there was by then very little unemployment in Chesham, it was still a town of extremely low wages. Many families in Chesham, even those with a number of children would only have half a pint or a pint of milk a day, and very often they could not even pay for that. This made milk distribution highly uneconomical. In no time at all we had a huge bad debt problem, but it was difficult to stop delivering to people who could not pay if we knew they had children. I felt at times that we were almost running a social service. We had to judge between those we could safely continue to supply because they would sort themselves out and pay when they got work, and those who had no intention of paying anyway. In those days, the moonlight flit was a very common occurrence and people used to go without a word. They would change their jobs and leave everything unpaid. This was particularly common in a place like Amersham, where most of the people were working as salesmen or office workers outside the area and could not easily be traced.

There was very little time off from work. In 1935 we never managed to get any holiday at all; that was the year that our first daughter, Penny, was born. In the following year we got away for a week to Carbis Bay in Cornwall, which had always stuck in my mind from the holidays spent there with my parents when I was very young. It was not disappointing. There were still the beautiful golden sands and the slightly rough, but very lovely sea. From time to time, we managed to get out in the evenings but not as much as people of our age would normally have expected to do.

Florence just twenty-one, Penny two weeks and me twenty-three.

Apart from the short-term and largely abortive efforts to go in for vegetable growing and selling, my major farming venture during the period from 1932 to 1939 was the development of the dairy herd. My first efforts to buy cows locally soon after I had taken over Grove Farm had only been partially successful. Of the four I bought, two were quite good milkers, one had died and the fourth was so difficult to deal with that I had had to get rid of her. The National Herd at that time was extremely unhealthy and our cows were no exception. Brucellosis – that is, contagious abortion – was rife and so was TB, so we had to do something about cleaning up our cattle and I was one of the first people in the area to make a start.

In the early 1930s, cattle breeding throughout Britain, but particularly in the Home Counties, was completely dominated by the Shorthorn breed. This had originally been developed in the eighteenth and nineteenth centuries, presumably driving out the inferior types of local breed which were popular before. Its main merit was its extreme adaptability. Within the one breed, specialist breeders were able to produce exactly what qualities they wished. In the more isolated areas of northern England and Scotland, they selected their cattle purely for their beef and produced a type of animal which became popular with beef breeders throughout the world. From the same origins, in the Midlands and southern England, nearer to the main centres of population where more

Before the Second World War the majority of dairy cattle in Britain were Shorthorns and had been for sometime. By the fifties they were declining in the face of the even more specialised Friesians.

dairy products were required, the breed was selected for its dairy potential and so developed into what was known as a Dairy Shorthorn, and that was what was popular in Bucks. Despite their name, they were not consistently good milkers, just reasonably good by the standards appertaining at that time. It was quite unusual then to have an animal which gave 1000 gallons or more in a year, whereas nowadays 2000 gallons are readily obtainable.

Almost all the cattle found in Bucks in 1932 would have been Dairy Shorthorns. A great number of them had been bred from stock bulls bought from one particular breeder, Mr Timberlake of Hastoe near Tring, who owned a nationally known pedigree herd, and every local farmer liked to boast that he had a bull from Mr Timberlake; George Larkin had worked for him before coming to manage The Grove. The breed could be any mixture of brown and white, either in patches or all brown or all white, or sometimes the hairs were all mixed up producing what was known as a roan. The brown ones were always known as red and in eastern England they were specifically selected to be all red, but within this breed colour was actually immaterial. You selected your cattle for what you wanted to produce.

Shorthorns were quite hardy and adaptable and easily managed, but by the early thirties most people engaged in milk production were looking for much higher yields, and they tried to achieve this either by improving their Shorthorn herd or by taking a short cut and going into another breed. The Friesian breed, which had been brought in from Holland and which was common throughout northern Europe, almost always gave much more milk than the Dairy Shorthorn but there was strong prejudice against it at the time. To start with, the milk did not carry as much butterfat as a Dairy Shorthorn's and in the 1930s people wanted fat in their milk, not like nowadays when many try to avoid it. Indeed because you could be prosecuted if your milk fell below the 3% standard butterfat content, which Friesians quite often did, there were grounds for prejudice there. In addition, as the breed then was, it was a very difficult animal to fatten once it could no longer be profitably milked and so it was not a good butcher's animal. The one other main objection people had against Friesian cows then was that they were supposed to be delicate, and since the first Friesian cow I bought, though a marvellous milker, died within months, this prejudice was reinforced in my mind. I therefore looked elsewhere for another breed which would give more milk than the Shorthorns I already had.

The herd of Ayrshires I built up – a good choice at the time.

The breed I chose was Ayrshires because my experience with just one Ayrshire was a good one and furthermore the disease situation in south west Scotland where they were bred was much better than elsewhere. The only other choice I could have made was one of the two Channel Island breeds, the Guernsey or the Jersey, but these are small animals and have other problems, or at least I thought they had, so I went for the Ayrshire. Nowadays an infinitely improved Friesian breed has even higher annual milk yields and much better butterfat percentages than before. What's more, the animals now fatten reasonably well when their milking life is over and their progeny fatten quite well too. So the dairy scene is now dominated by the Friesian and the Dairy Shorthorn has become almost a rare breed. In 1932, in the local markets of Tring and Aylesbury, probably 80% or 90% of the cattle would have been Shorthorns or Shorthorn crosses. Today 80% or 90% would be at least partly of Friesian breeding. So there you have a total change in the cattle population of an area in less than a lifetime. My choice of the Ayrshire was a good one at the time for they gave much more milk than the Shorthorn, you had no trouble with the butterfat, and they were hardy and easily managed. A choice made today would be quite different, for the breed has not been developed and improved to the same extent as the Friesian has.

There was only one Ayrshire herd that I could find out about anywhere near and that was kept by the National Society for Epileptics at their farm colony near Chalfont Common, and some while before I was married, I went over there to see their herd. The people who were running it indoctrinated me further in the merits of the breed and made determined efforts to sell their animals – but at a price which I felt I couldn't afford to pay. So I began going to Ayrshire sales at Reading. At that time the auctioneers at Reading were bringing down large numbers of cattle from Scotland and selling them in Reading market, all TB-tested. I started off by buying a bull and just one or two females and over a period of seven years changed my herd over from a mixed herd of Shorthorns to a pure Ayrshire herd.

During this period I sometimes went up to Scotland to buy the cattle myself and have them brought down by rail. I would go up overnight on a train to Lanark where there were big sales and get off at about six o'clock in the morning and have to wait in what seemed like the coldest and draughtiest station in the world until things opened up. I would then go to the sale, buy what I required, have the cows transported to Berkhamsted and we would then pick them up off the train and drive them through the roads from Berkhamsted station home. This would be quite impossible these days, of course, but there wasn't much traffic then and two men, or better still a man and a dog, could easily drive a bunch of cattle the four miles home to Grove Farm.

Gradually I built up contacts with a lot of Scottish breeders and dealers, in particular a big cattle dealer called Hendry Brothers who were responsible for a lot of the cattle coming to England at that time. One of the brothers would take me round to a number of farms, and as a result of that I met a man called Bertie Drummond at Bargower in Ayrshire who at that time was the leading exhibitor of Ayrshires at all the major shows, especially the Dairy Show in London. He was a bachelor absolutely obsessed with his cattle, who had, apparently, little other interest in his life. He had inherited, along with his brothers, a number of herds from their father who had been something of a genius in selecting animals which, when mated together, would produce good results; this is known in the breeding world as 'nicking'. At that time the name Bargower dominated the Ayrshire breed.

Every year the Drummond brothers had a sale of their bulls which was one of the top events of the cattle breeding year, and around about 1938 I went up with a view to buying a bull and

Bertie Drummond being presented with his portrait by the President of the Ayrshire Society at the time, Monty Sellars.

stayed the night with Bertie Drummond at Bargower. I was fascinated by the fact that he kept questioning me about my two years of marriage, which had already resulted in one child and another one was on the way. 'Where did you find your wife,' he asked. 'Was she a farmer's daughter?' When I said 'No', his face fell somewhat. His next question was: 'Is your marriage a success?' and when I replied, 'Well, I think it is', he said, 'Well, surely it's just like animals, you've got to choose something which nicks'! It astonished me that he should apply to his own life the rules which he applied to his cattle breeding. But obviously he never made up his mind as to what would 'nick' because he died quite recently still a bachelor, a genius in his work as his father had been before him. The experience I gained in this period was to be of some advantage to me in business later in my life when I was commissioned by a number of other people to buy whole herds of cattle for them.

During all this period, land was still extremely cheap in the area and in 1932 or 3 I had rented the balance of Shepherds Farm, the one that had been ruined and abandoned after Mr Ford went bankrupt, for 10 shillings an acre. Most of it was covered with wild rose bushes which looked extremely beautiful and amongst which I grazed my young Ayrshires. It didn't carry much stock but at least those it did take didn't cost me very much; they just wandered around among the bushes in the summer getting a reasonable living. Of course, they were extremely hard to find at times – it was like looking for cattle in a jungle! But so long as the perimeter fence was kept sound it wasn't too bad, and I was able to use a small part of it that was under separate ownership and which had been kept cut every year for hay. In fact, for several years I got the hay for nothing which eased my feeding problems.

The man I rented the field from was a local speculator named Jim Long. He had originally been a boot manufacturer in Chesham, but in the early twenties had fallen out with his employees over a strike, closed down his factory and gone in for land speculation instead. He gradually built up what in later years would have been called a large land bank, but his plans did not apparently develop as quickly as he had hoped and by the mid-1930s he was sailing close to the wind of financial trouble.

None of this need have concerned me had it not been for the fact that during Ascot week in 1936, on a hot day on the way back from the races, Jim Long, who could not swim, went for a bathe in Marsworth Reservoir and was, a very short while afterwards, found upside down and dead. This led to considerable complications for very many people in Chesham if they banked with the same bank that he did – the National Provincial Bank. I was one of those people. By this time my capital was stretched to the limit. We had a milk delivery business, a greengrocery business and two shops. I was twenty-four years old and it had never occurred to me that a shortage of capital would limit my actions. You had vegetables to sell, so you opened a greengrocery shop; you had milk to sell, so you started a milk retail business. And if you had to borrow money in order to do something, you borrowed it. Actually my calculations were quite good and it would all have worked out if it hadn't been for Jim Long's death. In those days bank managers had a lot of latitude and the manager of the National Provincial in Chesham at the time had lent large sums to Mr Long which appeared, on his demise, not to have been well secured. In the event, the inquest found that he had died accidentally (i.e. it was not suicide), so his insurance policies held good, and his many debts were covered. But by that time the old manager had been retired early and his replacement had set about calling in all poorly secured loans.

At that time, I owed the bank a miserable £500 or so. I was told that, notwithstanding the fact that there was an agreement that my loan should be repaid over two years, it was required at once, and that, in principle, all overdrafts were immediately repayable on demand. This was obviously very difficult to accept, but I had no choice. My first reaction was to go to the only three wealthy people I knew to try to borrow from them. The only person to come up trumps at once was my godmother, Alice Warrender, still a maiden lady and still living at Bayman Manor. She immediately lent me a hundred pounds, guaranteed me a further hundred and told me not to pay her back until it was easy. In fact it remained lent to me until her death, when under her will the debt was cancelled. This got over my immediate problems, but more had to be done, unfortunately. It was impossible to run a growing business without any real facilities from the bank.

I left the National Provincial Bank and moved up the road to the Westminster. They made it quite clear that they knew what had happened and they would not give me any facilities until I had entirely paid off the National Provincial. So some of the retail milk business, which had been built up with such effort over the previous few years, had to be sold. In the end we sold off the Amersham half of the business and were left with only a small round in Chesham, which our own milk was sufficient to supply. We were more or less back to square one – a much smaller business but with virtually no debts.

The business was so much smaller by this time that I had to try to achieve a larger income somehow. Then an opportunity occurred to do something which I had never contemplated doing before – working for a short while in what had been my father's silversmith's business at 177 New Bond Street in London. It had fallen on hard times and the trustees who were managing it were, by this time, fairly happy to have somebody from the family to go in and see what was happening.

So I commenced working there as a very junior member of the staff; I was expected to sell when nobody else was available to do so and generally learn about the business. I never had any intention of staying there long, but just looked upon it as a short-term method of augmenting my income. Before I left on the 8.30 a.m. train to go to London, I still had either to do the milking or deliver milk – one or the other. Frequently, I had to change clothes in the train with the door to the compartment protected by some friends of mine who I travelled up with. When I got home in the evening, if it was still daylight, I had to go back to work on the farm.

In all I spent a year leading this double life and it was in some ways quite a fascinating experience, something that I had no previous knowledge of, although my family had been in the business for two generations. The customers were a curious

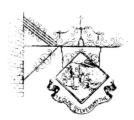

The firm's sign painted by my aunt, Ruth Harman. Obviously we always had a tendency to do things within the family.

HARMAN & C⁰ Lᴛᴅ
GOLDSMITHS & SILVERSMITHS
SPECIALITIES
CHOICE ANCIENT SILVER
OLD SHEFFIELD PLATE
PEARLS JEWELS &C.

mixture of the aristocratic, even royal, and the extremely sleazy, and by chance the sleazier episodes seemed to predominate when I was there. But fascinating though it was, I had no real interest in it. I don't even like silver or jewellery, and I certainly don't ascribe any particular value to things just because they are old. So temperamentally I was entirely unsuitable. But coming in from outside as I did, with no prejudices, I was at least able to help sort out the finances and personnel and eventually leave the management in more capable hands. I then returned to farming a little bit better off financially and left the business, I think, a little bit better organised.

In the period immediately before the Second World War, when it was fairly obvious, or should have been to everybody, that a war was imminent, we ought to have been preparing for a much more intensive campaign of food production on every farm in Britain. But we were not. There was no sense of urgency, either on the part of the authorities or on the part of most farmers. Confidence had been so diminished by the long years of depression that few dared to take much action to increase production. A good many, like me, badly wanted to but had not the capital. And an approach to the bank for more capital produced absolutely no assistance whatever. I did, however, manage to get capital from two sources outside of either farming or the banks but they were very short-term. In order to cater for this situation, we turned the farm into a company for the first time, A. S. Harman Ltd, which lasted until the war broke out.

There was one way in which production on an individual farm in an area like the Chilterns could be increased. This was by taking advantage of the large amount of vacant land around. There were considerable tracts of land which had either been earmarked for building and not used or were part of untenanted farms. Much of it had not been cultivated for some years and had fallen down to grass. You could get such land for a purely nominal rent for grazing stock or cutting for hay. With capital in such short supply it was cheaper to take advantage of this grass than it was to try to improve your own by fertilisers or cultivations. So each summer we were able to get a bit of free or almost free grass somewhere close by in the area. My only regret is that I did not take a great deal of it on a more permanent basis. Most of it was subsequently cleared, ploughed and put back into arable production and some of it was quite good land. I should have taken advantage of it when it was freely available, but I simply couldn't find the money to do so.

There was still lots of land vacant in the middle of the thirties but we didn't have the money to buy it. (From Around Chesham in Camera by Clive Birch/S. H. Freese collection.)

About this time, 1937 or 1938, I found that it was absolutely necessary to get a tractor and the implements to use with it on the farm. This was partly in preparation for what I felt would be the inevitable increase in cultivation that would be necessary in the event of war. The only way I could finance buying a tractor was by the sale of the remaining milk retail business that I still had in Chesham. This was done and I bought a standard Fordson tractor, which was a crude, heavy, simple machine, giving no trouble but very unsophisticated and very uncomfortable to drive. It had remained almost unaltered in design since the First World War, but nevertheless was still by far the most common tractor on farms in Britain in the thirties. It had to be started with a starting handle on petrol and then you switched over to a type of paraffin when it got warmed up. The seat was a simple metal plate, shaped to fit some average man's back end and not comfortable for mine at all. Furthermore, the exhaust either came out on your feet so that they cooked or, if it had an upright exhaust, just in the face of anybody fairly tall like me. Altogether, it was a very uncomfortable machine to use, but extremely reliable and quite effective.

This was the period of the great boom in au pair girls, of whom most of us had heard nothing previously. Very large numbers of people in Britain, who either had large families or enough income to afford it, employed refugee girls from the areas of conflict in central Europe. It gave at the same time relatively cheap labour and a glowing sense of self-righteousness at the thought that you were helping people in difficulties. We had an obvious need for help in the house since Florence was working a great deal with me outside, particularly before we sold the milk retail business, and we had two children growing up. (Hannah had been born in the March of 1937.) So we had two girls to work in the house and one on the farm. We also had a German refugee neighbour, Hans Jörgen Roeber, who settled down in what had been the two cottages belonging to Grove Farm. These had been allowed to become derelict, but Hans and his wife converted them into one very nice house. They had a little land and started some farming there on a very small scale, and we became quite friendly with them.

In 1938, we found that we could afford a short holiday in France. We crossed to St Malo in Brittany, then across the river to Dinard and, with the aid of a French bus driver, we found ourselves a cheap hotel. There we had a very relaxed holiday with no other English people in the hotel and the usual long delicious French meals. It was extremely interesting for me because I had

The old Fordson tractors lasted a long time. This one, being driven by my brother-in-law, was still going strong in the middle of the war when we also had the big tractors from America.

never been out of Britain before and now had a chance to look at the farming in another country, which at that time in France was very primitive. There was not a tractor in sight and we saw quite a lot of ploughing still being done with oxen, or even cows, instead of horses. We arrived back in London with no money at all and had to take a taxi to where my mother was living and ask her to pay for it. When we got there we heard that the Munich crisis was going on. From that moment it seemed obvious to me (but apparently still not to everybody) that soon there would be a war.

Despite this, there was little or nothing I could do to increase production on the farm. I had tried to increase our income by growing more vegetables to sell in our retail shop in Chesham and, subsequently, when we disposed of this in 1938, to sell wholesale. We were at a permanent disadvantage because in those days there were no chemical weedkillers and all crops, other than grain crops, still had to be hoed by hand. Hoeing on stoney Chiltern clay is a great deal more expensive in labour costs than almost anywhere else in Britain. It is extremely hard work, your hoe bouncing off the stones all the while, and in the summer when the ground is dry it is not even very effective.

The only avenue which seemed to open for me to make some more money was through a firm in Northampton called Willett & Bartram, who made ropes for the Navy. They had concluded that if there was going to be a war they would not be able to get the flax from Belgium and France to make their ropes as usual and so were offering contracts on favourable terms to farmers anywhere in Britain to grow this crop. I duly signed a contract to grow flax in the next season – that is, the summer of 1939 – 7 acres at a price per acre which seemed to be much higher than any of the grain crops we had. I naturally asked about methods of harvesting flax as we had never grown it before and was told that a Belgian-made machine would be sent round to all the people under contract to pull the crop, because it was difficult to cut with ordinary farm machinery. It had to be pulled up by the roots and we were told that this machine would do it effectively. The flaw grew very well indeed. We put it on a bit of clean land and it looked absolutely beautiful, completely blue when in flower and then quite a nice greeny-gold colour afterwards, when we were told it was ready for harvesting. The idea with the particular variety of flax that we grew was that we would harvest both the straw for Willett & Bartram's ropes and the seed for seed merchants, so it had to be harvested when it was nearly ripe.

A crop of flax being pulled somewhere where they must have had different bloody hands to Mrs Batchelor's!

The time came when the crop was exactly ready. I telephoned the firm, only to be told that not only had the machine from Belgium not arrived but it would arrive too late anyway to come round to our farm and that we should have to harvest it in some other way. The man cheerfully told me that an ordinary binder would cut it if the knife was very sharp. Well, we sharpened our knives as sharp as it was possible to sharpen them and started cutting, but at the end of less than 100 yards, we came to a complete stop. The knife had been blunted by the tough fibres of the flax. I put through another telephone call to Northampton and was told, 'Your fibres must be of a very good quality. You will have to pull it by hand like people do in other countries.' We duly mobilised everybody on the place – the men who worked on the farm, their wives and, of course, myself. We started pulling and at the end of the second day we had pulled about one acre. Then everybody went on strike. One of the farm wives, Mrs Batchelor, when told that the Belgians and the French pulled it by hand, said, 'Well, they've got different bloody hands to mine then – I'm not doing any more'. Our hands were all more or less raw.

So only one seventh of the crop was ready to be sent to Northampton. The firm expressed disappointment and I expressed something rather stronger in that they had misled us as to the ease of harvesting. The remainder of the crop was left until it eventually rotted, which took nearly two years and interfered with all the cultivations in the meantime. The tough, long fibres wrapped themselves around ploughs, cultivators and everything else, making ropes, in effect.

Just prior to our problems with the flax, I had decided to bring a bit of extra land into cultivation at short notice. We could not manage this with our one tractor and the horses, so I reverted to the method used by my father some twenty years before and got a set of steam ploughing engines in from a contractor, Boughtons of Amersham. The men duly started with two big engines and the plough, able, I thought, to plough 8–10 acres a day at least. I thought wrong. The trouble was that most of the men had been out of practice for many years, and they got in a terrible muddle. In the first hour one driver mistook a signal from the other and pulled the plough too soon. They had an accident. Then they were so slow on the job that all the rest of the farm staff had to spend a whole day carting water and coal for them. After a full day with very little achieved, I rang Boughtons of Amersham up and told them it wasn't on. 'We can't possibly afford to have your engines for ploughing', I told them. 'Your men don't know what they're doing'. The Boughtons are a most pleasant family, and immediately Mr Boughton said to me, 'Right, we'll take them away again'. 'What about finishing the job?' I asked. 'Well, if you're not satisfied, you don't want it finished', came the reply. So we were forced to finish their work and clear up by whatever means we could.

Harvest in 1939 was fairly early. After it was over, we arranged with our neighbours, the Roebers, to go on another short holiday in France. Madge Roeber knew France very well and was to be our guide in Paris and in Normandy. Everywhere we went in restaurants, hotels, shops, the French people would recognise Hans Jörgen as being German and he got a very hostile reception. Waiters were disobliging to all of us, rude remarks were made under their breaths and one heard 'Sale Boche' muttered everywhere. One could hardly get up and explain that he was a refugee from Hitler's Germany and probably a damn sight more reliable in any conflict with the Germans than they were going to be. We arrived home just in time to hear the declaration of war.

'They Need Us Again'

Two days after war had been declared, whilst walking along Chesham High Street, I met Mr White, the manager of the National Provincial Bank, who three years before had caused me such awful difficulties by calling in my overdraft. 'Oh, Mr Harman,' he said, 'I wish you would make your account active again. We don't like losing customers,' and I thought to myself, 'My God, at last farmers are wanted. People only want us when a war is on.' At that stage nothing on earth would have persuaded me to go back to the bank which had so interfered with my plans, which had almost stopped my farming in mid-stream, and which had quite stopped my retail business. But the fact that he had approached me did give me more confidence to ask the other bank that we were then with, the Westminster Bank, for greater facilities and, because there was a war on and farmers were once more regarded as good risks, they were granted immediately.

After a few weeks, the government set-up for helping and supervising agriculture during the war came into being. There were to be county and local War Agriculture Executive Committees (which came to be known as War Ags), consisting of farmers and a few farmworkers and landowners, who were to co-ordinate the drive to bring as much land into cultivation as possible. They were to have authority to order farmers and landowners generally to plough up grazing fields, parks and even golf courses and, at the same time, to give assistance so that they could do what they were ordered to do. Machinery pools were set up whereby farmers who had not got a particular piece of machinery could hire it, and labour pools were organised, which in the first instance consisted of gangs of girls who opted for agricultural work rather than service in one of the armed forces, and conscientious objectors who objected to military service but still had to be called up. In our area, a hostel was set up just outside Chesham for conscientious objectors and they were available at a very early stage to help with farm work. Most of them were townsmen but some adapted very readily to country life and were quite useful. Some subsequently finished up in the machinery side of the business and did very well.

In the following spring the authorities set about finding people to cultivate the vacant land in our area, both the abandoned

Top: German POWs working on Grove Farm during the war.

Bottom: Many town girls like these chose to work on the land for their war service.

building sites and the untenanted farms. Most of the farms acquired new tenants fairly quickly because it was becoming obvious that farming was now going to be at least slightly more profitable than it had been, but it was often quite difficult to find the owners of the building sites, who deliberately made themselves scarce in order to avoid having to do the necessary work. Consequently the War Ag. itself started to cultivate land or it got people from nearby farms to look after abandoned areas.

One problem with setting up the War Ags was that in those days there were very few people qualified to help and advise in agriculture who were not already working in it. There was not the vast reservoir of people with agricultural degrees and diplomas that there is now. So the staff of the local agricultural executive offices were an odd mixture. Some of them were elderly colonial agricultural officials who had probably been trained in British agriculture in their youth and whose ideas were well out of date; others were land agents interested in estate management; and others were people who had been involved in activities which were ancillary to agriculture. So it worked out that the Amersham office, under which we came, was run by a Mr Lillywhite, who had been the secretary of the local Milk Recording Society and so had built up quite a knowledge of dairy farming, and a Mr Hurst who had had some agricultural training in his youth but who had for many years been, in the words of his colleagues, 'working as a seaside landlady'. Nevertheless they did the best they could under difficult circumstances and, in any case, agriculture was in such a low state that almost anything one tried was an improvement.

This is the way we went into a war in which we were constantly told that the supply of food was critical to the success of our struggle and that lack of food was more likely to beat us than anything else. Agriculture, demoralised by twenty years of depression and disorganised thanks to the total failure of peacetime governments to plan ahead, was suddenly of maximum importance. The Buckinghamshire County War Ag. was headed by Lord Addison, who had been a Minister of Agriculture in the 1929 Labour government and, I suppose, was rather more capable than the average county chairman may well have been.

By the first spring of the war, Grove Farm and all the farms around were looking just a little better because we had that little bit more confidence and were trying to do the work a little better and spend a bit more money on our operations. But there was nowhere near as much improvement as could have been made had

Lord Addison, chairman of the War Ag. for Bucks.

there been proper planning in advance. Although the countryside was looking a little better, the war was looking much worse and the need for us to increase production was becoming acute. In the end this led in 1941 to American equipment being fed into this country under the Lease-Lend scheme and it was this that began to make a really dramatic improvement in our farming. In the spring and summer of 1940, however hard we were working, however much we were concerned with doing our jobs well, our minds were really on what was going on in the war – the threat of invasion and the failure of the British forces in France, Belgium and in Norway.

In the late spring of 1940 we were ordered to plough out about 66 acres of Shepherds Farm which we had rented for some years as rough grazing land. (These were the fields that we had rented from the notorious Jim Long.) The owners had previously refused to let us plough them up so we were quite glad when the War Ag. over-ruled their objections. I remember I ploughed the land myself after Will Barnett had first cut down the tremendous tangle of wild rose bushes that covered it. The weather was cold and wet and it was already too late in the spring to plant a proper crop, so I had to get the work done as quickly as possible in order to get anything growing at all. Every lunchtime Florence used to

Will and I cleared land the hard way by hand. This land girl has got a lot of power under her to do it with.

Hoeing sugar beet. This was a crop we had never grown before, but were urged to grow once sugar was rationed.

bring me over a full cooked lunch and I used to sit in the hedge to eat it. This, combined with a Labour Member of Parliament's wife who lived nearby – Mrs Barstow – bringing me out coffee, was the only thing that kept me going, working, as I was, something like twelve or fourteen hours a day to get the job done. I remember each of them would also bring me the latest news from the radio of what was happening at the various war fronts. It was not very cheering news.

It was only by taking more land into cultivation in this way that production could be increased, because there were still no adequate supplies of chemical fertilisers available then. Also, the varieties of grain we could grow were the same as we had always grown and there was a limit to the amount they would yield. But there were changes of a sort in the type of crops we grew. Nobody had thought previously of growing potatoes on any commercial scale in the Chilterns because it was not suitable land. But because it was anticipated there might be transport difficulties as the war progressed, we were encouraged to grow a small acreage, and so, for the first time since my boyhood, I planted potatoes. I suppose if there had been an absolute breakdown of transport, it would have been an advantage to have potatoes growing everywhere instead of only in certain areas, as these were a staple part of our diet.

The other crop we were encouraged to grow was sugar beet. Again, this had previously only been grown in specific areas, mainly East Anglia, but once people woke up to the possibility of there being no sugar because cane sugar could not be brought in from abroad, there was a drive to increase sugar beet production and we started growing about 18–20 acres a year. It grew quite well on our land and we were able to produce as good a yield as anybody in the country, with a high sugar percentage. The only snag was that the stones tended to get lifted up with the beet, get transported to the factory and damage the refining machinery. So we were always getting rude notes about the amount of flints we sent in with our beet.

Sugar beet is a crop which, certainly in those days, needed far more hand labour than we had; in addition to hoeing, the young plants had to be singled out about a month after they were up. There was no seasonal labour available in the district, no gangs of wandering Irishmen as they had in East Anglia, no large numbers of gypsies around to do the hoeing once a year as a regular thing. So, in order to get the work done we had to make use of the labour pools set up by the War Ag. At first we had 'land girls' who were boarded out in the area, and some of the conscientious objectors from the hostel at Chartridge. Much later on we also used German and Italian prisoners-of-war.

All these groups were administered by the War Agriculture Committee to work on different farms. I suppose this was the only way to get the work done but it was not very efficient. To begin with, the workers had to be collected from different points in the morning, driven to the farms and then driven back and dropped off at night. This took up about two hours of the day in travelling time and used up precious petrol. Also, the workers we had couldn't always do the work very well. I mean no criticism of the people involved, but it is very difficult for people outside agriculture to adapt to its tremendous variety of work. It is very hard physical work too, which the Italian POWs, in particular, weren't at all keen on. They tended to be very relaxed and spent rather a lot of time cooking delicious lunches using the herbs they found growing locally. On the other hand, the Germans were excellent labour. I remember one group we had arrived with an armed guard. The guard, once it had been explained to the prisoners what they had to do, calmly walked into the next field, lay down and got out a book to read. 'Aren't you supposed to be keeping an eye on them?' I enquired. 'No need,' he answered, indicating the German corporal who was part of the group, 'that bugger will never let them get away.' Sure enough, the corporal marched up and down all day, barking commands and keeping his troops hard at work. He made even more of an impression on us when, having been given a cigarette by one of the farm hands, he promptly turned and divided it between the four prisoners nearest to him.

The first year we grew sugar beet we had about ten land girls, who came on the lorry every morning to do the hoeing and help with other work on the farm. A lot of them were not very good but some settled down quite well and we even took two on regularly, both girls who had spent all their lives in Shepherds Bush. The furthest they had ever previously been from London was Brighton on a day trip, so it was quite an experience for them to come out into the country. They stayed with us for more than three years, some of the time lodging in Chesham and some of the time living with us. One of them, a rather attractive blonde girl called Evelyn Hawkins, we still hear from. She – inevitably – married an American serviceman who was stationed at Bovingdon and finished up in some windswept place in Montana.

Not all that consciously, I rather liked working with Evelyn. We used to work in pairs, a man and a girl, as this seemed to be the most efficient system, the man to chop out the weeds with a hoe and the girl to single the bunches of young plants by hand. My constant preference for having Evelyn working with me caused her,

POWs harvesting a crop of rape on Grove Farm. In those days it was grown for fodder, not for oil seed to make margarine as now. The soldier who was supposed to be guarding the German prisoners as they worked was asleep in the hedge. He knew their own corporal wouldn't let them escape.

I discovered later, to be referred to as 'the boss's blonde'.
Fortunately Florence did not seem to object too strongly! When,
finally, after the war, Evelyn went off to America to join her
husband, we had a short letter from her which I thought spoke
volumes. In England she had married a man in uniform who, I
suppose, looked tough and glamorous. Her letter from America
said, 'Bill met me at the station – he had glasses on and a Stetson
hat. Somehow he looked different.' However, she adapted well to
the climate out there and we hear from her every Christmas about
her children and grandchildren and she seems to have become a
typical American farmer's wife.

The emphasis on the farm during the war was inevitably on
arable cropping. It produced quicker results in food for human
beings and also, I suppose, because meat and butter take up less
cargo space, this is what supply ships were loaded with – those that
got past the German planes and submarines. So there was a
tendency for livestock on farms all over Britain to be reduced. At
one stage, there was even a subsidy paid out for slaughtering cows
in order to reduce dairy herds. This is paralleled by the same thing
now, though today it is done for entirely different reasons. Then it
was to produce more arable crops; now it is to reduce the European
butter mountain. In any case, dieticians had already worked out by
then that we could do perfectly well without butter and that it was
not actually very good for us. So milk production was reduced and

*The new cowshed in 1944.
Now it is no longer used for
milking but for rearing beef
calves.*

what wasn't left as milk was made into cheese. I suppose people who kept other forms of livestock may well have been subject to similar cuts. Certainly pig-keeping was a problem because so much of pig food is the same as human food and it must have been very difficult to provide enough. Sheep were the odd stock out. They were kept largely on pasture or its by-products so I imagine the sheep population must have kept up pretty well.

We continued to produce milk at Grove Farm throughout the war and, even though we no longer had a retail business, it still had to be got away very early in the morning. I did most of the early milking sessions myself, which still took place in the same dilapidated cowshed. By this time the building had started to slip into the moat and for several years it was held up solely by ropes of baling wire which we attached to another more sturdy building nearby. When, in 1944, it eventually slid into the water and we had a new shed built, our two town girls acted as hod carriers for the bricklayer.

I made one not too determined effort myself to join one of the forces when the war first broke out. I went to a recruiting office in St Albans to be told firmly that, if I described myself as a farmer, I would only be eligible for flying duties in the RAF and no other service would take me. I did not make a false declaration, which I suppose I could have done, and I was certainly not brave enough to wish to fly. Consequently, when, during the summer of Dunkirk in 1941, Anthony Eden came on the wireless and announced the formation of what was at first called the Local Defence Volunteers and subsequently called the Home Guard, it was with a certain amount of relief that I rushed down, along with lots of other men, young and old, to the local police station to join. How effective a part of the defence of the country the Home Guard ever was, I have no idea. It has become subsequently a bit of a joke as 'Dad's Army', but at the time it did not quite seem that way. It was certainly a great personal relief to me to feel I could do *something*.

I remember, to start with, we were only given arm bands and no arms and were immediately told to patrol the countryside in our area and to report anything we saw. It was thought that parachutists and enemy agents might land in the country at any time and, indeed, in some places they did. Having people out on the look-out all night must certainly have increased the chances of these people being found. The first night I went out, I went with a boy called Fred Puddephatt (no relation to poor Arthur), who was about seventeen and so not yet eligible to be called up. He and I

had one shotgun and a few cartridges between us and we patrolled for the whole of the night all the Whelpley Hill area. If Fred and I had run up against any German parachutists, the plan was that I should hold them at the end of a shotgun whilst Fred, who we reckoned would be quicker than I was, ran to get help. It was probably just as well nobody ever did land in our area because I think my nerves would have compelled me to discharge both barrels of the shotgun at any suspect before he had a chance to shout 'I surrender!'

I subsequently became the leader of the Home Guard Platoon for Whelpley Hill, Ley Hill and Ashley Green and even went on a couple of courses to learn about explosives, guerilla fighting and how to mount a defence of an area in the event of an invasion. Our duties were principally to patrol our assigned area every night, to maintain a guard post on the highest point at the back of Grove

Whelpley Hill Home Guard – young boys and old men, nearly all of whom worked on the land. Will Barnett is third from the right in the back row. Mr Oldham, the Boer War veteran, is seated on my left.

Farm and to train one evening a week in the local village hall. Initially, because we had no weapons, the training consisted of practising parade ground drills which were taught to us by an old Boer War veteran called Oldham, and a cowman called Forey who had been a sergeant in the First World War, but gradually we were equipped with rifles and grenades, and we even devised our own 'mortars' out of steel tubing with which to fire the Mills bombs that we had been issued. The crowning glory of our eventual armoury was a proper full-sized Lewis gun which I managed to buy from a dishonest soldier in a regular unit in the area. It used the same ammunition as our rifles and would have been a very useful weapon had we ever been called into serious operation. When the war was over and the authorities announced an amnesty for people to turn in any unauthorised weapons to the police station, the Chesham police were absolutely astonished when I arrived with an army-issue Lewis gun and two fully loaded magazines.

As the war went on, the possibility that the Home Guard might be of some use dwindled. In the very early days, when the likelihood of an invasion seemed quite real, we might have been useful in delaying the enemy or at least have had some nuisance value. But as D-Day approached, I imagine we must have become increasingly irrelevant, at the same time, ironically, as we were becoming more efficient and better equipped. Nevertheless the authorities continued to tell us that we were important and maintained that, when the Allied invasion of Europe took place, there might well be counter attacks or enemy agents dropped in this country and, therefore, we had to train to deal with them. When the actual Normandy landings took place, either for morale-boosting purposes or because it was really thought necessary (I will never know which), one or two selected Home Guard units were sent to positions on the coast, ostensibly to help to deal with sporadic German landings which might have taken place. One unit was called for from our area and, possibly because I was the youngest officer by that time, I was sent out to a position on the Essex coast with nearly a hundred men from the Chesham and Amersham area. We were quartered in an empty yacht club on the River Blackwater at Stone in Essex and stayed there just over one week while the Normandy invasion took place. Needless to say, we were not called upon to do anything.

I have to admit that the physical horrors of war barely touched our area. Chesham was only bombed once during the entire war, despite the presence of Bovingdon airfield nearby, which had been built early on in the war and which was occupied by the American Air Force around 1942. It was used by high-ranking American officials, including General Eisenhower, but was never attacked – I assume the Germans simply never knew of its existence. Some bombs also dropped harmlessly in open fields nearby.

So the war was not a dangerous experience if you were living in Whelpley Hill. In fact, in many ways, it was an exhilarating one, because people were nicer to each other during the war than at any other time. We were extremely lucky. The bombing went on around us and particularly to the south east of us in London, and on one occasion in June 1940 I was caught up in such a raid in London while Florence was at home giving birth to our first son, Dan. But bombs seldom fell in this area itself. I remember once seeing German planes overhead on the way back from a big raid on the General Motors works at Luton and feeling that I was slightly detached from it all.

Expanding and Diversifying

The popular theory is that farmers make a fortune in time of war. This was certainly not my experience. In the first and second year of the war, as a result of the expense of winding up the company of A. S. Harman Ltd when my backer pulled out and starting up again as an individual, we made a loss. During that time, we drew for our living just £5.00 a week. I was also being paid £4.00 a week from the business in London for going up twice a month to keep an eye on its progress. (I had long since finished working there full time but was still a director.) Of course £9.00 a week sounds impossible to live on now, but then it was not quite as little as it sounds, especially when you were living on a farm and having food and so on off it.

By 1943, we were at last making a proper profit, having taken advantage of our new credit-worthiness at the bank and a government scheme to buy new machinery to become more efficient. Even so, by 1945 our income from London had ceased because the family business had been sold, our income from the farm had only risen to £9.00 a week, and the capital stock – apart from what was on Lease–Lend which was still being paid for – had only risen from £3000 to £4000. So it hardly looks as though we were desperately prosperous profiteers. It may be that some people who consciously went into the black market and sold meat, for example, on the side, did extremely well, but in straight farming the price of what you sold and what you bought was so controlled that your income did not go up any faster than anybody else's.

You heard a lot of talk about the black market and farmers engaging in profiteering, but I doubt if quite as much went on as people imagined. Certainly, relations and friends and near neighbours of farmers who had poultry got extra eggs, but there wasn't much butter or cheese being made in our area so there was little opportunity of getting hold of these yearned-for commodities. A certain amount of meat was sold on the black market, it was said, although I never saw any of it. There was a strange rumour that somebody in our immediate area who had a big cellar in his house kept it flooded so that nobody would venture into it. On the other side of the cellar, away from the hatch entrance so the

The Goods and Services scheme started me off with big machinery. Once I'd started, I continued with ever bigger machines – this is our second combine.

story went, he had sides of meat suspended above the water, which his sons would ferry across the cellar in a small punt when buyers came. I saw the cellar in question once and it was just about technically possible, but I looked upon it as rather a tall tale myself. Just once and once only I was approached by somebody attempting to buy extra eggs. He was an officer in the local Home Guard and I got all stuffy with him about it and said I didn't go in for that sort of thing. He said he only wanted just an extra half a dozen for his old mother who lived in a flat in London all by herself and was having a hard time. He still didn't have the eggs.

After the war, of course, farmers' attitudes altered considerably. They rather resented the tight price controls and the fact that they couldn't take advantage of the shortages in the way that indeed everybody else in every other sort of business seemed to. This, combined with the feeling that they were going to be let down sooner or later by the government, whatever party was in power, once there was no longer a war on made them a bit cynical. In the event nobody let them down at all and the guaranteed prices continued for a long time.

Certainly where Grove Farm is concerned we made no *real* progress until after the war. Then we did come into a period of

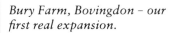

Bury Farm, Bovingdon – our first real expansion.

very rapid development and opportunity and very good farming. The great regret of anybody who lived through that period, myself included, is that they did not strike out more and take on more land as it became available in the immediate post-war period and during the war itself. Although our expansion only really got going after the war, I can pinpoint its beginnings to one particular day – 15 July 1943. On that day, I went to Bovingdon to see the directors of a steel design company, who had had their offices evacuated into a big Georgian house there and who also owned Bury Farm. Bury Farm was behind the church in Bovingdon in a fold in the land – an attractive place, running away from the village, with a nice house and modest buildings. It had been advertised that the tenancy was going to become vacant and I wanted to become the new tenant. I negotiated with the directors all afternoon in the house, more or less losing sight of the fact that Florence, nine months pregnant, was sitting in the pick-up truck outside, waiting for me. The reason the date is so memorable is that when I finally emerged with an agreement, Florence informed me that the baby was on its way and we had to rush home. Andy, my fourth child and second son, was born early that evening, so that day is never likely to be forgotten.

Having negotiated with the owners of Bury Farm, I then had to go and talk to the tenant who was giving up. His name was Mr Adey and he was a minute Scotsman, who, in fact, was hardly willing to talk at all – a really taciturn little man, who was extremely difficult to negotiate with. This wasn't helped by the fact that, before I met him, I had heard that he had once found a dead body hanging in his barn at six o'clock in the morning when he went out to milk. He did absolutely nothing about it – just left it hanging there, milked his cows and went back to have breakfast. He then told his wife, who thought she had better telephone the local policeman. When asked by the police why he had done nothing about the body when he had first found it, he said in a broad Scots accent, 'Well, he was dead anyway. There was nothing much I could do about it and I had to get on with the milking.' They asked him how he knew the man was dead and he replied, 'I felt his feet and they were cold.' It struck me that he must be an extraordinary sort of person to be able to continue with his milking with a dead body hanging there, which he had just felt to be cold.

Ultimately, and with a certain amount of difficulty, I negotiated taking over the farm, and on 29 September 1943, we took on this additional land. It was quite a good farm, but because we were not able to take the house too (a senior employee of the owners lived in it), I probably did not make as much of my tenancy as I ought to have done. I always had it in the back of my mind that, sooner or later, the man who occupied the house would want the farm as well, especially when I later heard that he had bought the house from his employers. Anyway, we had five or six years in Bury Farm and were able to use all the machinery we had at Grove Farm there too, which made the whole venture very efficient.

I had a rather bizarre adventure in connection with Bury Farm. It was the summer of 1944 and by that time I had a little Austin 7 car in which I used to go over to inspect the cattle at Bovingdon at night, especially if the man we had living there happened to be away. I went over one evening to look at the cattle, parking the car at the end of the drive as usual and not locking up, which I suppose I should have done, especially in wartime. When I came back about half an hour later, the car had gone and I started rather miserably to walk home. When I had got about half way, a friend, Mr Bryant, passed in his van and offered me a lift. I accepted gratefully, having already reported the missing car to the village constable, PC Lord. As Mr Bryant and I drove home via Ley Hill, we saw the Austin 7 parked, with two young men not far away from it. I got out of Mr Bryant's van and into my car, politely offering these youths a lift back into Bovingdon; they were foolish enough to accept. As soon as I got to the village I reported to PC Lord what had happened, who immediately grabbed the two boys, put them either side of the road and, by the most unorthodox methods, got confessions out of them that they had 'borrowed' my car. He did this by questioning one boy on one side of the road and, on getting nothing out of him, walking across the road to the other and saying, 'Your mate has told everything, you might as well,' and he did. PC Lord then went back to the first lad and told him the same story.

By this time it was getting late and I started off for home in my little car. What I had not realised, however, was that PC Lord had informed the American military police, who were then present in great strength in Bovingdon, that the car had been stolen, on the grounds that it might have been stolen by an American serviceman. As I reached the crossroads at Bovingdon, two military police jeeps, each with four men, fully armed, moved in on me, one cutting across the road in front, the other coming alongside. They shoved their Tommy guns at me and said, 'We have orders to stop this vehicle and apprehend the driver.' I, of course, tried to explain that

it was perfectly all right, that it was my car and it had been stolen but I had recovered it. They did not believe a word. It just did not seem a likely story to them. So I was duly arrested and taken to the pen that they had at Bovingdon aerodrome.

The pen was a sort of prisoner-of-war-type cage which had been prepared for the possible arrival of any high-level German prisoners at Bovingdon, who would then have been taken to a nearby interrogation centre at Latimer. It consisted of a high wire compound with a small hut in the corner, surrounded by searchlights, which were all turned on for my benefit. I was duly imprisoned in the hut and surrounded by armed men. By this time, I was feeling extremely miserable and uncomfortable. They would not believe a word I said and I did not know how long I would be there. Florence was not expecting me to be out so long and I thought she would be worried to death. Then, quite suddenly and oddly, things started turning in my favour. The compound had never been used until that date and the field telephone in the corner did not work. The Americans kept desperately trying to get on to the headquarters of their own unit and the village policeman, but

Bovingdon Aerodrome – a huge bit of countryside spoilt. X marks the spot of my brief imprisonment; now a proper prison is being built here.

there was no reply whatsoever. Gradually the whole thing began to
strike me as funny and they began to lose their confidence and
think that perhaps they had made a mistake. In any case, what
were they to do, since they could not report to anyone that they
had me? I proposed that we should go down to Bovingdon, find the
village constable and get him to put the matter right. We duly
started down the road, one military police jeep in front with three
men, a fourth man sitting beside me in my little Austin with a gun,
and the other jeep behind, also containing fully armed MPs. By this
time, PC Lord was out about his business and it was half an hour
or so before we tracked him down and I could be released. I got
home to find Florence not unnaturally a bit alarmed because it was
well after eleven o'clock and she had been expecting me at about
eight. As far as I know, I am the only person to have been
imprisoned in that cage at the American base throughout the war.

The only reason I had been able to contemplate taking on
Bury Farm was because earlier that year I had taken advantage of
the government's Goods and Services Scheme to buy some much-
needed American machinery. It is amazing, when I look back, how
primitive our machinery was up until that point. There had been
barely any development at all in British-made farming implements
in the twenties and thirties, and even after the war had started, the
agricultural engineering industry was at such a low level that it
couldn't get itself geared up to produce anything new. All it could
do was increase its manufacture of ordinary two- and three-furrow
tractor ploughs, old-fashioned reapers and binders, and threshing
machines built to a pattern which had remained identical for many
years. The larger and more sophisticated imported machines which
were available just before the war seemed terribly expensive to
us and, until the early 1940s, I never even contemplated buying
any of them.

But then two things happened simultaneously. In March 1941,
the Americans provided a Lease–Lend system to this country
whereby the British government was supplied with everything it
needed to fight the war against Hitler in return for the lease of
American bases on British territory, especially in the West Indies.
Of course, among the things that were needed to keep the war
effort going were agricultural machines and larger quantities of
these were shipped over. Not all American machines were entirely
suitable for British conditions, but most of them were and all of
them were far in advance of what we had had up until that point.
At the same time as more of this machinery was becoming

A crawler tractor similar to the first one I bought. It never got stuck and made easy work of our hills.

available, the Ministry of Agriculture set up a scheme whereby farmers, even those with very little capital, could get hold of the new equipment. This was the Goods and Services Scheme. The government got the machinery from the USA for nothing and the farmers bought it on extended credit terms payable out of their subsequent harvest over two and sometimes three years. The only proviso was that they had to prove that they could use the stuff efficiently.

Like many other people I took on as much as I could afford – an American-made crawler tractor and a British-made plough to go with it, a combine harvester and a drier and pick-up baler to go with that, and, later on, an American wheeled tractor which was much faster and more advanced than any tractor I had had previously. The crawler tractor, a Caterpillar diesel, cost just £784. Nowadays, a similar tractor would, I suppose, cost £17,000. I remember thinking at the time it was terribly expensive. Track-laying vehicles of the Caterpillar type were particularly suitable for our area because of the steep slope of many of the fields. The Caterpillar had a very big output and, unlike the horses, never got tired so we could have two people working it in shifts and so plough three or four times as much as we had previously.

Part of the conditions under which I financed its purchase from the Ministry of Agriculture was that I should use it for contract work in the area. Consequently, we employed a full-time driver, David Powell, who spent his whole life working that crawler for me and for other people. When he was on holiday or resting I took over and in the busy times of the spring and the autumn we did hundreds and hundreds of acres of ploughing. I remember for three days solidly ploughing some extremely steep ground at Hockley Farm, which is between Ley Hill and Latimer, on contract for the War Ag. I was always a bit nervous on slopes anyway, but the extreme angles on this land worried me tremendously. I kept thinking it was going to roll over with me in it and was very glad when the job was done. At that time, rules about safety on the farm generally were not very strict, and when we wished to move this tractor we used to drive it on to a two-wheel trailer with somebody (very often me) holding the draw bar up until it had reached the point of balance and then letting it down on to a block and hitching it to another tractor. This was actually terribly dangerous, but we had to move it cheaply from site to site to do the work on our own and other people's land and running it on the road would have damaged the tracks.

The first combine harvester to come to this district via the Goods and Services Scheme was bought by a man called Hugh Sampson, who was a very up-to-date farmer over near Chartridge. He was mainly an arable and poultry farmer and grew very good corn crops. I went up with Will Barnett to see his combine at work, and we decided – jointly of course, since I needed Will's co-operation – that we ought to have one. So, the following year, our first combine arrived and with it, all the ancillary pieces of

Even the earliest combines could deal better with a laid crop than binders could. This type had a sacker whereas we dealt with the grain in bulk from the start.

equipment you have to have. The advantage of a combine harvester
is that it cuts a grain crop and threshes it at the same time, which
completely eliminates the earlier procedures of stooking sheaves,
carting these back to the farmyard, building and thatching ricks,
and threshing the grain in batches. As the combine moves across
the field, the cutter bar cuts the whole crop and delivers it to the
threshing drum. The threshed grain is then delivered into a holding
tank for subsequent unloading into a trailer or lorry. The straw
drops out of the back of the machine in a trail and can either be
picked up by a baler and tied into bales, burnt where it lies, or,
occasionally, chopped up for incorporating back into the soil. The
ancillary equipment we needed was therefore a pick-up baler and
also a grain drier to dry the grain because in about two years out
of every three the grain is not dry enough to store in bulk
immediately it is harvested.

The grain drier we bought was an extremely primitive affair,
made by a firm called Kennedy and Kemp in this country. It was
made of sheet steel with a huge, coke-fired furnace, and it was
more of an art than a science to keep the fire going at exactly the
right level so that you could control the temperature. This was
done by moving a series of flaps in the sheet metal ducts, which
carried the hot air from the furnace over the corn as it fell through
slots made from steel mesh so that the hot air could pass through.
It was really a very crude device and not very pleasant to work
with because of the grain dust and coke fumes. However, it
enabled the harvest to be dealt with, dried and sacked up much
more quickly than previously. In those days, we had no bulk bins
in which to store the grain and it was all sacked up in $2\frac{1}{4}$ cwt sacks
which took quite a bit of handling. We sacked the grain off the
drier, not off the combine. You could sack directly off the combine
if you wanted to, but there was not much point when it
subsequently had to be dried.

The baler we bought was an American machine which baled
the straw into big 1 cwt bales. Like the combine, it had to be pulled
by a tractor but had its own engine on board to drive the baling
mechanism and to ram the bale; the baling wire had to be knotted
by hand. The baler had a seat on either side and two men or land
girls used to sit on these, one passing the wire through a slotted
board to the other person, who was responsible for dropping the
boards down into the bale chamber as the straw was rammed in,
threading the wire round the bale and returning it to be knotted.
The resulting bales were heavy and the wire cut into your hands as

A Kennedy and Kemp grain drier. It gave off fumes and dust and was rather basic – but it worked.

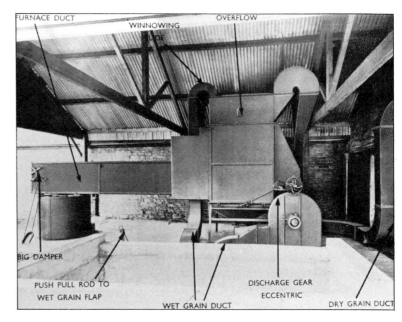

A John Deere baler needed three people to operate it and produced heavy bales tied with wire.

you lifted them. Looking back and comparing it with a modern baler, which is self-operating, knots and all, it was an incredibly crude affair.

When the combine arrived from America, it came in two or three huge packing cases and was of a new type which had not been available in this country before. It arrived with a book of instructions and, the next day, two agents from the manufacturers, the International Harvester Company, were to come and put it together. Will Barnett and I had a good look at it and I did not understand it at all. The next day, Will Barnett worked with the two fitters to put the machine together and, at the end of the day, the man in charge said to me, 'This machine will work well here and you won't have any trouble at all, not like in some places.' I asked why he thought this and he replied, 'Your man must have read the book through from start to finish because he understands it as well as we do.' 'Well, that's very strange,' I said, 'because the man cannot read.' Will Barnett could not read at all but, because he understood what this combine had to do – that is, perform the functions previously carried out by a cutting machine of one sort or another and a threshing machine whilst moving across the field – he knew how it all went together. This was probably the case with quite a lot of relatively uneducated, old-fashioned farm labourers who knew the processes very well and probably had better ideas about how the new machines should function almost than the manufacturers themselves.

Acquiring a combine harvester meant that the small, awkwardly shaped fields we had were doubly difficult to farm efficiently. The obvious solution at the time was to do away with some of the hedges and create bigger units for the new machinery to 'get its teeth into'. Consequently, within three years I removed about a quarter of our hedges by hiring a bulldozer, pushing them out and burning them. I even organised a demonstration under the auspices of the War Ag. in 1944 to show how effectively it could be done. Now I count myself rather lucky that I took these hedges out at a time when I was applauded for bringing more land into cultivation in the national interest, rather than being slated, as I would be now, for damaging the local ecology.

Hedges have always been a source of trouble, but before the 1970s this was usually because of boundary disputes. In this, I suppose, they are like the frontiers between different countries, a frequent cause of war. They have probably caused more arguments between farmers than any other single thing and, in days gone by,

Left: Not having a blade for my caterpillar tractor as this one does I had to hire a bulldozer to carry out my hedge removal.

Right: This is where I arranged a demonstration of hedge removal for the Ministry in 1944: six enclosures (and, way back, two complete farms – Wethereds and Two Dells) into one huge field.

they would fight each other through the courts and, occasionally, physically about who owned a particular stretch of hedge, which in many ways was more a liability than an asset. Of course, when large numbers of hedges were planted, enclosing the open fields in the eighteenth and nineteenth centuries, there were riots and pitched battles between the employees of the landlords who were doing the enclosing and the commoners and their friends who were opposing it. Now, if the same hedges are taken out, there is very nearly as much trouble, only it takes the modern form of letters to the papers and demonstrations and people chaining themselves to bulldozers.

The hedges on Grove Farm are not in straight lines like the enclosure hedges were. This is because, in common with most of the Chilterns area, our fields were never in the open field system and so the hedges pre-date the enclosure movement. They form all sorts of weird field shapes with funny little corners, sometimes following the contours of the land but, more often, taking a route which seems to have no significance at all these days. Very many of these hedge lines are exactly the same as they were in the sixteenth century.

Because they have been there so long, our local hedges consist of a great number of different species. Modern hedges and enclosure hedges are mostly thorn, which forms a useful barrier for stock, but ours are predominantly nuthazel, mixed with every sort

of tree and shrub which is native to the area. As a result, few are
stock-proof since cattle eat nuthazel, and they have to be reinforced
with barbed wire. Many used to have a great many large trees,
mainly oaks and elms, which belonged not to the tenant of the
farm, but to the landlord. The trees fed through their roots off the
tenants' fields, which he cultivated and manured, but when the
trees were ready for harvesting, it was the landlord that had them.
It was, therefore, not surprising that when, in the early twenties, a
great many farms were bought by their tenants and ceased to be
part of estates, the first thing they did was to remove the trees.
Consciously or unconsciously they realised that they had been a tax
on their efforts in the past, but were now a useful saleable
commodity in the Depression years.

Of course, part of the economy of hedges originally was that
labour was permanently available on the farm to look after them.
So, in the winter months when there was nothing more profitable
for them to do, the farm workers would keep the hedges in order
and provide some income from the various by-products. Nowadays,
it is quite different because we employ so little labour. The farm
hands we have would never get round to making and laying hedges
by hand the way they used to, so now we cut the hedges back with
a machine every year. This modern method keeps them within
bounds and enables as much land as possible to be cultivated. But
gradually, over a period of years, it changes the balance of species
in a hedge because nuthazel does not take kindly to being cut
annually. Slowly it will die out and its place will be taken by
blackthorn or quickthorn and hornbeam, which do not mind being
cut frequently. Blackberries, wild roses and wild honeysuckle,
which have always abounded in hedges, are almost unaffected by
trimming or cutting and still remain everywhere where they always
were. In our area now there are only a few people who can still
demonstrate the art of hedging, men like Maurice Brown who lives
at Bovingdon. He is one of the few people round here to have
farmed his acres in the traditional way all his life, despite
technological advances and increased scientific know-how, because
he maintains it is the right way.

I was one of the first people in this area to begin removing
hedges during the war, but in the country as a whole, most were
taken out in the 1960s and, of course, it is still going on. Apart
from any damage it may do to the local balance of flora and fauna
– it will cause a decrease in the thrush population, for example, but
on the other hand may well result in an increase in larks – the

Maurice Brown, the neighbour who has stuck closest to traditional methods.

most obvious effect hedge-removal has is to change the look of the landscape. It is this that sometimes causes me to regret my earlier enthusiasm which, albeit in a small way, has made part of Bucks look more like part of East Anglia – a terrible fate. But in 1944 I only felt pleased with myself for increasing the land we had for cultivation, improving our grain yield and raising our income. With a war on, a family of four to feed and years of depression still prominent in my memory, I had to decide my priorities.

The final venture I undertook in the latter years of the war in an attempt to respond to shortages was growing crops for seed. A number of quite simple crops which would grow in a temperate climate like ours had normally been imported and, after a period of years, these had become extremely scarce – bird seed, for example, such as canary grass and millet. These were not needed in enormous quantities, but as stocks began to run low towards the end of the war, there was an opportunity for farmers to make quite a lot out of growing such seed on small plots of land. There was no objection by the authorities so long as it was not grown on a scale which would interfere with the production of food.

I did not interest myself in bird seed, but I grew flower and vegetable seed for a while, and also sunflowers. Then, as, indeed, now under the Common Market, there was pressure to find crops from which you could extract edible oil. Pre-war, most edible oil had been imported from Mediterranean countries in the form of olive or sunflower oil and once hostilities began, supply more or less stopped. So there was a need to increase oil production in this country, both of linseed oil for animal feeding and veterinary purposes and sunflower oil for human consumption.

It was some of the local advisory people who first invited me to consider growing sunflowers on contract. We knew that they grew perfectly well in people's gardens but had never tried to grow them on a field scale. There was a particular reason for growing them in our district. A retired business man living at Bovingdon, called Mr Music, who was of Russian extraction and could remember fields of sunflowers in the Ukraine when he was a boy, had set up a plant for drying and processing sunflower seeds. So we duly set out to grow about 6 acres.

We found them quite easy to cultivate and, of course, they also looked very beautiful. The snag was that in this country there is an enormous bird population and the sunflower is perfectly designed for birds to be able to help themselves to the most enormous meals with the minimum of difficulty. The seed head of the sunflower is shaped like a plate and the birds can settle on it without ever having to move again until they are full. We were warned that the last thing you needed in a field where you were growing sunflowers was either telephone or electricity wires anywhere near, because the birds would sit on the wires to digest their meal and then come down for another one without even

Maurice bringing order out of chaos on his farm without the aid of any machine. The farm opposite here used to have the lovely address: Few Onions, Pudds Cross.

Combining sunflowers was easy enough – the problem was the birds.

bothering to move out of the field. We found it quite difficult to find a field that was nowhere near any wires, but did our best. The crop grew magnificently and we were instructed that when the seeds were beginning to ripen, we should cut the plants off at ground level and hang the flowerheads over strings suspended between stakes all across the field. In this way, the seeds would be hanging down and would not be so tempting to the birds, the crop would be protected from the weather by the back of the flowerheads and the seeds would dry perfectly underneath. Of course, the people who advised us did not take into account the inventiveness of some birds, who simply sat on the back of the flowers and picked holes through to the seeds; or the athletic abilities of other birds who would merely hang upside-down underneath and peck upwards.

The crop had to stay like this for about two weeks because the weather was not all that hot, after which time, amazingly enough, there were some seeds left. When it came down to it, however, Mr Music's plant at Bovingdon was far too busy dealing with his own crops and those of nearer neighbours to deal with ours. So we were told we could, if we really persevered, thresh the sunflowers with our own combine and dry them with our ordinary grain drier. We threshed them with the combine without too much difficulty and proceeded to get them into our drier for drying. Unfortunately, nobody had told us that sunflower seeds, when they get warm, are very sticky. As soon as we got the seeds in, we were quite unable to get them out again. They simply stuck together like a mass of toffee and dried in that state, then caught fire and nearly ruined the drier. It took me half a day to fill the drier, which should have taken half an hour, and two days to empty it again after it had been considerably damaged.

I then went over to Bovingdon to Bulstrode Farm where Mr Music farmed and persuaded him that he would really have to put his machine on overtime and do our drying for us. His machine was quite a different type, specially designed by Ransome of Ipswich to deal with oily seeds and so there would not have been the slightest difficulty in drying our relatively small amount. But Mr Music was an extremely eccentric old gentleman who kept trying the machine out in ways the designers had never intended so he had little time left for ordinary seed drying. He really wanted to make a contribution to Britain's war effort and to feed people in difficult times, but I strongly suspect that some of his colleagues sold all the sunflower seeds he dried for oil extraction to make black market toilet preparations, although I could not prove it. Anyway, finally he did dry our remaining seeds for us and we never grew them again.

I then took up the growing of other types of seed on contract: grass and clover seeds on a very large scale; vegetable seeds on quite a large scale; and flower seeds on a small scale. Every one of these crops demands a different sort of technique in growing and harvesting and none of them had been grown in our area before, so it was a very demanding business, but also very rewarding and interesting. I would never previously have imagined that in the same year I would be harvesting sweet williams, antirrhinums, Shirley poppies, marigolds, runner beans, vegetable marrows and carrots for their seed. They are all of different sizes, have a different character and require different methods for harvesting, threshing and drying. Some are extremely easy, once you know how. For instance, when you grow sweet williams on a field scale you have to tie them into sheaves and stook them up with their heads upwards, just as you previously would have done with corn, and wait for a nice sunny day. Then you go along with a dustbin, hold the sheaf upside-down over the top of it and, if the air is hot and dry enough, all the seed comes out of its own accord. So that is a very satisfactory business. On the other hand, marigold seeds are similar to sunflower seeds. They have to be dried very carefully because they are sticky.

Carrot seed, as produced in the field, is not as you would buy it in a packet in a shop. For seed, the carrot crop takes land out of the farm rotation for nearly two years. It has to be sown one July, left over the winter and harvested the following August or September. As with sweet williams, it is cut with an old-fashioned binder, allowed to dry in stooks and threshed out with an old-fashioned threshing machine. But it is only, so to speak, half-threshed out. The result is a very light, woolly seed, which has to be sent away in large bags to a seedsman who will reduce it to a relatively small seed yield with special machinery that rubs off the whiskers. I remember we sent away two railway trucks of enormous bags of carrot seed but the whole lot weighed only a ton or two.

Quite a lot of flower seeds come from the Far East, from Japan or places where special conditions suit a special crop. So to try to grow this great variety in Britain obviously presented considerable problems. One of the very worst types is nasturtiums. The seeds are stuck together in threes and have to be picked up off the ground by hand. I imagine that normally they must be grown where there is a lot of cheap labour because they are not all that expensive to buy.

After the end of the war, all this rather exotic seed-growing faded out as communications with the rest of the world were

Marigolds, Shirley poppies and other flowers grown for seed. Every single one needs a different technique for harvesting.

restored and things could be imported again. The one thing which we were able to carry on with, and still can for that matter, was the production of grass and clover seed. That previously had largely been done in other countries and was then imported into Britain, but under the joint stimulus of wartime shortages and the experimental work in varieties of grass and clover carried out by the University of Wales in Aberystwyth, the industry in this country grew. There was a special effort to grow grass and clover seeds in Bucks, and a seed-growers' association was formed with the encouragement of the Ministry of Agriculture Advisory Services. This worked quite well under controlled conditions during the war, but immediately there was a chance of getting slightly more by selling on the open market farmers, as is their wont, started to break their contracts. So the whole scheme for an organised seed production in Bucks collapsed and people were left to their individual efforts.

If there is ever a shortage of the more obscure seeds again, I should think I am the only man in the Chilterns who would know how to contend with them and harvest them. Perhaps I ought to record the different methods in more detail – every flower that you can think of and every vegetable that you can think of requires a different technique in the handling of its seed.

For me the Second World War actually represented a period of very interesting and therefore very enjoyable farming. The variety of crops we grew, the acquisition of new machinery and our expansion geographically all added up to a challenging and rewarding experience. Of course, not everyone felt like this. I remember taking a lady who worked at the Bond Street shop out for lunch the day after war had been declared. 'Nothing will ever be the same again,' she kept saying in a rather emotional way, and doubtless many people all over Europe were saying the same thing. But quite a lot of people, myself included, did not want it to be the same. I did not want there to be widespread depression, unemployment and the gross inequalities I had been aware of throughout the whole of my life up to that point. I had become considerably involved with the local Labour Party from 1932 on and was even considering going into politics myself. When the war ended and farmers weren't immediately dropped, as they had been after the First World War, but continued to be supported by the government, my confidence increased still further. It seemed to me, at that point, that everything was possible.

'Will They Still Need Us?'

In 1945 when the war came to an end, what was the state of agriculture and what was the mood of the farmers? Certainly among the majority of older farmers who had experienced what happened after the 1914–18 War and had somehow survived, there was a feeling that the same thing would happen again. The politicians would let them down because nobody wanted to support farming in Britain except in time of war. Those of us who were a bit younger had more hope, but we were nevertheless looking to new ways of surviving in what we thought would be a more difficult climate. For five years we had been under a considerable amount of control; we had had to cultivate our farms fully or we were thrown out of them. We were given advice and loans to buy machinery, and by 1945 land under wheat had risen by two-thirds.

As far as I was concerned we had now got not just Grove Farm but Bury Farm at Bovingdon as well, although I knew I wouldn't keep that long. At The Grove we had maintained our dairy herd, slightly reduced in numbers but with an increased production of milk. Gradual selection of the cows and encouragement from the government to sell off the less productive ones had helped us to do this. We also had a much improved set of machinery and a number of sidelines. With everybody going around wringing their hands and saying 'We shan't be wanted now the war's over' it seemed obvious that you had got to do as many different things as possible. My seed-growing sideline had been reasonably successful. The grass and clover seed crops were good because we grew the Aberystwyth varieties bred by the University of Wales, which were highly productive. We had some truly magnificent crops of rape too, which in those days was not grown as an oil seed crop but as fodder for sheep, and we grew the seed on contract to supply other farmers. We planted it following early potatoes and got some of the best crops the seed firm had ever known. I think really we farmers were all holding our breath, the most optimistic of us thinking that the world was still short of food and therefore prosperity would continue for a little while at least, and the old and the cynical thinking that it would only be a matter of time before we were dropped.

The end of the war found me with more land, a family of four and everything looking marvellous.

Then, in 1947, everything changed. It was a year as important
in my life as 1921 had been, or 1931 when I took over Grove Farm,
or 1934 when I got married. The reason everything changed was
because Tom Williams, the Minister for Agriculture in the post-war
Labour government, brought in the 1947 Agricultural Act which,
for the first time in peace-time, incorporated a system of
guaranteed prices into the law of the country. This was the most
effective means ever devised anywhere for ensuring that food was
produced at the most reasonable price possible for the consumer,
but which allowed the farmer to grow the maximum amount he
could. In the case of every crop except potatoes it was still the
farmer's responsibility to market his produce (quite unlike the
current Common Market system). A price for each product was
fixed at annual negotiations between the National Farmers' Union
and the government each February. After the harvest for that year
had been sold, the average price that each crop had fetched
nationally was calculated and farmers were paid the difference
between the average price and the fixed price. That, perhaps, is an
over-simplification but it is basically the way it worked.
Consequently it paid you to produce good-quality grain and market

*Tom Williams: originally a
coal miner, he became the
most popular Minister of
Agriculture ever.*

it well since if you got more for it per ton than the fixed price, you were still paid whatever the difference was between the fixed price and the average price realised nationally.

Almost from that moment on the whole aspect of farming in Britain changed and instead of being a country which could only produce a very small percentage of its food requirements, it became able to produce almost all we needed and indeed to export quite a lot too. I don't believe this was envisaged at all when the Act was being debated in Parliament. All that was envisaged was that it would keep some sort of agriculture going in peace time. I am sure Tom Williams had no idea that his work was going to alter the face of Britain to the extent that it has. Now, of course, his system of guaranteeing prices has gone, to be replaced by a different one imposed by the EEC. The supervisory system of Agricultural Executive Committees, born out of the War Ags, has gone too, as has the government's subsidised farming advisory services which these committees channelled through to the industry; it's all gone. But the huge surge in agricultural production which has carried us to our present situation of embarrassing surpluses all started from that day in 1947 when this Act was passed.

At the time it wasn't opposed by anybody. The Tory Party dare not oppose it because they felt that it was popular among farmers (most of whom voted Conservative), so they advocated it as a sort of non-party piece of legislation, though it wasn't. The Labour Party tried to take advantage of this by arranging conferences all over the countryside with invited audiences of farmers, farm workers and even landowners to discuss the Act and to ensure that it was going to be instituted effectively by the people appointed to do so. I took part in a lot of those conferences. I never found anybody who opposed what was being done, nor do I remember anybody who visualised how it would all develop.

The Act provided for increased funds to be made available for research and an advisory service to be set up under the guidance of the local Agricultural Executive Committees (the word 'War' was dropped). Under their guidance, the technical knowledge obtained by the scientists was passed on swiftly to farmers and this produced a very rapid growth both in our total production and in the efficiency of our production. As soon as the Act was passed I was myself appointed to the Bucks Executive Committee and made the Chairman of what was called its Technical Organisation Sub-committee. The duty of this committee was to spread the information as it came through from the research establishments and make sure that people used it, and you had certain sanctions you could use against farmers who refused to improve their methods. After all, this was still a time of food rationing and shortages. In fact, two major things that had not been rationed at any time during the war were rationed immediately afterwards, one being potatoes and the other, for a short period, bread.

My appointment to the Agricultural Committee caused quite a bother. The Chairman designate for Bucks was a Colonel Ashton and immediately he was told that I had been proposed he said that he would resign if my appointment was confirmed. This was apparently because he considered I was far too young at thirty-five to have the experience for the job and, in any case, he had another candidate he favoured for the appointment – a man in his seventies. The Minister responsible for these appointments was the Parliamentary Secretary to the Minister of Agriculture, George Brown. He stuck to his guns and I was duly appointed, so a new Chairman had to be found for Bucks. A farmer called Frank Hartop was chosen and the Vice-chairman was Lord Carrington, whose subsequent career in Conservative politics is, of course, well known.

Chairing the Technical Organisation Sub-committee had quite a profound effect on my own farming. First of all it took me all over the county so I saw what other people were doing, but more importantly it seemed in my mind to impose a duty on me to do rather better than other people, so that nobody could point a finger at me and say I had no right to be in the position I was in. At the same time, I was closely in contact with all the technical people who were drafted in to advise on the best methods of doing every conceivable form of agricultural operation within the county. Supervision of how other people farm is not in practice very easy. I had thought a lot and talked a little during the war about it being all wrong that people occupied the nation's land and didn't produce all the food they could upon it. But when it came down to dealing with the man who wasn't producing what he should, it was almost always some dear old fellow who had been born on the place seventy years before and, perhaps, whose father had been born on it as well, and to threaten him with eviction because he wouldn't adopt modern methods was not all that simple. Fortunately, most people responded to advice and in any case there were machinery pools whereby it was possible for us to move in and actually *do* things that required doing, charging them up, of course, to the farmer at harvest time.

I set to on my own farms to improve and expand in every area I could. The restrictions on livestock numbers which had existed during the war because of the shortage of animal feed started to diminish and I increased the number of cows we had by several considerable leaps. The new cowshed we had had built towards the end of the war held about thirty cows and two or three years after the war we added stalls for another eighteen, making the number up to nearly fifty. It wasn't long before that building became inadequate too and we put in a proper yard and a herring-bone milking parlour so that we could milk a hundred.

The varieties of grain we grew were still much the same as those we had been growing before the war, but as more artificial fertilisers gradually became available so we used more and more and improved our yield. Sometimes, however, using such fertiliser had a disastrous effect on the crops because the old-fashioned varieties were very long in the straw and the fertiliser caused them to become top heavy with grain, so that they got terribly laid if the weather was bad and were then very difficult to harvest. However, under the stimulus of government backing, scientists in this country, and also in France, began to develop new varieties of wheat which could yield what before the war would have been unthinkable crops of grain. The new types had a shorter, stronger straw to allow the applications of much heavier dressing of fertilisers without them collapsing under the strain.

At the same time as better types of grain were being developed, other scientists were improving the quality and reliability of artificial fertilisers and were developing sprays to eradicate weeds and pests and diseases. The first agricultural herbicide had been tried out during the war years in the form of a powder called Agroxone which you spread on the crops. It would kill annual weeds of certain types and left the corn intact. It was particularly effective against charlock or wild mustard, which had been a very difficult weed in the past, and so changed the appearance of the whole countryside in early June when the charlock would have been flowering. For as long as anybody could remember, spring barley had always been a mass of yellow at the beginning of June, almost like rape fields are nowadays, and the only way to deal with the charlock was to pull it up by hand which was far too expensive in labour costs to do. But the first and simplest and crudest of all the herbicides wiped the charlock out. It was so effective on broad-leaf weeds that we were all told that if the secret of the stuff got into the hands of the Germans they

Chemical sprays have entirely eliminated charlock from the countryside.

would drop a bagful over Lincolnshire and ruin the entire potato crop of Britain. Whether that was really true or not, I don't know, but it started a formidable train which has now led to a situation where weeds have largely disappeared from land that is carefully farmed and crops are cleaner than we could ever then have believed was possible. This particular trend upsets some people who are concerned about the environment because what are weeds to us are wild flowers to them, but I'm sure there must be a way of growing good crops and still maintaining wild flowers in reserved areas.

During the whole of the fifties, artificial manures were subsidised by the government as were a number of other farming operations. Alternate husbandry, or ley farming, which meant having your farm partly in grass and partly in grain crops and then changing over every three years, was also subsidised in order to encourage this practice. Ley farming had long been practised in some parts of Britain. By giving land a short break under grass, the structure of the soil is improved, the clover fixes nitrates in the soil and animals fertilise the ground as they graze. (This is different from the traditional fallow system where land was kept completely clear of any crop for a whole summer.) At the end of each three-year period farmers were paid £10 per acre for ploughing the leys up and the other half of the farm was then sown down. This system, which has since been largely discontinued, led to a big increase in farm fertility and efficiency during the 1950s and '60s.

The application of lime to land was also fairly heavily subsidised as was land drainage. Not much of the land on the Chilterns requires drainage because it is such a dry area, but some at Grove Farm did, and during this period we carried out the first bit of land drainage that had probably ever been done on our fields. At the same time the lime balance of every field was corrected in a way that hadn't been done since the old days of bulk chalking in the eighteenth century.

Suddenly, after a very few years, we realised that our yields could continue to rise far higher than we had ever previously imagined and I suppose it began to sink in with the authorities that, far from merely fostering a permanent stability in agriculture, they might have started something which would create, in the end, the enormous surpluses we now have. Gradually the administrative machinery which had started it all off began to be broken up. The Conservative governments of the period first of all weakened, then totally dismantled the Agricultural Executive Committees. Nobody minded very much by then, but it had been these committees that had got the increasing scientific knowledge through to farmers quickly, had more or less insisted upon them using it and so had conditioned them into using technical advances voluntarily in the future. So by the early sixties we all had quite a different attitude to the job than we had had even immediately after the war. Instead of nurturing strictly limited ambitions about what we could achieve, almost anything seemed possible. Yields that had gone up from under a ton to over two tons to the acre showed every prospect of going up further. Costs which had come down in real terms through mechanisation could be held down by further mechanisation, and every February the National Farmers' Union, which by then had become a very strong and efficient bargaining organisation, went into increasingly acrimonious battle with the government to set the prices that would be guaranteed to farmers that year. The NFU nearly always came out on top of these negotiations until that was altered by the Common Market and an entirely different form of price fixing.

Looking back, it is quite extraordinary to think of the technical changes that took place because of the Second World War. When we went into it, a great many people were still using horses for ploughing. Practically all the corn in the country was harvested by a tractor-drawn binder and handled in sheaves the hard way. But by the end of the war, most people were using tractors for ploughing and a substantial amount of the grain

To drain farming land, earthenware pipes were laid end to end in trenches and covered with a porous material such as ashes or shingle. The water seeps into the pipes via the joints and is carried away to an outfall – either a brook or a larger drain.

Modern combines protect the operator from the dust and have instruments rather than levers with which to control the machine and monitor the quantity and flow of grain.

The technique of sowing seed by hand remained the same from the first farming right up to this century. We used the same action to spread the early fertilisers.

harvest was being handled by combines. Those horses which had not disappeared by 1945 had disappeared by about 1950 and the whole industry became mechanised. With full employment after the war, a lot of people left the country to work in towns and we used the technical advances in machinery to make do with far less labour. British manufacturers started to follow America's lead and began to turn out machines for us which were in some ways better adapted to our particular climatic conditions. Herbicides cut out the need for hand-hoeing; mechanised dairy parlours cut down on the number of farm hands we needed to do the milking. In 1932 we needed two people to milk thirty cows. Once our milking parlour had been installed we needed two men for 100 animals. In the late 1930s, in addition to the milk, Grove Farm produced barely 40 tons of grain with three men. Now we produce over 800 tons of grain plus a lot of beef when the staff is again only three men, plus a boy. (At one point in the intervening years it went up to nine.)

But does that mean that the physical work of farming is any better now than it was in 1939? Harvest now is somebody sitting on a combine advancing steadily across the field hour after hour, day after day, in a great cloud of black dust. He has to wear a face mask to keep the dust out of his lungs because it contains various sorts of mould which irritate your throat and nose like mad if you breathe it in. Then in a good part of Britain most years the grain has to be dried. Nowadays drying grain is not as bad as it was in the forties because there are augers and conveyor belts to help you move it about in bulk so you do not have to handle it too much. But still, whoever is supervising the drier has to do it in a cloud of dust wearing a face mask and possibly goggles as well.

It is not just milking, ploughing and harvesting that have become totally mechanised since the war, but nearly all jobs on the farm. Spreading artificial manure, for example, had been done when I was very young by a horse pulling a fertiliser drill. It was only 8 or 9 feet wide and so it took a long time to cover a field. Then, during the war, I discovered that it was quicker to do the job manually so, for several years, I and Will Barnett spread an ever-increasing quantity of artificial manure by hand. We used the same action as that shown in pictures dating from the Middle Ages, taking a handful of the granules and scattering them with a sweeping action of our arms. It was not an unpleasant task, especially as it could only be done in fine weather, but it involved a lot of walking – miles and miles to do a single field. This was also the way we sowed grass seed, despite the fact that seed barrows

had been invented in the late nineteenth century that were supposed
to speed up the process, but didn't. Nowadays, all such jobs are
done with big machines, most of which just have a hopper and a
disc at the bottom with fins on it which spin the seed out as it
dribbles through from the hopper in almost the same sort of action
as we scattered it ourselves by hand.

All this mechanisation has of course led to the decline in the
traditional country crafts which used to be handed down from
generation to generation. Thatchers, for example, were no longer
needed to thatch ricks once combine harvesters threshed the grain
and the straw was baled out in the fields. As less labour became
needed on farms, so the old method of laying and trimming hedges
became less practical, and once hedge-cutting machines came on the
market, it more or less died out.

Hedging used to be a very satisfying activity because you could
see the results of your labour as you worked along, and if you were
trimming a neglected hedge it was very pleasing to bring order out
of chaos. Another job I always enjoyed was ploughing. There is
something at the same time soothing and also stimulating to
thought in seeing a furrow turning over in a way similar to the way
it has done for thousands of years ever since man began to till the
land. It was always a satisfactory job and also a relatively clean
job, and has remained so.

But the thing in farming that I enjoy most is the continuing
job of watching livestock. Half the success of a herd of cattle or a
flock of sheep or, I imagine also, a herd of pigs, depends on your
observation of them: to notice immediately if they are slightly ill, to

The horse-drawn seed drill was introduced in the mid-eighteenth century. The tractor-drawn equivalent in use nowadays is basically the same machine but bigger and stronger.

Our hedge-cutter at work on an overgrown thorn hedge at Grove. The hydraulic arm can be moved to cut the top as well.

notice when the calf is about to come or a mating is due, or an animal is beginning to show signs of a deficiency, or there is not enough grazing in a field, or that it is becoming too cold for them to remain out in the field. There are a hundred and one things of that sort to look for and, still, no matter how far science advances, all cattle have got to be seen every day to be effectively looked after, so have all sheep and so have all pigs. This has a special satisfaction and no matter how long you have been doing it, you still get enjoyment from seeing the results of deciding the mating one year and seeing the calves nine months later. This satisfaction science can never take out of farming.

On the other hand, during the last sixty years the methods of treating animals when they are sick have changed quite drastically. Right up to the end of the Second World War, agricultural papers were full of advertisements for patent medicines for livestock and every farmer had a vast range in stock and had no idea whether any of them were of any use or not. They were generally described as 'Red Drenches' or 'Black Drenches' and had no indication or scientific declaration of what they contained. The range of drugs available was really quite small, and the vets, when you called

IN
FINE
FETTLE

Thanks
To—

ELLIMAN'S
ROYAL EMBROCATION

The recognised Standby of Farmers and Livestock Keepers the whole world over is **Elliman's** Royal Embrocation. In every emergency of sickness and accident the prompt application of Elliman's

Royal Embrocation has a wonderful effect and in the more serious cases the lives of valuable animals are often saved. Keep a bottle always handy and be prepared to meet Emergencies.

ELLIMAN'S ROYAL EMBROCATION (for Animals), 1 6, 2 9 and 4 6.

ELLIMAN'S Universal Embrocation (For Human Use) 1 3, 2 - and 4 -

ELLIMAN ATHLETIC RUB For Sportsmen and Athletes 1 - and 2 6

From all Chemists and Stores or direct from Elliman's, Slough.

This embrocation, advertised in Farmers' Weekly *in the 1930s, seemed to be able to do rather a lot of very different things.*

them, came almost entirely to do physical operations on animals. They might recommend to you dietary changes and that sort of thing, but they mainly dealt with physical injuries. They were as good as surgeons at this although they had no antibiotics then with which to treat infections.

In my view, vets could largely be dispensed with now but for rather severe regulations governing the buying of drugs by farmers. I do not know whether this is done to avoid a real risk or whether it is done to protect the vested interests of the vets but, nominally at any rate, you cannot get any antibiotic or any one of a number of other drugs except through a vet. Therefore, vets have really changed their status on the farm; they have become almost mobile chemist shops and, if you have a cow that you suspect has a certain condition which you know will require a particular drug, you have to ring up the vet to bring it even though you might well be able to treat the animal yourself. This has caused a certain amount of annoyance among farmers who feel their vets' bills are unnecessarily inflated.

Perhaps one reason why farmers feel they could take over many aspects of veterinary work now is that since the war people have specialised far more in the type of livestock they keep; in fact they have specialised more all round. Nowadays people tend to go in for arable cropping or dairying or pig or poultry keeping (which have both developed into factory enterprises), and we have done the same on Grove Farm. When the war ended and the Agricultural Act was passed, we had a dairy herd, some beef cattle, pigs, poultry, seed crops, sugar beet, potatoes, wheat, oats and barley. Now we have been educated and progressed out of all that to the things which we perhaps do best: beef cattle, wheat and barley.

All the changes brought about by research and mechanisation – the expansion and the specialisation – all that was gained by them and all that was lost – were set in motion by the war. They were all inevitable from 1945 on. I suppose if there had not been a war, they would have happened anyway, but they might well have taken half a century instead of just a few years. In 1947, of course, when the Agricultural Act was passed no one foresaw this – I certainly didn't. My main priority was to get more land, more space, in order to use my machinery more efficiently and to put the new technical advice into operation.

I was reasonably sure that it wouldn't be long before the owner of Bury Farm at Bovingdon would want it back to farm it himself. Consequently I always had it in the back of my mind that somehow or other I should try to rent at least one of the two smallish farms with elderly occupiers next door to us. One of these was Mattesdon Farm at Lye Green, about 70 acres of particularly good land occupied by an elderly man called Harry Robbins. Harry kept a pet shop in New Oxford Street, London, and was not really a full-time farmer at all. He had no machinery or plant to deal with modern farming conditions and I felt that, sooner or later, he was bound to give up. I also felt that my neighbours, the Mashes, although good friends, were likely to want this additional land too, and as they had more money than I had and had more prestige than I had, I thought the Robbins were more likely to want to sell to them in preference to me. However, I started going to see Mr and Mrs Robbins whenever I had a chance and, in the end, I used to go along regularly at about half-past ten in the morning once a week. Mrs Robbins would give me a large piece of currant cake and a cup of tea and we would discuss their farming and our farming and all the local gossip.

Slowly the Robbins became more and more friendly and I was able to help them out quite a lot. Jessie Dell, who ran the Rover Bus Company nearby, and I did all the work for them one winter.

This was just about the point at which they were making up their minds finally to sell out and I think they still would have given first offer to the Mashes, except that Mr Robbins went down to do some shopping in Chesham one day and the secretary of the Mashes' company, Mr Bucknell, met him in the Broadway and, in public, asked him when he was going to sell up. The old man, who was vague about most things, was absolutely outraged that people should try to discuss his private business in the middle of a busy street and that ruled the Mashes out finally. When he decided to move out, he agreed to sell the farm to me and the farmhouse to Jessie Dell, the two people who had helped them out. Consequently, when, as expected, the owner of Bury Farm, Bovingdon, wanted it back for his own use in 1952 and there was no way we could go to the expense of fighting him for possession, we only had a reduced acreage for about a year before we were able to buy Mattesdon Farm. It seems incredible now that I bought the 70-odd acres of Mattesdon Farm for £7000, immediately sold £900 worth of timber off it and only had to have an extra mortgage of £6000 for enormously increased efficiency.

Looking back to this particular period in the late 1940s and early '50s I wonder how on earth I managed to get everything done. I was still doing a high percentage of the farm work myself, serving as a magistrate on the local Bench, going every Friday to Stoke Mandeville to meetings of the AEC and spending very many nights a week on Labour Party activity throughout the county. But, of course, thirty-five is a good age to be. My service on the Agricultural Executive Committee actually only lasted three years. It came to an abrupt end in the 1950 General Election because I stood for Parliament for the first time and the Act laid down that parliamentary candidates could not be members of an AEC. I was quite sorry to drop it, since it had given me a much wider view of farming than I'd ever had previously and quite a privileged view, in a way, because you had access to all the economics of a whole lot of farms and saw different methods of a very large number of farmers at first hand.

Though I did not get elected in the 1950 election, I never returned to the AEC, but I did continue to serve as a magistrate for the next twenty-three years. My arrival on the Bench in Chesham in 1946 had been somewhat comic. I was walking up the side of Chesham Police Station where the Court used to be held, feeling rather nervous about my first morning's sitting, when I heard, literally, a roar from across the road behind me. It was Doctor

Cunningham, a remarkably outspoken ex-naval doctor who at that time practised in Chesham. He roared: 'What the hell are you doing going up there? What have you done?' I walked back to him and said rather nervously, 'I haven't done anything, I've been appointed to the Bench.' He let out a tremendous guffaw and then said: 'Well, I don't like your politics but at least you know your arse from your elbow which is more than the others do.' I went in feeling somewhat embarrassed by this because some of those elderly ladies and gentlemen who didn't know their arses from their elbows, according to Doctor Cunningham, were walking up the yard beside me when he roared out.

I suppose people's view of the immediate post-war years is coloured by their political attitudes. To me they seemed the most wonderful years. The Labour Party that I'd supported all my life was in power and seemed to be providing more of everything than one had thought possible. There seemed to me no reason why both my industry and the country generally shouldn't continually advance to a higher standard of living, a higher standard of production and a higher standard of service than ever before.

It was through my involvement with the Labour Party that I became friendly with Jenny and Nye Bevan and when in 1953 Nye became interested in buying a farm in the Home Counties I was one of the people he asked to look out for one for him. I took him to see several farms in our area, none of which was particularly satisfactory. On one of these at Radnage near High Wycombe the owner had planted a lot of fir trees of which he was very proud. He was roundly denounced by Nye for planting fir trees instead of oaks and beeches because, he said, 'nothing grows under fir trees', and of course he was right. Finally, I went down to see a local farmer called Alan Crawley at Cuckoo Farm because he had mentioned that Asheridge Farm, next to his brother's, near Chartridge was coming on the market. It seemed to be absolutely ideal for the Bevans' purposes, not too big a farm and a nice house in a fairly isolated situation. They took it.

From the moment they came to live up there at Asheridge Farm and so for the last few years of his life I saw quite a lot of Nye. Frequently on Fridays, when Florence went to her Co-op meetings (she was by then a director of the local Co-op), Nye would ring up and ask me up to dinner. We would talk over the farm and, of course, lots of politics as well.

In the autumn of 1955 Cowcroft Farm at Ley Hill became vacant to let and the land agent approached me to see if I was interested in taking it. That night I had to go up and see Nye about something and I mentioned the business with Cowcroft Farm to him. He started to upbraid me saying: 'Why are you so unenterprising – what's the good of an entrepreneur without any enterprise? Under the system under which we live people running businesses have got to expand – that's the only way it works.' I replied that I didn't think that I could raise enough capital. 'Have you asked the bank manager?' Nye demanded. I had to admit I hadn't, so for that I got denounced again for my timidity. 'Here's a man who won't do something he knows he ought to do because the bank manager won't give him a loan he hasn't asked for!' mocked Nye, and by the end of the evening he had helped to persuade me that if it was a sound proposition to rent Cowcroft I ought to try to do it.

The next morning I went down to the Westminster Bank in Chesham to ask the manager for a loan to take Cowcroft Farm. Before I had opened my mouth he said: 'I've just had a distinguished visitor here talking about you,' and I'm afraid my heart sank a bit because I wondered what had been said. 'Yes,' the manager continued, 'I've been told that if I don't give you a loan you haven't even asked for I don't know my job as a bank manager so I'd better listen to what you've got to say.' He then listened to what I had to say, submitted the scheme to his area bosses and the loan was sanctioned. We took Cowcroft and have had it ever since.

When Nye came to Asheridge a lot of locals were hostile and suspicious. When he died four years later everybody was upset. I had more telephone calls from local Tories and people of that sort, asking kindly after him because they had met him and talked to him in the road, than ever I did even from Labour supporters. He may have had some faults as a politician, but he was marvellously entertaining company and a very good friend. What's more, in my view, most of his ideas proved right in the end.

Nye Bevan had strong views on everything from politics to farming to my lack of self-confidence.

The Godfather

The Charolais Success Story

All my life until 1954 I had been a dairy man and an arable farmer, but had never had anything to do with beef at all. In that year everything changed and changed in such a way which was to lead me into an entirely new aspect of farming. In some ways it has turned out to be the most interesting part of my farming life in that it has been the only part that has affected the course of agriculture in this country generally.

In 1954 Berryfield Farm at Aylesbury, a large grass farm, came up to rent by tender and I tendered for it and succeeded. It had for hundreds of years been recognised as one of the best grazing farms in the Vale of Aylesbury. It was famous for its ability to fatten beef cattle and sheep in the summer, but because it was such a wet farm the bulk of the land was unploughable. Since it would have been a very expensive operation to drain it, I had to start thinking about going in for types of farming which I had never previously touched. I immediately acquired a flock of sheep through my sister's brother-in-law who was a sheep farmer at Carter Bar on the Scottish borders. He sent me down 150 elderly ewes who had had several crops of lambs, knew all about the job themselves, but who could no longer find an adequate living on the hills and wanted something easier. This proved to be a very workable system straight away. We had very few difficulties, a good crop of lambs and because these good old ewes knew as much as we did about the job, we didn't lose very many and the lambs fattened extraordinarily well on the Vale of Aylesbury grass.

But grazing an area with sheep alone is not practical because you get a build-up of parasites on the land. To avoid this you have to alternate with cattle and I decided to get some beef cattle. I tackled it in two ways. I had understood from the farmers I had met through my Agricultural Executive Committee activities that the type of land at Berryfield was ideal for fattening cattle which were already fairly old and which were big animals – the bigger the better. So I went down to Devonshire and bought a lot of South Devon bullocks which had come off Dartmoor at the end of the summer and were probably already about two and a half years old. The South Devon breed was the largest breed then available in

This photo of me was taken at the Royal Show on a very hot day and inscribed by Alastair Mackay, the Secretary of the Charolais Cattle Society at the time.

Berryfield Farm was a mile west of Aylesbury on the Bicester road – about 17 miles from Grove.

Britain and the idea was that I would winter them through and then fatten them at Berryfield for sale the following autumn.

This worked fairly well, but, of course, the capital required to buy enough bullocks in order to use the whole of the farm in this way was far more than I had and, in any case, there were not adequate buildings at Berryfield to winter very many. (Traditionally farmers in the Vale of Aylesbury had bought weaned calves in the spring, turned them out into the pasture and then sold them before the next winter.) The landlord agreed to put me up adequate buildings for the subsequent years, but in the first year they were woefully inadequate for what I needed. I therefore also adopted a second strategy which was to buy the surplus calves from dairy herds and to rear them at Berryfield. I would then re-sell the heifers (females) to dairymen who had what are called flying herds, which means they didn't rear their own replacements, and fatten the males up for beef on our grass.

At the same time, I tried to integrate the arable system at Grove Farm with the system at Berryfield. There was a small acreage at Berryfield under wheat and, because the land was different, I anticipated that the grain would ripen at a slightly different time from on Grove, so I would be able to use our combine and baler for the harvest on both farms. On the whole this system worked, but because we had no drying facilities at Berryfield, we had to cart the grain all the way home to Chesham to be dried, which wasn't particularly efficient.

By now the dairy herd at Grove had grown to nearly 100 and as we didn't require all the female calves for replacement, I decided to look for some way of producing beef calves from my surplus Ayrshires which could be fattened up successfully at Berryfield. We tried crossing every native British beef breed that there was on the Ayrshires in the hope of producing a good beef animal. We used an Angus and the result was very small and slow-growing. We used a Hereford and the males were fairly good, but the females put on too much fat long before they were of any size whatsoever. The Beef Shorthorn was even worse. Friends I had met in the West Country through buying the South Devon bullocks persuaded me that I should use a South Devon bull, which I did, and this produced, yes, enormous animals, but animals that wouldn't fatten until they were maybe three and a half or four years old. To have had so long a period between calving and selling would have made the enterprise very uneconomic.

The male calves that I bought from dairymen that I tried fattening up were either pure Friesian or Friesian crossed with a beef breed. In theory, the beef crosses should have been better beef animals than the pure dairy animals, but, in practice, when we came to sell them, although the beef-crossed animals graded better and people paid more per hundredweight for them, they were so much lighter than the pure dairy animals that they actually came to less money. There seemed to me to be something quite ridiculous in a pure dairy animal when fattened for beef fetching more money than recognised beef breeds. Perhaps I should explain a little more about how the different breeds of cattle developed in this country in order to understand how this situation could have arisen.

Originally, domestic cattle were kept for three purposes: they were used for haulage, the females produced milk and the young males (and the females when they had done their work) were used for meat. All these functions existed in the same animal. Very gradually, from the Middle Ages onwards, farmers became less concerned with self-sufficiency and purely local consumption and began to supply the developing towns, so they started to want more specialised animals. In certain areas of Europe, particularly Holland, the cattle were selected and bred with the emphasis on milk because they were in a good geographical position to sell a lot of dairy produce. Other areas further from centres of population

Left: the South Devon is our biggest native breed and the nearest in the 1950s to the continental breeds. But it still did not carry the same percentage of meat.

Right: A foreigner to Britain, the Friesian is such an efficient milk producer it has nearly destroyed our native dairy breeds.

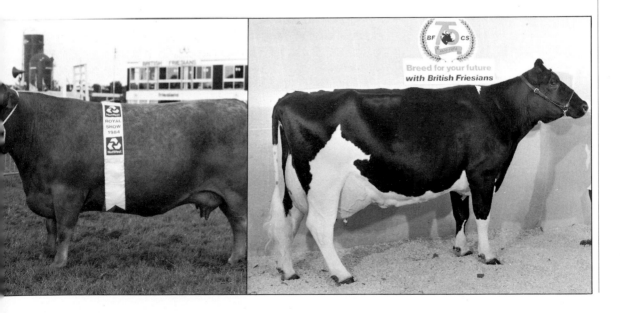

concentrated on producing meat because there wasn't a big enough market for perishable dairy goods nearby. Gradually, the haulage function of cattle in this country faded away and horses took their place, but in France and other parts of Europe, cattle continued to be used for this purpose.

All of this led to a situation where, before the Second World War, British cattle were for the most part either specialised dairy animals, such as the Friesian or Dairy Shorthorn, or specialised beef animals, such as the Hereford or Aberdeen Angus, most of the latter being reared in remote areas on the hills of Scotland, northern England and Wales. These beef breeds were specialised in other particulars as well. They were for the most part quite small because small cattle do better on hill land and also because everybody in between the wars argued, erroneously it turned out, that because families were getting smaller, the joints of meat they would require would be smaller, therefore the animal needed to be smaller too. This was a universal doctrine in those days. Presumably nobody thought about simply cutting a larger animal into smaller joints, which is what has happened since.

Another factor which resulted in the type of British beef animals we had then was that people actually liked fat on their meat, so the beef breeds had been selected to put on a lot of fat as well as lean. That was what the market wanted. In France and some other countries in Europe, however, it was entirely different.

Draught oxen went out of use in Britain long before the rest of Europe.

Because the people there use a lot of oil in cooking they had no taste for fat meat. They wanted their animals lean and the more lean meat the better, therefore the bigger the better, and it so happened that the haulage breeds of animals they still had exactly fitted the taste of the Continentals for beef since haulage cattle have plenty of muscles and muscle equals lean meat.

Then, beginning just before the Second World War and accelerating after it, people's taste in meat in Britain began to change (partly because of health propaganda) and they too turned against fat meat. But by this time three-quarters of all the cattle in Britain were of the one Friesian breed which had arisen in Holland the previous century and which had been selected entirely for milk. Some of these Friesians were crossed with the British native beef breeds in an attempt to go someway towards meeting the new demand and this produced an animal that wasn't too fat and carried a fair amount of lean meat. But it didn't go far enough. In particular, the females from these crossings still acquired too much fat before they got to any great size and carried any great amount of meat, as I discovered at Berryfield. They were fattened either by being fed indoors during the winter on the surplus products of an arable farm (this mainly took place in East Anglia), or on the better grasslands in the rest of Britain during the summer time.

This whole process of producing beef was very slow, which made it difficult for breeders to achieve the advances that had been

Aberdeen Angus – specialised high-quality beef animals but slow-growing compared with continental breeds.

Pigs lend themselves to mass production of meat because they have so many progeny a year, whereas a cow only has one.

made from the twenties onwards in the production of meat from poultry and pigs. These are both animals which breed very very quickly. It is possible to get two generations of chickens in a year and one hen will lay hundreds of eggs, so if you get a hen which carries a particular characteristic for meat purposes she can produce hundreds of similarly endowed progeny in a year. A sow can produce twenty or more piglets in a year and so therefore selection can make rapid changes in that species too. All over the world farmers and geneticists were working to improve these meat animals between the wars and onwards, so that by about 1950 pork and chicken were beginning to become very cheap whereas beef, which took a long time to produce, was still expensive. Under the old system of producing beef the *minimum* time from mating to slaughtering was two and a half or three years, and what's more an enormous amount of the finished animal was wasted. Whereas about 80% of the body weight of a pig is usable meat, with a beef animal it's rarely more than 60%.

With each generation taking so long – three to four years – to replace itself, the geneticists and farmers would have needed a lifetime to alter the confirmation and characteristics of a breed of beef cattle. So the atmosphere was ripe to find existing breeds elsewhere in the world which more nearly approximated to what the market now required in Britain – a large, lean, quick-growing animal that would give a good return in a fairly short time.

At the time when I was first looking for a more suitable animal to cross with our dairy cows I had no conception that importing breeds from other countries would prove to be possible. But when, in the spring of 1956, Florence and I went on a short holiday to France with John Mackie and his two brothers-in-law, who were also farmers, and their wives, we decided we would take a look at the French Charolais breed, originally a haulage breed, just to see if it would answer our problems. What we saw astonished us and immediately converted us to the idea that we had got to do something about bringing the breed in. Not only did the animals which we saw obviously grow much faster than British breeds, but also they had so much more lean meat on them and meat in all the right places where the most expensive cuts are. Of course, we only had time to see one or two herds on that holiday, but within a year or two the French, realising that they had a chance of developing an export market, put on a big show at Vichy in 1961 and invited us and many other foreign representatives to come and have a more thorough look at the breed. There they laid

The Charolais we saw in France astonished us. They grew so quickly and carried so much lean meat in all the right places where it's worth most – the loin and hind quarter.

on demonstrations of the killing out percentages of the animals, their rate of growth and everything else one could want to know – all mixed up, as you would expect in France, with a lot of pretty good eating, drinking and entertainment. I remember on one occasion being served champagne and caviar in a municipal slaughter house. However, that was a bit later.

We came back from our holiday determined to start a campaign to get the breed in. The first step was to summon everybody who had shown any interest in the breed to a meeting – people who we knew personally, people who had written to the papers, people from the farming press and people from the Milk Marketing Board (one of whose jobs it is to provide an insemination service for all the milk producers in the country) – we wrote to them all. The upshot was that a rather mixed bag of people joined together to form a committee to conduct a propaganda exercise aimed at getting the breed in. It included no regular beef breeders at all; they were too prejudiced in favour of what they were already doing. Instead there were a number of dairymen like me, arable farmers like John Mackie, one or two butchers and one or two landowners. Not one regular beef breeder expressed any interest until almost ten years had gone by and we had already got the breed into the country.

Ultimately, after several years of campaigning, the then Minister of Agriculture, John Hare, set up a committee under Lord Terrington to enquire into the problem. The committee reported that the breed should be tried out in this country and so an extended trial, planned to last perhaps twenty years, was set up whereby bulls imported from France were to be crossed with British dairy breeds to see if they would really result in any benefit for agriculture generally. There were to be no females allowed in, and no attempt to establish the breed as a pure breed in Britain. This compromise was arrived at primarily because although the Minister's scientific advisers agreed that foreign breeds generally should be tried out, there was a strong lobby against it from breeders and certain farming organisations who didn't want any change. The breeders' organisations were obviously opposed to the scheme because it threatened the dominance of their breeds in Britain, and the farming organisations objected because they had swallowed propaganda which claimed that it would be very difficult to bring in a breed from the Continent without introducing foot and mouth or some other disease. In point of fact, that particular problem never really existed. Live animals can be quarantined, tested and cleared of any possible infection whereas carcasses, which were then being imported on a huge scale from South America, could not be tested in any way at all and could and did bring in foot and mouth from time to time.

The first importation of bulls coming out of quarantine. They were chosen by Ministry officials and the French, not by we breeders, but they did a good job.

The first importation consisted of bulls born in the year 1961 and they arrived in Britain just about New Year 1962. They were immediately used experimentally on a great number of farms, and I, along with some of the other interested people who now formed a Charolais Breed Society (which the Ministry would not then recognise), started a grading-up scheme whereby, since they wouldn't allow us females in from France, we crossed calves repeatedly with imported bulls until such time as we had a virtually pure female. I started this grading-up programme using South Devon females since this was the biggest native breed and also a non-dominant breed; other people tried different ones. Although subsequently we have had pure animals in from France, many of these up-graded animals still remain within the breed in Britain.

The herd of cows on which I tried out the bulls was kept principally not at Berryfield but on the 220 acres of grassland over at Tring which I had taken on in 1958. Tring Park was laid out by Lord Rothschild in the last century with a great many trees in situations that made it impossible to plough most of it, even during the war. It was where, in my extreme youth, my godmother, Miss Warrender, had taken me to Tring Show. Over the years it had become neglected and overgrown, but its attraction from my point of view was that it was very dry land, a good deal of it sloping, and had plenty of tree shelter, so was an ideal place for wintering cattle. You couldn't winter cattle at Grove because the ground is

Cross-bred cows with their second-cross calves in the shelter of trees at Tring Park. The calves already look almost like pure Charolais, the breed is so dominant.

*Immediate and unexpected
success with a cross calf in a
Tring show. The judge was a
butcher.*

heavy and the farm is exposed to cold winds. You couldn't winter
them out at Berryfield because the land was very wet indeed and
we hadn't enough buildings, so Tring was very attractive from that
point of view. Furthermore, because a lot of the grass had been left
down for many years it was possible to sell turf, which gave an
immediate return and which I shared with the landlords. So we
started using Tring Park purely for wintering cattle which were
fattened at Berryfield the following year and for surplus store cattle
from Grove Farm. Then I established the suckling herd there on
which the Charolais bulls were tried out. (Suckling herds are herds
of cows that do nothing but rear their own calves for sale.)

The first imported bulls sired calves which were born in the
severe winter of 1962/3 and some died. This was immediately
hailed by parties who wanted to stop us bringing the Charolais in
as evidence that the breed was delicate and difficult to rear. This
was rubbish; we had no special problems. Interestingly, the first
friends we had were not breeders but butchers who immediately
recognised that Charolais carcasses were what they had been
looking for for years. We had the pleasant experience of entering a
cross-calf (Shorthorn/Charolais), at one year old, in a fatstock
show at Tring and winning all the championships. This astonished
me as much as it did everybody else within the market, but the
judge was a butcher and, being at the practical end of meat
production, butchers are far less prejudiced than farmers.

The appointment of Christopher Soames as Minister of
Agriculture, who was thought to be a dedicated European, made
absolutely no difference to the situation. He was just as much tied
to protecting what he saw as the legitimate vested interests of the
breeders as his predecessor had been, so we had to wait until the
Labour Party got in in 1964 and John Mackie, who was the
Charolais Committee Chairman at the time, became Parliamentary
Secretary to the Minister of Agriculture for a change in attitude.

In March 1965 I was in Paris at the Annual Paris Show. I even
remember the date since it was my birthday, 6 March. I had been
instructed to telephone one of the Permanent Secretaries to the
Ministry of Agriculture on that day, which I did, and learned that
we had been given permission for a further importation of
Charolais into Britain, this time to include up to 200 females. Since
these had to be allocated fairly to all the interested parties this
meant that none of us was going to get very many because, by
then, the interest in the breed had grown and we had some forty or
fifty members wanting to import. The Ministry added further

complications by stipulating that we had to cater for Northern
Ireland and the Isle of Man too, who had very few members but
were allotted a considerable allocation. By this time the Ministry at
least recognised us as an established breed society and it gave us
the job of dealing with the importation. Since I was now the
Chairman and since also I was the only member of the Society with
any regular secretarial assistance, it fell upon me to organise this
first mass importation of Charolais. It was not too easy.

The Ministry's veterinary officers laid down stringent
conditions as to how the animals were to be quarantined, and since
there was no quarantine station available, we had to find one. After
a considerable search, we found a building that fitted the bill in the
Naval Dockyard at Plymouth – a disused storage shed which was
about to be pulled down. We also had to arrange for the buying in
France ourselves and pay all the costs, both of the buying and the
quarantine, and of two Ministry Inspectors to go with us to
observe the buying. Fortunately one was Tom Alsop, the Ministry's
Principal Livestock Inspector, who was a broad-minded and
sensible man and very helpful in everything. However, the
veterinary people at the Ministry were, in my opinion, not helpful
at all. Every possible obstacle was put in our way: overlong
quarantine periods, testing for non-existent diseases, or diseases
which didn't affect cattle, or diseases which they said were not
present in Britain but which we discovered were present in quite a
large number of British cattle. And all the time the same officials
were pointing out to me 'off the record' that there was actually a
much greater danger of disease from the importation of meat on
the bone from the Argentine which was then allowed.

However, in the end all these obstacles were overcome and, of
course, the fact that we did overcome them altered the whole
atmosphere of the imported cattle trade in Britain. Now it is
possible to buy animals anywhere in Europe with only quite
reasonable testing and quarantine requirements, and great benefit
has accrued to the agricultural industry, the meat trade and to the
British meat-consuming public.

During the year 1965 I made no less than thirteen visits to
France to organise various aspects of what we were doing, to
arrange trips for our members to be shown around farms to buy,
to arrange for bulk-buying of animals to be picked from the
quarantine in England for those who didn't wish to go to France
themselves, to co-operate with the Milk Marketing Board in buying
additional bulls for their use, and many other things. During all

Cowcroft Emperor at six months.

Cowcroft Emperor was sold to New Zealand and from there his semen was widely sold in Australia.

that time, contrary to what one may have been led to expect, and certainly contrary to what some of our members say, I found the French extremely helpful and, on the whole, no less honest than British farmers. Over a period of four or five years from 1965 on, I personally dealt with several hundred French farmers and only a tiny proportion of them ever tried anything on whatsoever. I really don't think a foreign buyer visiting England would have any better experience than that. The French farmer is also, in my experience, extremely hospitable and much more friendly than your average French townsman. Since he often lives in quite an isolated situation, he expects to entertain people who visit him on business and does so sometimes on quite a lavish scale which rather surprised me.

Over many years the French have produced not just the Charolais, but several beef breeds which are far more suitable for the modern market than any of the British ones. It could be said that while the British breeders with their world-wide reputation for stock breeding were ruining our breeds, the French with their down-to-earth practical attitude were building theirs up, so that in the end we had to have them.

For the next eighteen years a good deal of my time was taken up by the work of the British Charolais Cattle Society, which in time grew from a part-time job in our office in Chesham to a full-scale operation with a secretary and numerous staff. During this time the breed grew in Britain so that, at this time, in 1986, it is the second most numerous beef breed in Britain after Herefords, and in fact there are more Charolais bulls in use than bulls of any other breed, especially on hill cattle in the north of England and Scotland, and in Wales. So it is a colossal success story. Maybe it could have been done better, but nobody had any experience of how to do that sort of thing at the time; as importers we were all amateurs. As an adventure it is now more or less over since the whole thing has become established and conventional. Perhaps if there were now a proposal to bring in some other breed from the other side of the world the Charolais breeders in Britain would oppose it just as the British beef breeders opposed our entry back in the 1950s and '60s. Certainly many of the Charolais breeders who have benefited so much from past innovation are now very hostile to new methods such as embryo transplantation and breeding programmes to eliminate the horns on Charolais cattle and things of that sort. In my view, such people are portraying the same self-defeating attitudes that almost prevented us from getting the breed into this country in the first place.

My involvement in the Charolais story has taken me not just to France but all over the world. For a few years after we brought the breed in we experienced a demand for our cattle from all sorts of places world-wide. This was because everybody was suspicious of the disease situation in France, but because we were able to test the imported calves and then rear them in Britain, our stock had very high health standards. So the Americans and New Zealanders who wanted the breed had to come to us for them. The Australians were only allowed to buy animals born in New Zealand and New Zealanders could only buy animals born in Britain, so it took more than two generations to get the animals into Australia, but they still felt it was worthwhile. I went out to New Zealand to see animals that I had sold and also managed to combine it with a trip to Australia to sell semen from one of my bulls, and to Kenya, Mauritius and Thailand sightseeing.

Attending meetings of the International Charolais Organisation, which meets in different countries each year, took me to Mexico, which I certainly wouldn't have visited otherwise, and to the USA where, in any case, I sold animals. In fact, for the very first time it got me thoroughly off my own dunghill and gave Florence and I a chance to travel for genuine business reasons. The only problem was that we tended to visit only those countries which had got Charolais cattle and when one winter it was suggested that Florence should spend a few weeks in the West Indies for health reasons, we had to find an island that had some Charolais for us to have a look at.

Amongst the people in America I sold Charolais bulls to was a man called Paul Wyndham who lived in a little town called Elba in Southern Alabama. Elba is a town that has a memorial in its centre to the boll-weevil, an insect which destroyed the cotton crop and drove the local farmers to grow peanuts which proved to be far more profitable. When I was in the States one time in the early seventies, I visited Paul who gave a party for me and some visiting Charolais breeders from another state in a big wooden hut out on the farm. At the end of the evening Paul was in such a terrible state that he had to be carried off to bed by a large black servant called Spike. I was all right and somebody took me down to the travel lodge where I spent a good night in my cabin.

The next morning I got up fairly early and went out to organise myself some breakfast in the town. At the end of the row of cabins, I came across a large room with some people in it who were eating. I took it to be a café of some sort and so walked in and asked if they would serve me breakfast. The lady who was there told me to sit down and we started to talk. She gave me a cup of coffee and was about to serve me some hominy grits when I noticed that she was in a dressing gown and that all the other people having breakfast were children. Just at that moment a man came in in his stockinged feet carrying his boots and I realised I had walked into a private house, had asked myself to breakfast and they were giving it to me. I was covered with confusion and apologised profusely, but they didn't seem to mind; that is one thing about the southern states of America – they are very hospitable. When I got back to England I wrote to the people and said that if they were ever wandering around in the Chesham area and wanted breakfast, they were to come in and help themselves.

The Charolais have now become our sole livestock enterprise. We produce some thirty bulls for sale each year and, of those, the very best go to Scotland and the north of England to be sold at auction sales in the autumn and winter. Others are sold in Wales for use on Welsh Black and Hereford cows, and some are sold locally at the farm door for use on dairy herds and on the few suckling herds in Buckinghamshire and Hertfordshire. We keep most of our females for replacements but a few are sold for breeding and any cattle which don't measure up to the required standards are fattened for beef and sold in Banbury market, as are the cows which cease to breed or don't breed well. Very often they go back to France again as carcasses where their grandparents or great-grandparents came from.

Beef cattle is an expensive and low-output type of farming. For this reason it is really more suitable for the poor hilly land and the wetter areas of the north and west rather than the good arable land at Grove Farm. In fact it could be said that The Grove is not a suitable livestock farm at all. Because of its northerly and easterly aspect, it has too short a grazing season to be an ideal dairy farm and being in the home counties the land is too expensive to devote completely to beef. But now we have built up our reputation and experience we will stick with it and it will continue to make up an important part of our income. For a long time to come, the fields on Grove Farm will be full of white cattle instead of the roan, brown, or brown and white cattle they had when I was young. This represents a change as big in the beef industry as the increase in yields of 18 cwt of wheat to the acre to 70 cwt to the acre in arable farming, because the Charolais produce beef at the rate of almost a kilo where a pound would be produced by the traditional British breeds.

Berryfield, the farm which started me off on all of this, has gone. I gave it up in 1968 in favour of taking over a small piece of land nearer to Grove Farm. Since then I've seen all the land there drained by my successor and it is now growing good crops of wheat. I can't help regretting that I wasn't more enterprising and didn't keep it. Certainly I shall always think of it as the farm that encouraged me to help change British farming.

Expanding and Specialising

My involvement in the Charolais adventure all stemmed from that day in 1954 when our tender for Berryfield Farm was accepted. Another enterprise which I began in the same year had absolutely nothing to do with farming, but it too has proved successful and is still going – building. In the summer of that year, I had been faced with a possible labour crisis. We still had quite a large staff then and two valuable men announced that they might have to leave my employ because of housing problems. Will Barnett's son, known universally as Young Will, who had been working for us for some years, told me in June that he was going to get married the following January and if I couldn't house him he would have to move away. At the same time, our other tractor driver, George Scott, had an eviction order served on him where he lived in Whelpley Hill. It appeared that the only thing I could do was to build two cottages for them.

At that time, getting planning permission for a pair of agricultural cottages was a relatively straightforward business. I submitted plans that had already been prepared for somebody else by an architect I knew called Richard Lewellyn-Davies and permission was given early in July. I then tried to find a builder who could build the houses for me. It proved to be totally impossible. No builder would start before October which meant that they couldn't possibly be finished before January which was our deadline.

Over a cup of tea at a meeting of the Amersham Labour Party I put my problem to several people and one man, a bricklayer by trade called Len Bolton, said, 'Why don't you build them yourself? I'll do the brickwork for you.' And just as a result of that chance conversation I decided to build the two houses at a site in Lye Green by direct labour. When I came to settle up the architect's fees with Richard, he pointed out that I had put up my cottages cheaper than the builder who had built the ones for which the plans had originally been drawn. 'You must be a better builder than a farmer,' he joked. 'You'd better change your occupation!' As usual I replied that I had no capital, and with that his wife, Pat, said, 'I've got a few hundred pounds and plenty of time to spare –

Ruined chapel or ruined great hall, I don't know which, but converting it into a house was a fascinating business.

let's start a building business.' So together we set up the firm of
Harman and Davies. After we had built several houses Pat decided
to proceed with her political career, so she withdrew from the
business and it became just Harman (Chesham). I carried it on on
my own until my second son, Andrew, took it over in 1966.

Perhaps the most interesting project I took on as a builder was
converting the ruined chapel at The Grove into a house – my
house. The chapel was one of the first things I knew about on
Grove Farm. Because it was so old and partly ruined people were
intrigued by it and when I was young many believed it to be
haunted. It wasn't for a long time that I learned that there was no
actual evidence that it had ever been a chapel, and it wasn't until I
had been looking at it for many years that I realised it had
previously had an upper floor and that it must originally have
been a house.

The first use I saw it put to was as a store for heaps of
walnuts. Later corn stacks were built all around it and it was used
for storing the sacks of corn when threshing was going on. It
wasn't particularly big or particularly useful as a barn. When I
started farming it got used variously for pigs and for cattle and for
storing and riddling potatoes. Year by year a few stones fell off it
and it became more and more derelict-looking. But it had been
there a long time and had got in the habit of being there and, in
spite of stones falling out and some walls appearing to be rather

*The interior of The Grove
showed clear signs of it
having been a house with an
upper floor at some stage.*

unsafe, it never actually fell down. Habit is a very powerful thing in buildings.

Then, round about 1957, when no use was being made of it at all except that there was a bull living in one little wing of it which was always known as 'the vestry', Mr Elliot Viney, a keen amateur archæologist, came round from the Bucks Archæological Society to have a look at it. 'It's a pity to let this fall down,' he said to me, 'because I think this is a fairly unique Tudor roof and, of course, the lower walls are much older. It's surrounded by a moat too so it's very interesting – you really shouldn't let it fall down.' 'I don't want it to fall down,' I said, 'but it's no good as a barn so what am I to do?' By the end of the afternoon we had both decided that the only long-term future for the building was to restore it to its former use as a house.

Because 'the chapel' was not just a scheduled building, but an ancient monument, as the law stood at that time the Ministry of Works had to be involved and in due course an official came down from that body with strong ideas about what should be done. 'Yes, we shall permit this conversion and encourage it,' he said, 'but you mustn't fake anything. Where things have fallen in you must replace them with purely twentieth-century materials and methods of construction.' He pointed to a wooden extension on one side: 'Where that Victorian extension is there, for example, you must build something completely modern – I'm not having any faking.' His was an original approach, but I could understand the logic.

The only thing that the Man from the Ministry would contemplate us completely renewing in a similar form to its original was the arch over what had been and was to be the front door. He took a sample of the stone, sent it away for examination and it proved to have come from Tisbury in Wiltshire. I found it quite astonishing to think that somebody in the Middle Ages had brought this stone from Tisbury to Chesham to make an arch over his front door. It must have been very expensive. Anyway, we sent somebody down to Tisbury and got suitable stone and, the plans having been passed, proceeded to restore the building to a house without any special thought about how we could use it afterwards. We didn't at first think about moving into it ourselves as it didn't make a particularly big house. It was fairly big downstairs, but the restrictions on what additions we could make made it difficult to achieve the same space upstairs and we finished up with a rather unusual construction: one very big living-room, a small study and what's known as 'the usual offices' downstairs and, at first, just

The finished job: no faking allowed which accounts for the strictly modern replacements of what had fallen in.

three bedrooms and a bathroom upstairs. By this time we only had our two youngest children, Matthew, born in 1955, and Mary, born in 1958, still at home, so bedroom space wasn't quite so important. However, we did subsequently fit another small attic bedroom in the high Tudor roof.

Originally I had thought that I would have to sell the house or, at least, if I could raise the necessary extra capital, let it out, but at the finish Florence and I fell in love with it and we sold Grove Farm House instead and moved into the converted ruins ourselves. Some years later I was reading about our area in the Bucks volume of the *Victoria History of the Counties of England*. Under the heading, 'Former Manor of Grove' the compilers had written 'Part of the great Hall still stands'. I suppose they meant us.

I continued my involvement in the Labour Party all through the fifties and was a Labour candidate in several elections without ever getting in. After the 1959 General Election, in which I had stood unsuccessfully as the candidate for Chigwell, Essex, I more or less decided that I didn't want to be a Member of Parliament, or at least that it was too late to be a Member of Parliament since I was likely to be fifty before I could get in. But I did not entirely give up my interest in politics and certainly not my contacts in the Labour Party. In 1961 Florence and I went with a delegation to look at farms in Czechoslovakia, the delegation consisting of Dick Crossman, who was a farmer as well as a politician, John Mackie, Wilfred Cave, a big farmer from Wiltshire, and their wives. In 1962

Left: Matthew, Mary and our first grandson, Richard, when I was just about to set off electioneering in Chigwell.

Right: Politics and farming. A vineyard in Slovakia with (from left) two Czech officials, John Mackie, Dick Crossman, myself and Wilfred Cave – all of us socialists as well as farmers, a fairly rare breed.

the same delegation went to see collective farms in Poland. I cannot say that I learnt much in either country which was of use to us here, but I did take a great liking to both Czechoslovakia and the Czechs as a race. Our visit took place just before the Dubček era and many of the people we met were Dubček supporters including a Mr Boruvka who was for a brief while Minister of Agriculture under Dubček.

In 1963 my eldest son Dan came down from university and decided to work with me on the farm. He immediately relieved me of quite a lot of responsibility because he had a great deal more aptitude for machinery than I have ever had and quite soon he was playing a major role in running the arable side of things while I concentrated on the livestock. Will Barnett, who was good at all arable work, was still with us but, being rather set in his ways by then, he was not all that easy for a very young man to work with. In retrospect I realise I probably delayed too long in handing the full control of that side of the business to Dan.

In farming the sixties was a decade of increasing specialisation in this country generally and at Grove Farm in particular. In 1959 we had two herds of dairy cattle, one at Grove, one at Cowcroft, a herd of beef cattle at Berryfield, store cattle at Tring, a herd of pigs first of all at Cowcroft and latterly at Tring, a poultry unit and a flock of sheep; we grew wheat, barley, kept up some seed growing and still had a small acreage of potatoes. By the end of the decade almost all of that had gone. Overwhelmingly we were into wheat, barley and beef cattle and little else.

The dairy herd went in 1968. I was very sad to see it go but Grove Farm is not an ideal dairy farm, and as Dan was not interested in this aspect of farming there was little point in keeping it going. The whole herd was sold in one lot to two brothers who had a farm in Cheshire. They were cheesemakers who had lost their herd in the last big foot and mouth outbreak in 1968. It was rather a painful day for me seeing those Ayrshires, which I had slowly acquired from 1932 onwards, all going away together thirty-six years later. I made a bargain with the brothers of a price per cow and they could leave 10% behind. In the event they took 118 of the 120 cows, leaving one because she had milk fever and couldn't get up and they thought she would die and the other because I couldn't guarantee her to be in calf. The one who was going to die in fact lived another eight years and finished up being probably one of the oldest cows in the whole of England.

My son, Dan.

It was a period of steadily increasing yields of almost every crop.
The work being done by the plant breeders seemed to be
accelerating. Almost every year a new variety of wheat would
either be raised in this country or brought in from abroad which
gave ever higher yields and had ever better standing straw so that
you could use ever more units of nitrate on it to produce larger and
larger yields. At that time the annual negotiations between the
National Farmers' Union and the government were still carried on
every year and the guaranteed prices for our produce were
maintained. We seemed to be under no threat at all except that,
towards the end of the decade, anybody who thought about it must
have realised that when we got into the Common Market (which
seemed more and more likely), the system of protecting agriculture
would have to be very different. Nevertheless we were confident
that there would still be a system of some sort and so we kept on
producing as much as we could.

Many people were by then arguing in the farming press and
elsewhere that crop rotations were no longer necessary. The sprays
you could use were so effective against all forms of disease that you
could grow crop after crop of the same thing if you wanted to –
barley after barley after barley – and still get a good yield. I
suppose that's the period in which the conception of the Barley
Baron in East Anglia grew up – a farmer who tore out all his
hedges and grew nothing but barley for which he received huge
government subsidies. I don't know whether he ever really existed
but he became a sort of popular villain in the eyes of the
environmentalists.

It was in this period that most of the hedge removal in Britain
took place, though not on Grove Farm since I'd done all that was
needed during the war. My neighbours in the Chilterns mostly took
their hedges out in the seventies and even in the early eighties and
attracted a lot of adverse publicity. Fortunately for me, a lot of
people in Whelpley Hill and Ashley Green didn't know that I had
ever pulled any hedges out and I've actually been congratulated by
some of my commuting neighbours for not having done so. In fact
I hereby confess that I have done rather more of that sort of thing
than almost anybody in this area and certainly did it long before
they did.

By 1967 the first progeny from our imported French Charolais
were ready for sale and over the next few years these played an
increasingly important part in providing our income. Immediately
they were available there was a big demand for the male offspring

Colossus: died of overweight in Tennessee and was there buried.

to be used for crossing with other breeds in this country. I regret that I didn't immediately appreciate quite what their commercial value was and sold the first male calf I had (called Charlie after General de Gaulle) in the spring of 1968 when he was barely a year old for £1000, thinking I was doing frightfully well. The next time I met my colleagues in the Charolais Society they all told me I was out of my mind and that people were prepared to pay much more. The second one that I had available for sale was bought by an American in Tennessee. There he grew into what at that time was the largest Charolais bull in the United States and his owner, Charlie Anderson, was very proud of him and proud of his size. Unfortunately Charlie fed him too much and at three years old he died of a heart attack, grossly overweight, weighing 1½ tons. Charlie Anderson put an obituary notice in the papers in Tennessee and sent me a copy. It said: 'Funeral by courtesy of the Nashfield Trucking Company'.

During the summer of 1968 we had the first international sale of Charolais cattle in this country at the Royal Show ground to which we hoped to attract a lot of foreign buyers. There were only ten bulls catalogued (which shows how small the scale we were operating on then was), including the one of mine that went to Tennessee. One week before the sale, an American rancher from

Jim Chittim with American domestic Charolais. They were far less meaty than the French breed, but much more active and so more suitable for prairie conditions.

Texas named Jim Chittim arrived in Britain, acquired a catalogue and went round to see all the people who were selling to try and buy the bulls beforehand and take the whole lot to America. We felt this would spoil our international event – a bull sale with no bulls – and so, as the Chairman of the Committee, I had to ring round everybody and try to persuade them not to sell. Sometimes I would ring up at the same time as Jim was visiting and occasionally our member would put him on the 'phone to me and he would drawl: 'Get off my back, Harman, and let me get on with my business.'

In the end Jim only succeeded in buying one bull before the sale and we became firm friends. He bought some more at the sale itself, which helped us, and I subsequently visited him on his ranch, south of San Antonio in Texas. He even ran a partnership for a few years with Dan, buying cattle in Britain and exporting them to the States. Visiting him in Texas was quite an event. He lived like some medieval baron near the Mexican border in scrubby mountain country full of wild deer of all sorts and flocks of wild turkeys. His ranch, complete with cadillac and helicopter, had a drive 28 miles long down which he had had to lay his two telephone systems. He invited me to fly with him in his helicopter but I refused and he was very offended. 'I'm the only one-eyed helicopter pilot in the United States still licensed to fly at over seventy years old,' he said proudly. Small wonder I didn't find the invitation very attractive.

It was also in 1968 that I gave up Berryfield when I bought a small farm directly next door to Grove Farm. It was known as Hemmings Farm and had about 90 acres of the very best land in the Chilterns. The farm had come on the market under the most unfortunate circumstances. It had been farmed by the Miles family for years – the family from whom I had had to retrieve some of my father's fields when I took over the The Grove in 1931. Each generation of Miles seemed to die at an earlier age: the grandfather at fifty-nine, the father at forty-nine and finally the son in his late thirties. It was very sad to see a family go out of farming in this way, especially a family who had been there since my youth.

Most of the families who had been farming in this area in my father's time had gone out of business during the Depression and had been replaced by people from other areas, mainly Scotland and East Anglia. One of the old Buckinghamshire families who had survived were the Crawleys and they had survived by being careful. When I was at school at Chartridge Hill House I remember old Mr

Crawley passing by twice a day on his bicycle with a can of milk on each side, delivering it from his farm at the far end of Chartridge into Chesham, a distance of three miles at least. He was carrying more than 1 cwt in weight and he did it twice a day every day of the week all his life, so he survived. He had two sons: one, Alan, came to live at a little farm called Cuckoo Farm or Lower Farm not too far from me, a small and difficult farm. The other one, Arnold, stayed in the family farm at Chartridge and they both prospered, after a fashion.

Alan was, if anything, more careful than his father had been. I remember that, in the fifties, because in Will Barnett I had an exceptionally capable combine driver, we were in the habit (after we had done our own harvest) of going out and harvesting difficult crops for other people on contract to help pay for the machine. One of the crops we frequently did was clover seed, which is a small seed that is harvested quite late, generally sometime during October. It was a very valuable crop but small in quantity. Amongst the people who asked us to do their clover seed was Alan Crawley and Will duly went down to Cuckoo Farm and combined Alan's clover seed with Alan fussing around all the time and looking on the ground to see if any was being spilt. When Will had finished, it was dusk, but Alan said, 'Now we must clean out the machine because any seed that's inside is mine, you know.' Will more less said, 'Bugger you – I'm off home,' and he went off home with his combine. Every week from then until Christmas Alan used to ring me up and say, 'Have you cleaned that combine out yet? Don't forget that seed in there is mine, whatever there is,' and from time to time I would say to Will, 'When we get a wet day, let's clean out the combine and take Alan his seed,' and I was generally met with some ribald remark. In the end, just before Christmas, the combine got cleaned out and we collected a little bag of dust and seed for Alan. He expressed disappointment when I gave it to him and said, 'I should have thought there would have been more than that,' but he was obviously pleased to have it. So Alan survived too; when times are hard it's the careful ones who make it.

By 1969 Dan was twenty-nine years old and was running all the cultivations on the farm, all the arable side of it, with the help still of Will Barnett until he retired in 1972. I took all the decisions relating to the Charolais herd except that Dan also had a small herd of cattle, first of all in partnership with Jim Chittim and then on his own. By this time we had not only given up milking, but potatoes, pigs and poultry too. The main reason for finally giving

Will Barnett, now in his seventies.

up potatoes was that the gangs of ladies we used to use to pick them were all by now fairly old and it was not work that younger people were interested in. The potato-picking machines that were available then did not work well on stony land like ours; in fact, if conditions weren't ideal you finished up with mashed potato. We gave up pigs and poultry because we couldn't produce the sort of results other people were obtaining in their highly scientific, factory-style units without laying out a large amount of capital for the same sort of systems. Seed-growing, however, is one side-line we have continued with most years, although on a much smaller scale.

With the increased arable acreage attached to Grove Farm itself and the substitution of a relatively small number of beef cattle for the large dairy herd, we dispensed with the alternate husbandry which we had been carrying on since the early 1950s (that is, half the farm in grass, half the farm in arable). Right up until this time the government had been paying out a subsidy on ploughing up short-term leys and in 1969 this was withdrawn. But that was not why we changed the system. It had simply become irrelevant. With a dairy herd there had been a great advantage having grass on the better land where it grew quickly in the spring, produced high-protein feed and resulted in the cows giving a lot of milk. With the beef cattle that wasn't so necessary, so we tended to leave the poorer land, the fields which are more difficult to cultivate in permanent grass from then on and kept all the better fields as arable.

So, the hangings and the small fields which all those years before my father had brought back into cultivation for the first time and had then sown down to permanent grass until they were ploughed up again in the war, went down once more for permanent grass and have remained so ever since. It isn't that these steep fields won't grow good crops of grain – they will. It's just that they cost much more to work. A tractor drawing a plough up and down a hill uses more fuel. It wears its tyres out more because they slip on the stony ground and the hangings were excessively stony. So I suppose the pattern of the steep fields and the awkward-shaped fields as grass, the level fields and the good rectangular fields in arable, will remain like this until war or shortage of grain or some other new circumstance stimulates the extensive cultivation of land once again.

So 1959 to 1969 was the decade of increasing specialisation and steady growth in productivity in agriculture in Britain. The next decade started off in exactly the same atmosphere but, in retrospect, this appears to have been based on a wholly unrealistic optimism. One of the first things that put paid to further expansion was the increase in the cost of land. By 1974 the freehold value of agricultural land in our area and in most other areas had gone up from around £600 an acre in the early 1960s to anything from £1500 to £2000 or more per acre – a price which couldn't possibly be justified by what it produced under any circumstances whatsoever.

To take an example, the land I had bought next door to us – Hemmings Farm – in 1968 went up in market value in the following six years to ten times what I had paid for it, and this had absolutely nothing to do with the prices of the foodstuffs we produced or the increase in productivity, both of which were rising steadily but not at that rate. It seems rather to have been caused by the professionals in the land business, the agricultural agents and valuers, and a lot of people in the city calculating that farm land in Britain must necessarily be worth at least as much as farm land in France, Belgium and Holland because we were going into the Common Market and so were also going to have the benefits of the Common Market Agricultural Support system.

During all this period the managers of city funds were being persuaded to buy farms to let at rents which only yielded perhaps 2% or 2.1% interest on the investment, on the strength of the fact that every three years they could get an increase in the rent by going to arbitration. This they apparently thought would go on for ever because it was a period of general inflation and ownership of agricultural land was advocated as a hedge against inflation. I could never quite see this because it seemed to me that the rent value of the land and the freehold value of the land had got to be tied to what you could produce from it. At that time our revenue from an average yield of wheat had gone up to something like £250 per acre per year maximum. How on earth you could pay a rent which represented a commercial interest on £2000 an acre, plus all your other costs, when your total yield from it was only £250, I couldn't see. Anyway, it meant that any thoughts of expansion of our farming further during this period disappeared completely. But the arable farming carried on as before with steadily increasing yields and the Charolais side of Grove Farm continued to prosper. The size of our herd was increasing all the time and the demand for the breed all over Britain for crossing with native breeds continued to be very resilient.

It was in the mid-seventies that the trade in Charolais with New Zealand and, indirectly, Australia sprang up. This lasted for only about five years because the New Zealanders simply wanted to make a quick financial killing by selling to Australia, and the Australians soon had enough. There is now only a small trade in semen from Britain. By the end of the '70s the trade with America had died down too, but for different reasons. The boom in Charolais in America was so intense that it really burnt itself out. Every new bull they imported, whether from England or any other country, was immediately publicised as being the biggest and best Charolais bull there had ever been. Of course, some of them hadn't been tested and gave difficult or doubtful progeny, so after a while the breed lost a lot of ground. In fact by the end of the decade the American domestic Charolais, which is something very far removed from the French Charolais, became more acceptable in the American market than the imported French ones we had, not because this breed is better in itself but because it was less extreme and hadn't been over-exploited so much. Then the Americans started selling *their* cattle to Australia and cut us out there through high-pressure salesmanship which was very effective.

By the time Britain entered the Common Market on 1 January 1973, most farmers who had originally been very suspicious of it had become convinced that it would be a good thing. They saw that the prices on the Continent for agricultural products were, on the whole, considerably higher than here and that the arrangements for buying appeared to take no account of quantity, so they could continue to produce as much as they wished. Nobody seemed to be aware of the danger of building up huge surpluses, but continued in an extremely optimistic mood through the whole of that period. I think probably on Grove Farm we were the same. We were full of confidence that we could continue to produce more and more each year and somehow it would always be bought.

The system that had operated in Britain under the 1947 Agriculture Act had had built-in safeguards against the accumulation of enormous surpluses. As far as the main products, such as grain, were concerned they all had to be sold before a farmer got his guaranteed payment, that is to say sold to a user or trader who would obviously never be anxious to build up huge stocks that they would have to finance. At the same time, the farmer had to make sure the quality was all right because he was only given the difference between the average price that everybody got and the guaranteed price, not the difference between what he got for his own wheat and the guaranteed price. Consequently if he sold wheat of below average quality he didn't get so much and anyway, the buyer wouldn't buy at all unless he could see an immediate use for the grain.

The only products for which there was a system remotely resembling what was imposed by the Common Market were potatoes and milk. The Potato Marketing Board would buy up any surplus potatoes themselves and attempt to market them for animal feeding or for uses outside the normal trade. But even that had two built-in safeguards: firstly, potatoes will not keep, therefore you can't store mountains of them and they had to be disposed of each year, and secondly, the Potato Board had a right and a duty to impose quotas so that not too many were grown. (This was always a difficult job because the yield of potatoes varies by a bigger percentage than almost anything else from year to year.) Dairy produce was all marketed by the Milk Marketing Board, but this had a built-in safeguard too in that the price received by the farmer was, broadly speaking, an average of the price of all the milk the Milk Marketing Board sold. So, if they had to sell surpluses cheap, the farmer got less, which made the system self-regulating. To some extent, in the case of milk, this still happens.

The old system of price bargaining between the government and the NFU was, of course, dispensed with and the EEC system of intervention buying introduced. This system, still in operation now in 1986, works like this. Intervention boards in each country offer to buy at the guaranteed price, fixed in Brussels annually, any grain offered to them. There is no limit on quantity and so, quite naturally, farmers who can't find a commercial market for their grain offer it to the intervention board. The system suits the French farmer fairly well because there is an intervention board store in almost every small town in France, therefore haulage from the farm to the store is a fairly easy matter. Here, however, stores had to be set up and a number of old aerodrome hangers and buildings of that sort were taken over. These are not evenly distributed throughout the country and often the grain has to be transported long distances to the stores.

Because of over-production, vast mountains of grain have now accumulated in these stores all over Europe since grain doesn't have to be used to be paid for There is a slightly different system for dairy produce and meat but it has the same eventual effect – the dairy and meat trade can also sell any surpluses to the intervention board at guaranteed prices.

In Britain, the EEC Agricultural Policy has resulted in vast amounts of grain being stored in widely dispersed, converted buildings, such as this aircraft hanger. The French, on the other hand, have the advantage of purpose-built co-operative stores in small towns all over the country. Wherever it's stored, if it's kept dry and free from insects, grain will keep for years.

Common Market guaranteed prices were straightaway better than we had been receiving and therefore were an added encouragement to increase production, together with the feeling at the back of our minds that if our grain wasn't wanted it would still be bought. This has led to the position now where the whole farming industry is under enormous pressure. The population sees itself paying out large sums in taxation to subsidise the production of grain that it doesn't want. The farmer has been led on to borrow money to finance the production of more and more grain in order to raise his income so that he is now on an escalator going the wrong way. He has to produce more and more and more in order to meet his obligations, and any reduction in the price he receives for his produce merely accentuates the problem. He either goes bankrupt or tries to produce even more.

We have now reached the point where a lot of land will have to go out of cultivation if our production is to be reduced to somewhere near what the market actually needs. Then the problem arises – how much land and where? There is widespread speculation now amongst farmers and in agricultural journals that a quota system of some sort may have to be introduced whereby we will only be allowed to grow perhaps three-quarters of the acreage of grain that we grew in 1984. In my view, this wouldn't work because we would all simply work like mad to produce from the reduced acreage at least as much as we had done from our previous acreage in order to maintain our standard of living. It would also perpetuate the practice of grain being grown in unsuitable places. Over the last few years there has been a tendency for barley, in particular, to be grown in the north of Scotland and Wales on land which is not really suitable for grain production. Presumably farmers in these areas would still be allotted a quota and would still continue to do it.

All of this is terrible for, say, a forty-five-year-old farmer who is too old to change his occupation and yet young enough to have to plan for another twenty years of working life. To an old man like me it is not so bad, except that, once again, I have that old uneasy feeling – now people have got enough to eat, they don't want us any more.

The Farming Conflict

With now, in 1986, the Harmans occupying and farming what were five separate farms in 1918, the Mashes what were at least seven farms and the Hunters, who moved down from Scotland only in the 1950s, what were four holdings originally, what has happened to all the people, all the families that used to farm these farms?

Well, some are still there, still surviving just as they were. Bill Stanbridge of Bury Farm, Whelpley Hill, is farming exactly the same area as his father was farming at the end of the First World War. It was the biggest farm in the district then by far – about 300 acres. One of the four Browns is left – Maurice, whose methods of farming are almost unchanged, and whose area of farming is just the same. Another family, the Newmans, farm just about the same area as they used to in 1918 (though not the same farm) and they do the same thing, they produce quite a lot of milk. But they've survived mainly by buying one or two big items of machinery and doing work for their neighbours. Mr Hobbs has survived in the same way.

The others have almost all disappeared. The nine Puddephatts have all gone. Of the many Batchelors who used to farm in the area, none are left here, although one, Hugh Batchelor, has moved to Kent and become quite notorious, being held by the national press as a millionaire who sweeps away hedges and spoils the countryside. There are two of the Crawleys still farming not much larger acreages than they had all those years ago. Their methods have been brought up to date, but they are still careful people, wasting nothing and therefore surviving. All the others have gone, either because they wanted an easier life, or because they failed at farming, or because somebody bought them out. They've all gone.

And what has happened to the farming since those difficult times in the thirties when I started on my own? Well, the period from the Second World War until today has seen a revolution in agriculture where Grove Farm has become totally specialised, as has almost every farm in Britain. The varieties of cattle we keep have completely changed as have the varieties of wheat and barley we grow. The plant breeders and chemists have enabled us to produce yields we never dreamed of in 1945.

This is the land I own now. The rented farms of Cowcroft and Dungrove, where Dan lives, are a mile to the south.

Young rape on Grove. As an oilseed crop it has only been grown on any scale in Britain since the 1970s. It has a major advantage over grain crops in that it is harvested quite early, around mid-July, and can be sold immediately. This means the arable farmer can re-pay some of his seasonal bank loan a month early.

Yet now, for the first time in many years, we are apprehensive. We are realising that nobody wants what we are producing, at least not on the scale that we are producing it. We have given up our own capability for doing a lot of different things and all this has changed the mood of unreasoning optimism of the early 1970s to a mood of considerable doubt. Although rents are continuing to rise because they are fixed by land agents who have a vested interest in keeping them up, the freehold value of farms has stopped going up and they are becoming more difficult to sell. Suddenly after only a year or two, it doesn't seem to be such a good idea to produce only wheat, barley and rape, however efficiently we do it.

In this atmosphere it became obvious to us that continuing to run the land at Tring, six miles away, was no longer sensible. It wasn't very productive land, only suitable for raising beef cattle, and everything we did there was expensive. The tractors had to run six miles there and six miles back on the road with a lot of wear and tear, so we decided to get out of Tring as soon as we could and try to obtain some extra land nearer to Grove. We couldn't actually do anything about this until 1984 when, providentially, at about the same time as the owners of Tring Park expressed a desire to repossess so that they had to compensate us for disturbance, Dungrove Farm, next to Cowcroft, came on the market. Dan did a deal whereby he bought the farmhouse and rented the land from the landlords, the diocese of St Alban's. So we are left with a slightly reduced acreage of between 800 and 900 acres but these are much closer together with something over 400 at Grove and something over 400 a mile and a half away at Cowcroft and Dungrove. In the long run this was bound to make us more efficient since more of our land is now available for arable (nearly all the land at Dungrove can be ploughed) and, of course, the moving of tractors and machinery and cattle between the two farms is much easier.

There now appears to be a possibility of growing crops we have not really thought about before. For example, we have been approached to grow evening primrose, the seed of which is used in pharmaceuticals. The drawback, of course, is that different crops and different seed require the acquisition of new techniques to manage them. Nevertheless it seems likely that in the next few years we shall turn our backs on specialisation and return to a more varied system of farming. At least this will be more interesting. The age of specialisation was a very boring age and I'm not too sorry that it appears to be over.

The turn-round in public attitudes towards farmers over a very few years is quite extraordinary. Ten years ago, farmers had a good press and most people saw their problems. Now they have a very bad press and it seems that everybody is against them. At the same time they find themselves having more difficulties than they have had for a very long time. Just recently, figures have been published which show that farmers' real incomes are lower than they have been for over forty years. I don't know how many people in other businesses would care to try and keep going on the same income they had in 1945. We were warned, over a long period, that we had got to produce efficiently; that, in the end, we would have to be subject to more strict market discipline, so a lot of farmers tried to increase the size of their holdings, buying land at high prices and agreeing high rents, only to be told in the end that they had made life impossible for small farmers just by being big. The strange thing is that the general population bemoans the decline of small farms and small farmers and at the same time does its shopping at Sainsbury's and Marks and Spencer's and not at the corner shop. The principles involved are just the same – if you want efficiency in terms of cheapness, you have to have big units.

So, for me, the whole thing is a conflict which goes on for ever. When people have not got a house they don't think too much that they are spoiling the countryside by building one; when they've got one, they do. When they are short of food, they do not think too much that they are spoiling the countryside in removing hedges. When they have enough, they cease to be bothered about producing more for other people, and the preservation of the scenery around them and the view from their windows becomes of paramount importance.

Because most of us in Europe are no longer hungry, many want to freeze the landscape as it is at the moment, disregarding the fact that there are people in the world who could do with the extra food that we could produce. But if cheap food from abroad became unavailable, as during a war, we would soon forget about the landscape and be prepared to alter it. It has always been like that. On the other hand a lessening in the pressure for production will mean that the countryside will revert to more beauty again. After the repeal of the Corn Laws in the last century and the influx of cheap grain from abroad, the decline in farming led to the countryside becoming more beautiful, to the planting of more woods and more land falling into a low state of cultivation with more flowers and more wildlife. The same thing will happen again.